Living on the Edge

Clive Calver and Peter Meadows

with additional material from
Steve Chilcraft

with assistance from
Stephen Gaukroger, Ernest Lucas
and David Jackman

LYNX

*Spring
Harvest*

Published by
Lynx Communications
Sandy Lane West, Oxford, England
ISBN 0 7459 2689 4
Albatross Books Pty Ltd
PO Box 320, Sutherland, NSW 2232, Australia
ISBN 0 7324 0747 8

First edition 1993

Acknowledgments

Unless otherwise stated, all scripture is taken
from the HOLY BIBLE, NEW INTERNATIONAL
VERSION. Copyright © 1973, 1978, 1984 by
International Bible Society. Used by permission of
Hodder and Stoughton Limited.

A catalogue record for this book is available
from the British Library

Printed and bound in Great Britain
by Blackmore Press, Shaftesbury

LIVING ON THE EDGE

Life is short. We only have one opportunity to make an impact on this world. Christians want to achieve something for God which will have lasting value both now and in the world to come.

We are concerned about people, our families, friends and neighbours. We want to see them come to faith in Christ if they are not already disciples of Jesus.

We are concerned about our environment, the planet we live on. We want God's creation to be well looked after and our children to inherit somewhere safe and pleasant to live in.

We also care about the value and standards of the society we belong to. Moral issues matter to us. We believe that the ethics outlined in the Bible are more than just good, they are the best, and that it is important that we say so for the good of all.

But for the Christian there is another dimension which gives us a very different perspective on life. We do not believe that death is the end. Heaven is a real place not just a metaphor. We anticipate living forever with God. That affects everyday life. We see things differently from those who only live for the present.

Living on the Edge will help us face four important aspects of life where being a Christian makes us different.

ENVIRONMENT—*Living in the Physical World*

ETHICS—*Living in the Moral World*

EVANGELISM—*Living in a Lost World*

ETERNITY—*Living in the Spiritual World*

As you work through these four days you will probably learn a lot. That is not the intention. This seminar series is designed to help us face some of the real challenges of our times and to make a difference. That requires action.

We will need to take risks. We must take our place in the front line. We must, together, live on the edge.

Using This Book for Group Study

This material has been written for use at the Spring Harvest main seminars, which are rather different from church study groups or home groups. But there is a wealth of information here, and plenty of stimulating ideas. So these notes can readily be adapted for any kind of group discussion.

One way might be this:

1. Taking one of the units (e.g. Environment), decide how many group sessions you will give to it and so which sub-sections you aim to cover each session.

2. Assuming each member has a copy of this book—it's packed with useful knowledge, so it would be unkind if they didn't!—ask them to study that sub-section on their own before next session.

3. Prepare discussion questions for each session. Some sections have questions in the margin, which may give some clues as to how to frame yours.

4. Remember these studies are meant to lead to thought and action, not just talk. Each unit ends with suggestions for action. So why not finish each of your sessions by looking on to the action section and choosing one or two ways members of the group could take action this coming week, before your next session. Then, next session, begin by sharing how that went.

CONTENTS

Environment
Living in the Physical World

CONTENTS

> **Book of the seminar day:**
> Tony Campolo, *How to Rescue the Earth Without Worshipping Nature*, Word

Introduction

There are some world events that you just can't miss. These are the high profile upheavals created by political or military uprisings and economic crises. Such violent and concentrated outbursts focus media attention.

In contrast continued gradual change can take place with hardly anyone noticing. The classic example of this truth lies in the field of ecological awareness.

Twenty-five years ago support for the Keep Britain Tidy Campaign was the pinnacle of ecological involvement. Today there is a totally different popular attitude to the earth and its resources.

Even more surprising is the fact that this transformation in public opinion has taken place on a global scale. A genuine 'people movement' is emerging:

▶ to voice popular concern about the current state of the environment

▶ to pressure those within the corridors of power to take appropriate action

The general public in the United Kingdom now have:

▶ a preference for environmentally-friendly products

▶ a strong antipathy towards pollution

▶ concern about the danger of damaging the ozone-layer and the threat of global warming

Specifically, there are fears about:

▶ nuclear proliferation

▶ acid rain

▶ the disposal of nuclear waste

▶ the destruction of tropical rain forests

▶ the potential extinction of rare plant and animal species

Not everyone voices the same concerns. Many retain a sense of apathy towards an issue they struggle to understand, and sense that they cannot influence. But a growing number of ordinary people are changing their lifestyle in subtle ways.

Green issues are no longer the province of those in open-toed sandals.

And the emphasis on green issues in schools will eventually provoke a generation of adults ready to create a greater environmental awareness, and a greener world.

To be 'radical' used to mean being politically 'Red'. Today it means being 'Green'.

But what is the Christian response to these developments? If anyone should be convinced of the need to support ecological involvement it would surely be those who believe in a creator.

Why Have We Missed the Revolution?

Evangelical Christian reaction to the modern Green revolution has been mixed. It has included:

▶ cautious approval about the need for greater environmental consciousness

▶ a strong sense of reservation—even suspicion—

towards a more public involvement on these issues

Why have evangelicals been slow to respond to the issues of the environment?

Evangelicals have seen the first duty of a Christian as faith-sharing rather than garbage disposal.

Evangelism is the heartbeat of evangelicalism. Any issue which deflects attention from the claims of Jesus Christ on the life of an individual is bound to arouse evangelical suspicions.

Evangelicals have always tended to concentrate on spiritual rather than bodily welfare.

Care for souls rather than the nurture and development of bodies has been the priority for the majority of evangelical Christians.

After all, one day our old bodies will be discarded in place of new permanent ones. So why concentrate on something with no eternal significance, at the expense of preparing ourselves for eternity?

Evangelicals also recognize that this planet is not permanent. One day it will be destroyed and its residents translated to their eternal destinations. So why put our energies into improving what will one day be replaced?

The conclusion is that our efforts should be concentrated on our eternal heavenly destination rather than our temporary earthly heritage.

Those who lead churches—and denominations—tend to be older and have missed the 'Green revolution' that has impregnated school, and children's media, in recent years.

Leaders have largely escaped the bombardment that has reached young people concerning the abuse of the environment. This ignorance has played a large part in isolating evangelicals from these issues.

The Green movement has been considered to be a lunatic fringe.

Only 'funny people' make a fuss about ozone and pesticides. Neither urban nor middle-class Christianity feels comfortable in the presence of—and with the ideas of—those who want to replace the car with the bicycle.

New Age thinking seems to be the motivation behind many within the Green movement, causing Christians to hang back for fear of being misunderstood or 'contaminated'.

Many Green supporters couple their interest in ecology with a desire to encounter Mother Nature. To them the issue is not that 'the earth is God's' but that 'the earth is God'—buying into a quasi-Buddhist view of life.

This mistrust has been confirmed by people like David Icke—a former spokesman for the Green Party—who announced himself to be the new Messiah.

A Christian Response

Irrational—or even rational—fears are not the basis on which Christians should approach environmental issues.

'Why do you talk to us on Green Issues? We never stop hearing about it at school. We've come to Spring Harvest to escape environmental issues not to learn even more about them.'
A SPRING HARVEST GUEST IN THE YOUTH PROGRAMME, 1992.

'Let the New Agers hang on to their fuzzy abstractions if they like, but as for me, I will explore the universe hand-in-hand with the Maker.'
NICK MERCER

KEY POINT

A truly Christian response to issues of the environment requires the right foundation.

It is not enough to say:

▶ we are spoiling things for future generations

▶ thousands will die if we don't do something

▶ endangered species will be gone forever

Such responses can be genuinely and sincerely made by anyone—Christian or not.

KEY POINT

But we need a firm Christian base from which to view our concern for the planet.

If this is truly God's world, made by him, then we need to approach it in the way that the designer intends. If God is creator then, as his people, we have a prime commitment to care for the creation in the way that he expects.

Does God the Creator Exist?

KEY POINT

If there is a personal creator behind the world—and all that is in it—this has overwhelming significance for the way we think and behave.

If the world came to pass as the result of a deliberate act of creation, rather than by accident, there must be a purpose behind its existence.

It is also reasonable to think that the creator has a view on the maintenance of that which he made. He must also know better than those he made how best to look after the world. So his instructions are to be taken seriously.

If this life is preparation for another world, then questions of eternity and a wider perspective will shape our priorities.

However, those who doubt the truth of the Bible argue that this world could exist even if God did not.

KEY POINT

Before looking at the environment in which God has placed us we must first face up to the question of whether, or not, the creator actually exists.

Any approach to the environment is quite different when based on a view that there is no personal God to whom we are accountable.

Christian thinkers have advanced important arguments for God's existence. These five arguments use:

▶ reason

▶ logic

▶ the evidence contained in the world around us

The arguments have been extensively debated. Some people have claimed they 'prove' the existence of God. Others more modestly believe they can claim merely to indicate the probability of his existence.

Some of the five 'proofs' are stronger than others. But each stretches the mind and can significantly help explain a belief in God.

1. The Ontological Argument:
If something is possible then it must exist

The philosopher, Anselm (1033–1109), stated that:

▶ God is the greatest conceivable being.

▶ What is real and actual is superior to that which is merely possible.

This means that a real God must therefore be superior to the greatest possible being we can conceive of.

Therefore, as we *can* conceive of God as being the greatest, the real God *must* exist. Otherwise we are left with being able to conceive of a possible being that is greater than the real one.

The weakness of this argument according to the German philosopher, Immanuel Kant (1724–1804), is that it only proves that *if* there is a greatest possible being, then he does exist. He did not believe that existence added to a concept. For example, an imaginary £100 banknote and a real one are worth the same in concept but not in reality. Reality is not a part of value.

But the strength of the argument is that it affirms that God is God. The world has meaning as God is indeed the greatest perfect being we can imagine. There can be no greater.

2. The Cosmological Argument:
The need for a first cause

The weakness of this argument is that it depends on the previous one. It is based on the principle of cause and effect.

Every effect can be explained in terms of a cause. That cause in turn can be explained by what causes lie behind it.

Take this argument back to its logical conclusion. What was the first cause? What or who caused matter in the first place? Every cause and effect to that point are inextricably linked together.

The ultimate cause *must* be separate, independent and self-determining or it is merely another step in the process.

For matter to exist there must have been a being who had a will and purpose of its own to create it. We call that being 'God'.

The question 'who created God?' makes no sense because, by definition, 'God' is the 'first cause'—the one not created.

This argument, classically taught by Thomas Aquinas (1225–74), was significantly developed by René Descartes (1596–1650), a devout French Catholic thinker often dubbed 'the father of modern philosophy'.

Descartes was sceptical about *everything*. However:

▶ He was convinced of his own existence because of his thoughts.

▶ Because his mind could conceive of the idea of God, he concluded that this could only be there because God put it there.

Therefore, he presumed, God must exist.

Descartes then investigated what he knew of this God, concluding that he is:

▶ All-powerful

▶ The creator

▶ Beneficial not detrimental to his creation

Therefore, Descartes argued, God could be trusted

KEY POINT

KEY POINT

'That the universe was formed by a fortuitous concourse of atoms, I will no more believe that than the accidental jumbling of the alphabet would fall into a most ingenious treatise of philosophy.'
JONATHAN SWIFT

'Posterity will some day laugh at the foolishness of modern materialistic philosophy. The more I study nature, the more I am amazed at the Creator.'
LOUIS PASTEUR

'We are not our own, any more than what we possess is our own. We did not make ourselves; we cannot be supreme over ourselves. We cannot be our own masters. We are God's property by creation, by redemption, by regeneration.'
JOHN HENRY NEWMAN

'At both theoretical and practical levels, Christians urgently need to develop a Christian environmental ethic. And that ethic needs to be undergirded by fundamental theological attention to the environment as a dimension of God's good creation.'
LAURENCE OSBORN

KEY POINT

and this God would aid his own use of logic to discover the truth and confirm his discoveries.

A hundred years later Scottish philosopher David Hume (1711–76), followed by Bertrand Russell (1872–1970), maintained that the argument was flawed. They challenged the process of *necessary* cause for effect. Just because something is seen to always behave in a certain way does not mean it always has or always will. They claimed that the universe simply had always been there. Russell put it: 'The universe just is, and that's all.'

Nevertheless, the law of cause and effect is a powerful pointer to a creator God.

3. The Teleological Argument: The argument from design

This is the most popular of the five arguments. Put simply it asks,

'How can anyone believe that such a beautiful and intricate world of plants, animals and natural wonders just happened? It is not reasonable to believe it to be the result of blind chance.'

The argument goes deeper than being one of mere mechanical efficiency, for which atheistic evolution attempts its own explanation. It is one of beauty—a design that lifts the human spirit and produces wonder and appreciation.

This argument is not exclusive to Christian thinking. It was first advanced by the Greek philosopher Plato (c. 427–347BC) who believed the universe required a designer.

The classic expression of this theory is in William Paley's book *Natural Theology* published in 1802. Here he describes discovering a working, ticking watch upon the ground. Should its existence be explained by:

▶ the chance forces of wind, rain, heat, volcanic activity, and so on, combining together in a billion-to-one accident?

▶ the deliberate actions of an intelligent watch-maker?

However, the philosopher David Hume suggested that:

▶ Given the vastness of the universe and unlimited time, probability alone means that this universe could exist by chance.

▶ Once it was in existence, natural adaptation would give the appearance of order and design. This is particularly true seeing that experience of this world is all we have—with no other system of order with which to compare it.

Additionally the teleological argument must cope with the existence of unexplained and potentially unexplainable processes in the universe which appear purposeless.

▶ Why does the duck-billed platypus exist? Is it God's sense of humour? A cosmic joke?

▶ How does the existence of evil fit in?

▶ How could a good designer allow the destructive forces—fire, flood, storm, volcanoes, and so on, into his world?

Many scientists are sympathetic to the argument that design needs a designer. They see a remarkable harmony in nature that is difficult to explain by

theories of chance alone. For Christians this is not least because it appears to be affirmed by scripture.

'The heavens declare the glory of God; The skies proclaim the work of his hands' (Psalm 19:1).

'For since the creation of the world God's invisible qualities—his eternal power and divine nature—have been clearly seen being understood from what has been made, so that men are without excuse' (Romans 1:20).

'He has made everything beautiful in its time. He has also set eternity in the hearts of men; yet they cannot fathom what God has done from beginning to end' (Ecclesiastes 3:11).

4. The Moral Argument: The sense of 'ought'

Human beings are not mere machines—which need to be programmed to make choices.

People have an inbuilt sense of right and wrong.

We know what we *ought* to do and it troubles us that we do not do what we should.

This sense of 'ought' cannot entirely be explained away in terms of social conditioning or self-interest. The fact that we recognize a set standard indicates that there must be a Being who establishes these values.

Worldwide, there is widespread agreement on basic moral principles:

murder is wrong, stealing is wrong, telling the truth is right.

The fact that we have a moral dimension—a concern for right and wrong—indicates that there is a creator, from whom these values come.

It is also argued that the universe has an end purpose to which our moral dimension points. Life is not pointless but has a purpose, given by a creator.

The argument has been criticized on the basis that:

▶ It is wrong to assume that moral behaviour can only be explained in religious terms.

▶ There is a wide diversity of moral beliefs in different cultures.

5. The Anthropological Argument: A greater mind, personality and will

Along with being a physical and moral being, humankind also has a mental dimension. We can think—following logically from an initial proposition to its conclusion.

Our ability to reason, imagine and take decisions requires, it is argued, the existence of an ultimate intelligence.

If this 'mind' does not exist then we would not be able to evaluate any thinking. There would be no reference point for the system of logic itself. Out tiny minds point to the mind of God.

Each of these five arguments may have a weakness individually—but together they present a strong case. We should also see these 'rational' proofs in the wider context of God's ways of dealing with humankind.

KEY POINT

KEY POINT

KEY POINT

KEY POINT

<u>Most significant is the human being, Jesus of Nazareth. Historians and philosophers alike must contend with the fact of his existence and his claims.</u>

One individual from an obscure Mediterranean town has influenced history—events and people—to an extent that defies normal reason. Here is a life that points clearly to a supernatural dimension and a God who acts in history.

The Christian's belief is rooted in the following convictions:

▶ The evidence of the Gospels can be trusted, despite widespread objections. The writers give first-hand evidence.

▶ The claims of Jesus to divinity—to be the Son sent from the Father—if accepted, 'prove' the existence of God.

▶ The evidence of Jesus' life, his perfect character and his miracle working.

▶ That the death, resurrection and ascension of Jesus actually took place.

▶ The effect of these events on the followers of Jesus and the subsequent emergence of the Christian church.

These are rational arguments based on history which do not require faith. That may follow.

KEY POINT

<u>The surest knowledge we can have of God is always what he says about himself, rather than beginning with man's search for God.</u>

It is here that we must give careful attention to scripture which claims to be inspired by God and a way of him making himself known to us.

God and Science

KEY POINT

<u>Despite the arguments for God, the contemporary world of science has often been seen to be in conflict with the concept of there being a creator.</u>

Confidence in a creator God must deal with the world of science.

The relationship between God and science has an interesting history:

For centuries science and Christianity rarely clashed. This was partly due to a deficiency in scientific knowledge. It also owed something to the penalties which existed for heresy!

Three hundred years ago the founders of the Royal Society saw nothing strange in dedicating their scientific research 'to the glory of God'.

Two hundred years ago new scientific discoveries were used to support the view that design needed a designer.

A hundred years ago the observations of Charles Darwin and others put Christianity on the rack.

For the past century it has often appeared as if science and the Christian faith were in a fight to the death.

Charles Darwin was not the first to suggest that species can change progressively in the course of time. But his book *The Origin of Species* in 1859 was the first to propose natural selection, or the survival of the fittest. By this view:

▶ Organisms adapt to their environment by natural selection.

▶ Through successive generations those which adapt and survive will be those best suited to their environment.

This, Darwin claimed, was the main means of evolutionary change. Darwin did not set out to attack Christian belief or the Bible. However, those hostile to the Christian faith—humanists and rationalists—seized on his material and used it for their own ends.In the years that followed:

▶ Scientists claimed that scripture was now redundant, if not irrelevant.

▶ Theologians claimed that scripture provided a theological explanation rather than a scientific analysis.

▶ Some Christians saw science as 'the enemy' and took an over-literal view of what the Bible said.

On this basis an uneasy truce was reached, as science and theology dealt with separate approaches to the question of creation.

▶ Science discussed the way creation took place.

▶ Theology dealt with the author of it all.

Some Modern Problems

KEY POINT

<u>Recently, the long-running truce between science and the scriptures has been broken over another issue.</u>

Hostilities have been provoked by:

▶ The amazing success of books such as Stephen Hawking's *A Brief History of Time*, Transworld Publishing, 1988.

▶ Events like the much-publicized debate between Dr John Habgood, the Archbishop of York, and Dr Richard Dawkins on science and religion.

The issues that these debates raise are hard to grasp even by theoretical physicists, thermodynamicists or cosmologists. For our purposes we need to keep the following material even simpler!

The origins of the universe—time and eternity—are at the heart of the debate. Two basic views are offered to account for the existence of the cosmos.

▶ *View 1.* It always has been, with no beginning or end

▶ *View 2.* It had a beginning and will probably have an end

Both views have had supporters. In the 1920s astronomers discovered that the universe is expanding. The great star systems, the galaxies, are rushing away from each other at a speed which increases the further apart they are from each other. What does this mean for the beginning and end of the universe?

In the late 1940s Fred Hoyle and others put forward the steady state theory. They suggested that as the universe expands new matter comes into being spontaneously. It does so at a rate which means that the average density of matter in the universe remains constant. As a result, on the large scale, the universe always looks the same.

One attraction of this theory for some people, including Fred Hoyle, was that it seemed to do away with any need for an act of creation and a creator.

At the time there was an alternative theory, the Big Bang theory. This explained the expansion by

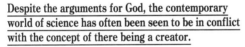

'*S*cience without religion is lame, religion without science is blind.'
ALBERT EINSTEIN

suggesting that the universe as we know it began with an unimaginably great explosion. This was the origin of all the matter and energy in the universe, and also space and time.

▶ In the beginning the matter and energy would have been extremely hot, at a temperature of millions of degrees centigrade.

▶ As matter expanded outwards it cooled.

▶ As matter cooled, matter as we know it eventually came into being, first as sub-atomic particles, then as atoms which formed clouds of gas, out of which the stars and planets were formed.

By projecting the process backwards from the presently known rate of expansion the Big Bang can be dated to about fifteen thousand million years before the present.

In the early 1960s two pieces of evidence led astronomers to adopt the Big Bang theory rather than the steady state theory.

▶ The study of galaxies which are strong emitters of radio waves showed that they are not uniformly distributed in space. This can be explained by the Big Bang theory but is contrary to the steady state theory.

▶ In 1964 the whole universe was found to be bathed in a uniform background radiation of microwaves at a very low temperature. This is readily explained as the 'after glow' of the Big Bang but cannot be explained by the steady state theory.

The 'ripples' in this radiation discovered by the Cosmic Background Explorer Satellite add further support to the theory. They represent the beginning of the formation of the gas clouds which eventually became galaxies and stars.

In addition, the steady state theory has been criticized for ignoring the Second Law of Thermodynamics. This states that whenever energy is transferred from one form or body to another, entropy (loss) occurs which is necessary to cause the internal disordering of molecules. Therefore, no state can be maintained indefinitely.

Many Christians welcomed the Big Bang theory. They saw it as being consistent with the idea of creation, because it is based on a universe which has a specific moment of beginning.

In the 1980s physicists began putting forward theories which tried to explain how the Big Bang happened purely in terms of the known physical laws. All these theories face a major problem.

▶ The Big Bang begins with a point of infinite density of matter and energy. This is called a 'singularity'. Unfortunately, the known laws of physics break down when applied to singularities.

Professor Hawking claims to have produced a theory which gets around this problem. It has arisen out of his work on 'black holes'.

▶ Black holes are also singularities, points of infinite density of matter and energy, produced when certain types of stars collapse in on themselves.

▶ Black holes are so called because no matter or energy can escape from inside them. This includes light, which is a form of energy. For this reason, no one will ever be able to see a black hole. However, there is some indirect evidence that black holes do exist.

Professor Hawking's theory presents the universe as 'self-contained, having no boundary or edge. With neither beginning nor end: it would simply be.' In fact it seems to present a never-ending cycle of expansions and collapses of the universe, each beginning with a fresh Big Bang.

In order to develop his theory Hawking has had to invent a mathematical quantity which he calls 'imaginary time'. He contrasts this with 'real time', time as we experience it. If the history of the universe is traced in imaginary time there are no singularities and so the laws of physics can be applied even to the Big Bang.

However, Hawking himself admits that it is unclear what imaginary time means or how it relates to our experience of reality, in which there are singularities, such as black holes.

Hawking's theory is still very controversial. He implies that it may leave no room for a creator. However, this is not so.

The central point of the Christian doctrine of creation is not how the universe came into being in terms of physics, or when it began, but why it exists at all.

Even if the universe has no measurable beginning—or end—it is still possible to take two views:

▶ That it has always existed and matter is eternal.

▶ That its existence is due to, and upheld by, an eternal creator who brought it into being.

After all, there seems to be no reason why an all-powerful and all-wise creator should not create a steady state universe or a Hawking-type universe if that was his wish.

▶ From the creator's point of view it would have a beginning.

▶ From the point of view of creatures within it, that

KEY POINT

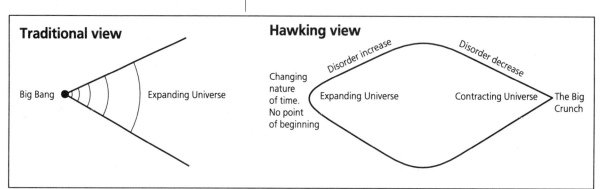

Traditional view

Big Bang — Expanding Universe

Hawking view

Changing nature of time. No point of beginning

Disorder increase — Disorder decrease

Expanding Universe — Contracting Universe — The Big Crunch

beginning would not be observable. But there is nothing in the Bible to say that it should be.

It is by *faith* that we believe the world was created at God's command (Hebrews 11:3). Such faith is compatible with the steady state theory, the Big Bang theory or Hawking's theory.

It is difficult for ordinary Christians to respond to complex issues such as these, especially as Hawking and others stray into philosophy and theology.

But scientific theories also change. So we should be wary of hitching our wagon to any particular notion—it may turn out to be wrong.

Helpfully there are some scientists who are Christians and who can make an intelligent response. An example is Professor Roy Peacock in his helpful book, *A Brief History of Eternity*, Monarch, 1989.

Christians who are not scientifically trained should neither ignore scientific developments in this area nor get too concerned. We can affirm that God created the world—which answers the question 'Why?'

Many scientists who dispute the means of the formation of the universe, are still concerned to affirm that it has both significance and purpose. Many affirm a belief in a personal God.

They would say:

▶ To believe in the creator who reveals himself in both nature and scripture is to believe that there is no ultimate conflict between the two. Our understanding of both is incomplete and fitting them both together may have to wait until we can ask the author of both face to face.

Today scientists are less confident that they have all the answers.

A greater humility recognizes that other disciplines such as theology and philosophy are necessary to provide full answers to the questions of our origins.

Science alone cannot be trusted. Careful evaluation is needed as to what is right and wrong, both in what it takes for granted and the conclusions that it reaches.

Science is not able to adequately explain other dimensions of life. In particular, it can offer no foundation for:

▶ ethics

▶ aesthetics—beauty, style, art

▶ relationships—love and bonding

Many have concluded, with Archbishop Ussher, that the generations and chronological details of Genesis mean that the act of creation took place in 4004BC.

But science hotly disagrees.

Creationists—those who do not believe in evolution between species—agree that much geological and biological data infers that the world is much older. However, they argue that just as the first trees created would already have rings in the trunk to indicate their age, so God could have created rocks in 4004BC which possessed an apparent age of 3,000 million years.

Similarly, fossils could be the product of a creator, not the residual remains of earlier organisms which predate 4004BC.

Creationists reject the verdict of geologists that

the earth is 4.6 billion years old. Not all creationists are committed to the precise date of creation. But they do believe the earth is 'young'. It is argued that:

▶ The rate of decay of the earth's magnetic field indicates a maximum age of about ten thousand years.

▶ The rate at which the sun is shrinking, and the influx of uranium in the oceans of the world indicate an age of less than a million years.

▶ The build-up of radiocarbon in the atmosphere is claimed to demand a date for creation within the last ten thousand years.

▶ Human histories only go back about four thousand years.

▶ It is only by ignoring the possibility of there having been a special act of creation that contemporary theories have become popularly accepted, and many of the methods employed to 'prove' the age of the earth can be demonstrated to be unreliable.

The Gap Theory

This concept was popularized by the Scottish theologian, Thomas Chalmers, during the nineteenth century. According to this theory, the six days of creation were days of reconstruction.

He senses a mysterious gap lies between the first and second verses of Genesis 1. He suggested that:

▶ A proper translation would read: 'and the earth *became* without form and void'.

▶ Elsewhere in scripture this expression designates the effect of destruction (Isaiah 34:11; Jeremiah 4:23), so a terrible catastrophe must have occurred.

▶ The presence of darkness is the symbol of evil, so clearly wickedness came into the world.

This passage therefore refers to the moment when Satan fell from grace (Isaiah 14:3–23; Ezekiel 28:11–19).

The death of animals, presumably also the dinosaurs, preceded the appearance of humankind on earth. This devastation swept everything away and God therefore took six days reconstructing the complete creation in which we now live.

This hypothesis lacks evidence but does provide a convenient explanation when responding to the onslaught of scientific criticism.

The Framework Theory

This was first suggested by Augustine, and has become popular in modern times. It argues that:

▶ The week of creation is a literary and artistic arrangement designed to explain *how* creation is related to God. It offers an explanation of how the sabbath emerged and its significance for humankind.

The author of Genesis is not intending to concentrate on an exact chronology of origins but uses the Ancient Near-Eastern pattern of six-plus-one. By this means he can emphasize the importance of the sabbath and the actuality of creation.

The events concerned actually took place, but Genesis 1 is intended to be a framework for

---

KEY POINT

Of 'determination'— a fixed mechanical universe, the product of a rigid process of cause and effect: 'God is reduced to a mere archivist turning the pages of a cosmic history book already written.'
ILYA PRIGOGINE, 'THE REDISCOVERY OF TIME' IN SARA NASH, EDITOR, *SCIENCE AND COMPLEXITY*, LONDON, 1985

KEY POINT

'You created something and that something out of nothing. You made heaven and earth, not out of yourself, for then they would have been equal to your Only-begotten, and through this equal also to you.'
AUGUSTINE, *CONFESSIONS*

'Through my scientific work I have come to believe more and more strongly that the physical universe is put together with an ingenuity so astonishing that I cannot accept it merely as a brute fact. There must, it seems to me, be a deeper level of explanation. Whether one wishes to call that deeper level "God" is a matter of taste and definition.'
PAUL DAVIES, *THE MIND OF GOD*, SIMON AND SCHUSTER, 1992

'To create is to bring a thing into existence without any previous material at all to work on.'
THOMAS AQUINAS

'For most of the time the universe has existed there has been neither man nor woman. We occupy just a tiny speck of space-time on one out of millions of planets. This makes me feel very humble. On the other hand it has taken an immense journey through time to produce us. God is the Master Mind who planned this great journey: that makes us something special.'
PROFESSOR COLIN HUMPHREYS

theology, not for science.

▶ This chapter is designed to reassert the truth of God's supremacy and creatorship against the claims of worshippers of chaos, sun, stars or any other created things. The effect on sun-worshippers in neighbouring territories, when hearing that the sun was only created on the fourth day, can be easily imagined.

This theory in no way denies the historical truth of the events it records. While the events did occur they are told in a theological, rather than a scientific, form.

Supporters of this idea would readily affirm that to attempt to use Genesis chapters 1–3 in order to derive technical scientific detail or a chronological order of events would be to misuse the passage. It would be a fruitless endeavour to acquire information that it was never intended to supply.

Putting it All Together

It is important to recognize that each of these theories is supported by a number of sincere evangelical Christians.

There is always the danger that one viewpoint will accuse the others of denying scripture, or deliberately destroying their integrity by ignoring current discoveries. In fact no single theory can be proved, beyond all doubt, to be correct.

Many scientists agree that it is a false assumption to say that because we now think we know what causes creation we can exclude God from it. It is possible to describe a painting in two entirely different ways:

▶ in terms of the chemicals that make up the paint and canvas

▶ the artist's technique and design

Both descriptions are true, but are totally different in the way that they relate to the creator.

The Bible and Science

There are ways to picture the relationship between the Bible and science.

Concordism: This stresses—with amazement—the harmony which exists between the Genesis accounts of creation and accepted scientific theories.

Anti-scientism: This focuses on the disagreements between these two disciplines and argues the need to build a substitute science of creationism to replace current scientific ideas.

Fideism: This separates the world of faith from issues of science. Scripture, it argues, teaches religious truth, science offers its physical counterpart. The two should be viewed as counterparts rather than opponents.

God the Creator

Scripture firmly maintains that this world is not a cosmic accident but the product of the activities of a divine creator.

The Bible maintains that:

▶ God is the maker of heaven and earth (Psalm 115:15; 121:2; 124:8; 134:3; 146:6; Acts 14:15).

▶ God alone laid the foundations of the earth (Psalm 102:25; 104:5).

▶ God formed the universe at his command (Hebrews 11:3).

▶ God spread out the skies above the earth (Job 26:7; Genesis 1:7–8).

▶ God is the maker of all things (Jeremiah 10:16; 51:19).

▶ God made the stars (Genesis 1:16; Nehemiah 9:6; Job 9:9).

▶ God created humankind (Genesis 1:26; 2:7; Deuteronomy 4:32; Job 33:4; Proverbs 22:2; Isaiah 51:13; Acts 17:28).

Scripture affirms that in the beginning God created both the heavens and the earth, along with everything which they contained.

Therefore creation is the energy of God's will. It is not just the energy of nature which has produced this world. (Isaiah 40:28; 45:12; 48:13; Acts 4:24; 7:50).

What God Created

God created this world out of chaos, not out of readily available raw materials (Genesis 1:2).

A traditional idea, which was popular in the early church, stated that God created the world out of nothing. This would make it only a sham world which would eventually dissolve again into nothingness. This is *not* stated in the Bible. The nearest specific statement to this view comes only in the Apocrypha.

'Look upon the heaven and the earth and all there is therein, and consider that God made them out of things that 'were not'; and so was mankind made likewise' (2 Maccabees 7:28).

The Latin Vulgate version translates 'were not' as '*ex nihilo*'. This idea originated in Greek philosophy and was repeated by the Shepherd of Hermes, Justin Martyr, Irenaeus and Athanasius.

This whole idea continued until the Reformation and has become popularized again by modern theologians like Paul Tillich.

Scripture affirms that God created by his Word (Psalm 33:6, 9; Hebrews 11:3).

▶ In Genesis 1 every deed of creation is accomplished by his creative Word. God's will is spoken, and with its proclamation the deed is done.

▶ The emphasis of the New Testament is on a Word through whom this world came into being. That Word in creation is Jesus (John 1:1–3; 1 Corinthians 8:6; Colossians 1:16; Hebrews 1:2).

Any understanding of God's creation must begin

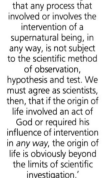

KEY POINT

KEY POINT

with an emphasis on the one who created—and how.

▶ *God the Father used his Son in creation.* So it is wrong to separate the activities of the Father in creation and the Son in giving his life to rescue it.

▶ *God did not merely bring about this world from nothing and then consign it one day to return to nothingness.* It will be replaced by a new heaven and a new earth similarly created by God.

▶ *God continues to hold this world in being,* therefore he is still concerned with his creation (Hebrews 1:3; Luke 12:22–28). He has not abandoned the world, but delegated responsibility for it to humanity (Genesis 2:15–19; 3:17–19). He will continue to send the rain but mankind must cultivate the earth responsibly.

▶ *God confirmed that his creation was good* (Genesis 1:4, 10, 12, 18, 21, 25, 31). He did not reject it after the fall—it was spoilt but not totally ruined.

The Quality of Creation

Arguments over how God created have tended to turn our eyes away from the central truths of the Bible's account of creation.

The emphasis of the creation story is on the God who created and the repeated confirmation that his creation was good (Genesis 1:4, 10, 12, 18, 21, 25). The conclusion is a simple statement that it was 'very good' (Genesis 1:31).

▶ The light . . . was good (v. 4)

▶ Land and seas . . . were good (v. 10)

▶ Vegetation . . . was good (v. 12)

▶ Sun, moon and stars . . . were good (v. 18)

▶ Marine life . . . was good (v. 21)

▶ Animals . . . were good (v. 25)

▶ All he made . . . was *very* good (v. 31)

Today there are sections of the New Age movement which proclaim devotion to 'Mother Earth'. However, the apostle Paul warned against the danger of worshipping the creature at the expense of the creator (Romans 1:25).

Even a quick glance at what God has made—and how good it is—should cause us to worship *him*, not it.

Creation therefore bears witness to God's power and love, as well as to his ability to sustain life. Indeed his creation bears testimony to these attributes (Psalm 50:6; 66:1–3; Acts 14:17; 17:27).

The Diversity of Creation

God's creation is distinguished by its diversity.

Only with the rise of modern science have we begun to appreciate the enormous variety of all that God has made (Genesis 1:20, 24; Psalm 104:24–25).

▶ A single tree in the Amazon rain forest has been found to host 43 different species of ant

▶ A total of 1,700,000 species of all kinds have been identified in tropical rain forests. It is estimated that 30,000,000 remain to be identified.

▶ A single spadeful of ordinary British garden soil teems with a huge range of minute life forms.

▶ In 1950 the island of Madagascar had 12,000 species of plant and 190,000 species of animal—60 per cent unique to the island. Sadly over 100,000 have since disappeared.

The earth still shouts out the awesome glory of its maker (Psalm 19:1–2).

This incredible biological diversity is expressed in literally millions of different species that are related by intricate webs of mutual interdependence.

The modern science of ecology investigates the profound interrelationships between species.

The Continuity of Creation

Scripture declares that creation is God's handiwork.

The greatest of God's achievements was not his creation of humankind. It was the moment of completion—when he finished the work of creation—and rested on the seventh day (Genesis 2:2–3).

God did not rest because he was tired but because he celebrated the task that was now over. He declared himself very pleased with what he had made (Genesis 1:31). The sabbath was therefore also to be a time of celebration (Exodus 31:15–17). The day of worship and thanking God comes from the seventh day when God also rested.

God is not finished with his world.

The bird and animal kingdoms rely upon him for provision of their food (Psalm 104:14–28; Luke 12:24).

Everything within creation depends upon the sustaining power of its creator (Genesis 7:15, 22; Psalm 136:25; Ecclesiastes 3:19–21; Colossians 1:17; Hebrews 1:3).

God is still participating in his world. This sense of God's involvement in both heaven and earth is picturesquely described in the powerful language of God to Job:

'Have you ever given orders to the morning, or shown the dawn its place?' (Job 38:12)

Nor is this just one-way traffic.

It is the duty of all created things to serve and praise their creator.

This is as it should be (Psalm 119:91; 148:7–13; Revelation 5:13). For a God who is still intimately involved in his world deserves the praises of his creation.

God and Ecology

The Garden

God did not decide to make humankind because he was lonely.

When God declared 'Let us make man' (Genesis 1:26) the use of the plural is not simply an illustration of the royal 'we'. The whole Trinity of Father, Son and Holy Spirit was involved in the work of creation (Psalm 104:30; Colossians 1:15–20).

KEY POINT

KEY POINT

KEY POINT

KEY POINT

God is not dependent upon his creation. The created order is the product of the activity of all three persons of the Trinity.

God did not create humankind purely for their own benefit.

God's creation is good even where it is independent of human beings (Job 38:25–27).

God created humankind because he had a job for us to do.

There is not a strong biblical basis to see ourselves as 'stewards'. To consider ourselves as such implies that God's creation is merely a resource to be *used* by us.

Rather, the biblical picture is one of us being caretakers. Genesis 2:15 says, 'The Lord God took the man and put him in the Garden of Eden to work at it and take care of it.' The words 'work' and 'care' are powerful here:

▶ *Work*, Hebrew *abad* is not work for man's sake but to serve, till and keep for the earth's own sake.

▶ *Care*, Hebrew *shamar* means to protect, guard or hedge about.

God also instructed man and woman to 'fill the earth and subdue it. Rule over … every living creature' (Genesis 1:28).

This verse expresses the superiority of human beings over the rest of the created order in the strongest possible terms. In particular, the two verbs used—'rule' and 'subdue'—possess powerful meanings:

▶ *Rule over*, Hebrew *radah*: tread the winepress, prevail against, have dominion over, reign over.

▶ *Subdue*, Hebrew *kabash*: conquer, bring into bondage, tread down, molest or even rape.

This means that when Genesis 1:28 is understood in the context of Genesis 2:15 a clear picture emerges. Our task of dominion over the created order is to take care of creation. We are to act as the servants of the creator who has appointed us to our task.

Thus, 'creation-care' is a more biblical way to describe our relationship to the non-human creation than 'responsible stewardship'.

Human beings represent the crowning-glory of God's creation.

▶ Made in the image of God (Genesis 1:27)

▶ Entrusted with responsibility (Genesis 2:15)

▶ Supplied with food from the rest of creation (Genesis 1:29, 30; 2:9; Psalm 65:9; Ecclesiastes 3:11–13)

▶ Given raw materials for use (Genesis 2:12; 4:17–22)

▶ Instructed to be fruitful and multiply (Genesis 1:28)

▶ Designed to rule (Genesis 1:28)

▶ Only slightly inferior to heavenly beings (Psalm 8:3–9)

Scripture teaches that privilege always involves responsibility. Given the privileges of being succoured and supported by what God has created, we are also responsible to look after it.

History shows how guilty we have been in failing to live up to that responsibility. Indeed many modern writers claim that much environmental mismanagement is the direct result of a Judaeo-Christian attitude of arrogance towards creation.

It is wrong to imagine that the world of the Garden of Eden was one for rest and relaxation.

The true biblical picture is of a situation where man must work to preserve his environment.

This task was to be a partnership between human beings and their maker—with every resource available to assist them. The job included:

▶ The naming of both birds and animals (Genesis 2:19–20)

▶ Working the land and protecting it from the ravages of natural forces

The guarantee of success lay in the continuance of a wholesome relationship with the creator. However, the rebellion in the garden—the fall—changed all that.

The Fall

The Bible shows a direct link between human rebellion against God and the status of planet earth.

When man and woman disobeyed God they denied their status as the creator's representatives on earth. The result of the fall was alienation and corruption. In one act of rebellion:

▶ They destroyed the tranquillity and completeness of their relationship with God (Genesis 3:24)

▶ They lost the garden (Genesis 3:23)

▶ Harmony was lost (Genesis 3:15)

▶ Personal pain—especially in childbirth—resulted (Genesis 3:16)

The effect of the fall went beyond human beings. The earth was affected as well. From now on:

▶ There would be difficulties in food production and the balance of nature was profoundly disturbed (Genesis 3:18)

▶ Adam faced a life of patient toil and the ground was cursed (Genesis 3:17)

The consequence of human sin and the welfare of the earth are related (Deuteronomy 28:1–4, 15–18; Hosea 4:1–3).

This means that:

▶ The earth's barrenness is not only due to bad land management or the over-exploitation of its natural resources. It is also directly linked to God's necessary judgment on human sin.

This same relationship between humankind and the creation is illustrated by God's words to Cain, following his murder of his brother Abel: 'When you work the ground, it will no longer yield its crops for you. You will be a restless wanderer on the earth' (Genesis 3:12).

Thus, this act did not go unpunished—but a new state of alienation between human beings and their land was emphasized.

The Land

Part of Israel's special relationship with God lay in their taking possession of the land he gave them. This was not a barren desert but 'a land flowing with milk and honey' (Exodus 3:8).

KEY POINT

The Promised Land was therefore a divine gift to a fallen people.

It was a land that was a temporary gift. Israel inhabited a land it did not create.

▶ God had given Israel the land (Deuteronomy 8:10), but only for a limited period.

▶ God remained the landlord. Israel was only the tenant (Leviticus 25:23; Deuteronomy 10:14).

▶ The land was never to belong to them unconditionally (Deuteronomy 6:10–13; 8:11–20), because the earth belongs to the Lord (Exodus 15:13–17; 1 Chronicles 29:14; Psalm 24:1–2).

Israel was often warned that they must not duplicate the actions of the Canaanites who were their predecessors in the land. The Canaanites had forfeited the territory by their wickedness (Deuteronomy 9:5). If Israel obeyed God then the land would be blessed by him (Deuteronomy 11:13–15).

It was a land God cared for. Moses emphasised this point (Deuteronomy 11:12). We need to be similarly reminded today that God still cares for his creation. Indeed he has promised that one day he will repair and restore it to its former glory (Romans 8:20–21).

KEY POINT

Undergirding all God's dealings with his people was the fact that he gave the land as part of his special commitment to Israel.

Possession of the land involved its responsible care, and faithfulness to God. Israel faced a choice: to live obediently and receive prosperity; to rebel against God and face ruin. This would include a polluted and infertile land (Deuteronomy 28).

This is not religious theory. It is about a successful lifestyle through fellowship with the creator.

The rules of tenancy

It was a land with conditions of tenancy. The Jews devised a kind of 'steward's manual' which included a set of legal requirements of conduct for the people. Many of these rules are found in the 'halakhic sources', a block of traditional Jewish legal material.

Wanton destruction of ecological resources was condemned. For example, when laying siege to a city, fruit trees were to be protected (Deuteronomy 20:19–20).

The Rabbis extended this principle to include:

▶ overgrazing

▶ bloodsports

▶ pollution of air and water

▶ wastage of mineral resources

▶ extinction of species

▶ destruction of cultivated plant varieties

▶ the overkilling of animals

These prohibitions applied equally to personal

property and the property of a neighbour.
Inhumane treatment of animals was forbidden.

▶ The taking of a mother bird from its nest (Deuteronomy 22:6–7)

▶ A muzzled ox treading corn (Deuteronomy 25:4)

▶ The removal of an animal from its mother before it was seven days old (Leviticus 22:27)

▶ Ploughing with an ox and a donkey yoked together (Deuteronomy 22:10)

Lack of human restraint was discouraged. A number of practical guidelines for land management were introduced. These included:

▶ Proper care of animals (Proverbs 27:23–27)

▶ Allowance for the needs of neighbours and their herds (Leviticus 23:22)

The tithe. This law demanded that one-tenth of all flocks, herds and crops were to be dedicated to God, because everything ultimately belonged to him (Leviticus 27:30–33; Deuteronomy 12:5–18; 14:22–29).

The tithe represented an act of thanksgiving from the people and provided for the disadvantaged. Widows, orphans, Levites and the homeless all received help from a food reserve which built up every three years.

The law of gleaning. This form of land management produced a sharing of resources with the poor and homeless (Leviticus 19:9–10; Deuteronomy 24:19–21). All produce and crops had a percentage left over for collection by those in need. One by-product of areas spared from cultivation was to produce useful refuges for local wildlife.

The sabbath was established as a day of rest (Exodus 20:10).

This provided relaxation, not only for the people but also for nature and domesticated animals.

The sabbatical year was established. For one year in seven the land had to lie fallow.

▶ No fields were to be sown or vineyards pruned and harvested (Leviticus 25:3–7).

▶ Storage was permitted, but only until wild animals could no longer find food for themselves in the fields. After that man had to take care of them.

This reminder of God's provision, emphasized the need not to exploit nature for greed and profit, and that God was the ultimate owner of the land.

The Year of Jubilee was established. Every fiftieth year was to be a special time of justice when debts were forgiven and land was returned to its former owner. This included neither sowing nor reaping.

Ecological need and the requirements of justice were both met in this special year. The land received rest, and the people found freedom and restoration of their rights and property.

Jesus and the Natural World

There were many ways in which Jesus expressed his relationship with the natural world.

▶ He affirmed the goodness of creation (Matthew 6:26; 10:29).

▶ He expressed care for something as insignificant as a sparrow (Luke 12:6–7) as an example of his

Repeated famines in Ethiopia have often been understood as being due to a failure of the rains. But 'it is a naïve analysis which places the blame on a God who "turned off the tap". This must be replaced by an analysis which also takes into account the gross political and economic mismanagement of the country involved.

'Even if there is less rain than in the past—and it is not clear that this is the case—the mass destruction of ground-cover due to decades of war in the main famine region must be at least partially responsible.

'Some account must be taken of the wholesale conscription of young men and women into the armies, on both sides of the battle-front, so that the farms are without labourers.

'There must be some significance in the fact that Ethiopia has the largest standing army in black Africa spending more than 60% of its gross national product on weapons despite being the poorest nation in the world.'

ADAPTED FROM PETER COTTERELL'S, *MISSION AND MEANINGLESSNESS*, SPCK, 1991

'All of creation reflects God's nature but only humanity is created after his image.'

STEVE CHILCRAFT

total care.

▶ He became flesh and blood totally identifying not just with the human race but the whole of creation. To many brought up in the Greek culture of the day, this was amazing as they believed that only the spirit was pure—the flesh and the whole material world was evil. Jesus contradicted this demonstrating that the material world was intrinsically good.

▶ He used many illustrations from the created order as the background to his parables.

▶ His miracles were changes to the material world—both healing of sick bodies, and the nature miracles, which included restoring order to the sea and meeting hunger. His care extended to more than the spirit alone.

▶ He exercised authority over the natural world (Matthew 8:23–27) in the same way as the creator himself.

▶ His physical death was the means of our salvation (Colossians 1:20). To save humankind—who are both physical and spiritual—and give them a new body (1 Corinthians 15:52) the process of redemption had to involve both dimensions.

▶ He came to re-introduce the principles of God's kingdom. By so doing he re-asserted God's rule over a corrupted creation and through his death on the cross reversed the alienation introduced at the fall.

The New Testament

KEY POINT

The relationship between humankind and God's creation is not limited to the Jews, the Promised Land and the Old Testament.

The New Testament paints a comprehensive picture. Paul affirmed the goodness of creation (1 Timothy 4:4), in the same manner as did Jesus (Matthew 6:26; 10:29).

Environmental issues were not seen as being of great importance in the Roman Empire. But the apostle Paul strongly stated the wider, creation-embracing, implications of the cross (Colossians 1:15–23).

KEY POINT

If it is sin that is at the heart of a damaged environment, on a cross there sprang hope for a new creation.

Some Christians see concerns about the environment as irrelevant because the world is soon to end. They see scripture as predicting the end of the created order (Hebrews 1:10–12; 2 Peter 3:10–13). But, in each case there immediately follows the suggestion of the transformation of creation.

The Bible also reveals the ultimate hope of a new heaven and a new earth (Revelation 21:1–5). This echoes the great hope expressed by Paul who recognized that creation:

▶ Was subjected by God to frustration (Romans 8:20)

▶ Will one day be set free from corruption (Romans 8:21)

▶ Will finally be restored to share our liberty (Romans 8:21)

He adds:

▶ In the meantime creation itself 'waits in eager expectation for the sons of God to be revealed' (Romans 8:19)

▶ We ourselves are already part of a new creation (2 Corinthians 5:17)

▶ We are renewed after the image of Christ himself (2 Corinthians 3:10) to share ultimate glory in his environment, for eternity.

▶ In his death Jesus reconciled *all things* to himself (Colossians 1:20). We do not know all that one day will be revealed—but there remains hope for God's world.

The State of the Planet

Any assessment of the current state of the planet needs to focus on four major areas:

▶ The destruction of ecosystems

▶ Pollution

▶ Population growth

▶ Resource depletion

However, to do so means entering a world with its own vocabulary. So we begin with some definitions.

Understanding the Words

Ecosystems: An interacting system of plants, animals and micro-organisms together with their physical environment.

Global-ecosystem: All the world's individual, interlocking ecosystems.

Bio-diversity: The full range of different plant varieties and animal species.

Global warming: The slow but constant rise in the mean temperature of the earth (estimated at 0.7–1.7° C higher by 2025 and 2–5° C higher by 2100 at current rates). This is due to a combination of increased radiation from the sun, the 'greenhouse effect' and the thinning of the ozone layer.

Greenhouse effect: The trapping of heat, radiated back by the earth after warming by the sun, by the gases in the atmosphere—like a garden greenhouse. For the survival of life it is essential to keep an average temperature of 15° C instead of an estimated 18° C.

Ozone layer: Ozone is a form of oxygen formed at ground level by naturally occurring chemical reactions mainly at the equator. It rises to the upper atmosphere (the stratosphere) and is distributed by winds to form a layer surrounding the planet. It provides essential protection from the sun's ultra-violet rays.

CFCs: Chlorofluorocarbons and halons, gases from refrigerators, aerosols, foam, chemical processes and fire extinguishers, which are highly durable and rise to the stratosphere. Here, the ultra-violet rays cause a chemical reaction leading to the formation of chlorine molecules which attack and destroy ozone. This primarily occurs where the temperature is lowest—causing the seasonal 'holes' in the ozone layer over both the Arctic and the Antarctic.

'*I* am convinced that the facts of science declare special creation to be the only logical and rational explanation of origins. "In the beginning God created . . ." is still the most up-to-date statement that can be made about our origins.'
DR D.T. GISH

'*H*eaven is the perfect environment.'
CLIVE CALVER

'*I*t might have been possible, we could say, before Christ rose from the dead, for someone to wonder whether creation was a lost cause . . . Yes. Before God raised Jesus from the dead, the hope that we call "gnostic", the hope for redemption *from* creation rather than for the redemption of creation, might have appeared to be the only possible hope.'
OLIVER O'DONOVAN

'*I*n Jesus Christ, God has restored the human pattern intended at the original creation.'
JÜRGEN MOLTMANN

'[*E*cology] is an academic discipline . . . Environmentalism is a popular response to the perceived threat to the natural environment . . . relatively few . . . active in the environmentalist movement [are] trained ecologists.'
LAURENCE OSBORN

Acid rain: Rain water which washes out gases (sulphur dioxide and oxides of nitrogen), which are in the atmosphere primarily due to the burning of fossil fuels, turning them into sulphuric acid and nitric acid.

The Destruction of Ecosystems

God put a system of checks and balances within nature—which scientists call ecosystems.

The loss of one element, plant or animal, has a knock-on effect. Certain insects depend on certain plants for their survival. Destroy the plant and the insects will also die out. It may not stop there.

Nature 'red in tooth and claw' means for example:

▶ An insect is part of the diet of a species of bird.

▶ If the bird cannot find its food it will fly elsewhere—to adapt or die.

▶ The bird may settle in another area where it 'steals' the food of a weaker species which would perish as a result.

▶ That species of bird may have been essential to control a certain pest which spreads disease amongst animals and humans.

▶ Man's response is to spray toxic chemicals throughout the area which not only kill the pest but other plants and insects as well.

▶ And so the process continues.

We should not be surprised. The Bible warns: 'A man reaps what he sows' (Galatians 6:7). Science now helps us understand how profound the principle is.

Generally, there is a level of loss of the population of any species which can be replaced naturally. Thus there is a level at which fishing, forestry and farming—which involve using up the earth's resources—are not harmful to the ecosystem as a whole.

KEY POINT

However, greed and lack of controls can easily destroy the fragile balance.

For example:

▶ 90 million tonnes of fish are caught each year. In 1958 it was only 30 million tonnes.

▶ In 1972 there were an estimated 2 million African elephants. Today only 600,000 survive.

▶ One third of the world's tropical rainforest has been destroyed. An extra 170,000 square kilometres have gone in the last year. It now covers only 7 per cent of the earth's total surface area.

▶ An estimated 625 million people live in areas (mainly cities) where the air is polluted.

▶ The largest forest in the Northern hemisphere, in Siberia, is threatened by unrestricted development to ease Russia's chronic financial problems.

▶ 50 per cent of all the world's plant and animal species live in the forests.

▶ Britain has lost 97 per cent of its wildflower meadows and 190,000 miles of hedgerows.

▶ 325–375 million tonnes of hazardous waste are created each year.

Past and present examples of the destructive effect humankind has had on the rest of nature include such examples as:

▶ The dodo

▶ The poaching of ivory with its destruction of the African elephant

▶ The size of fishing nets used by trawlers in the North Sea, overfishing of young fish and depletion of stocks

▶ The Winchester by-pass

▶ The indiscriminate felling of trees in North Africa and Arabia since 5000BC resulted in rapidly expanding deserts

▶ The burning of the Brazilian rain forest

▶ The pollution of the River Thames in the nineteenth and twentieth centuries which killed off the fish. Now salmon again swim up the river as its quality has been improved

▶ Intense farming in sub-Saharan Africa—including Burkina Faso—is eroding the topsoil and spreading the desert

The rate of loss of species has increased alarmingly and will continue to do so if action is not taken.

KEY POINT

It will be a tragedy if all that future generations could experience of the wonders of creation were scratched video images of highly-coloured parrots or exotic orchids filmed for twentieth-century television.

Jesus cares for the common or garden sparrow (Luke 12:6–7). It is implied that he cares for all creatures.

The earth belongs to God and *everything* in it

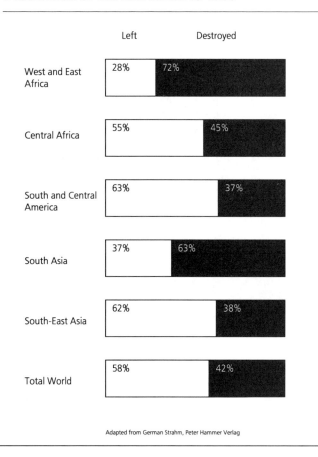

Destruction of the rain forest to 1985

	Left	Destroyed
West and East Africa	28%	72%
Central Africa	55%	45%
South and Central America	63%	37%
South Asia	37%	63%
South-East Asia	62%	38%
Total World	58%	42%

Adapted from German Strahm, Peter Hammer Verlag

(Psalm 24:1; 104:24). All of creation belongs to him. We have no right to destroy his property without good reason.

He watches over the earth (Deuteronomy 11:11–12; Psalm 104:24–32) with fatherly concern.

All of creation is a form of praise to God (Psalm 148). Destroying any part of this robs God of his due honour. Its very diversity reflects his greatness, like a full orchestra necessary to do justice to a symphony. If any instrument is missing the trained ear will notice.

Pollution

Once, 'Keep Britain Tidy' was no more than a call to make things look nice. Now it has become a matter of life and death.

It now stands as a serious issue alongside 'global warming', 'acid rain' and the 'greenhouse effect'.

KEY POINT

The seriousness of the pollution issue has taken many years to emerge but is now widely felt to be the most immediate threat to our environmental future.

Today, our industrialized society produces vast amounts of waste—in seemingly ever-increasing quantities. The list is endless:

▶ Commercial packaging of groceries and products

▶ Agricultural waste from intensive farming

▶ Insecticides and fertilizers

▶ Industrial waste

▶ Slag heaps

▶ Toxic chemicals and smoke

In addition to 'normal' pollution, serious accidents can occur. For example, at Seveso, Italy in 1976. Large amounts of dioxin—a highly poisonous and durable chemical—were released into the atmosphere, leaving the immediate area uninhabitable.

While at Bhopal, Northern India in 1984, 30 tons of another poisonous gas escaped, killing 3,500 people, leaving 300,000 people with long-term health problems through inhaling the poison, and destroying an unquantified number of animals and birds.

The use of highly dangerous chemicals to produce products (which may or may not be dangerous themselves) and the frequent production of equally dangerous by-products is generally highly controlled. No system can be totally safe and occasionally incidents happen which destroy man, beast and land alike.

Global warming

This is due to the greenhouse effect caused by pollution of the lower atmosphere by CO_2 and other gases. This will lead to a gradual melting of the ice-caps, raising world sea levels. The result may be:

▶ Certain Pacific island states disappearing altogether

▶ Much of Bangladesh's coastal area, home for tens of millions of people, being flooded permanently

▶ Transformed coastlines in East Anglia and the Netherlands

Pollution on a grand scale

1976	Seveso, Italy	Chemical plant explodes. Area polluted. 40% increase in local birth defects.
1978	Amoco Cadiz, Brittany, France	Supertanker runs aground. Releases 220,000 tons of crude oil. Pollutes 130 miles of coast.
1978	Love Canal, NY, USA	Town declared 'toxic ghost town' after leaking chemical drums buried in 1940s–50s polluted water supply.
1979	Three Mile Island, Pennsylvania, USA	Nuclear reactor accident. Core overheats with small discharge of gas. Plant contaminated and crippled. Major pollution of area narrowly avoided.
1984	Bhopal, Madhya Pradesh, India	Union Carbide pesticide factory accident. 30 tons of toxic gas escapes. 3,500 local people die. 200,000 injured.
1986	Chernobyl, Ukraine	Nuclear reactor overheats and large amount of radioactivity escapes. 30 die. Thousands nearby affected and likely to suffer resulting cancers. Pollution spreads across Europe. Sheep slaughtered in Wales and Lake District.
1989	Exxon Valdez, Prince William Sound, Alaska, USA	Supertanker runs aground. 11,000,000 gallons of oil escape. Arctic landscape and wildlife badly polluted.
1991	Kuwait	Deliberate spill of oil into the Gulf by Iraqi troops is biggest in history. Pollutes vast area. Followed by igniting of oil wells releasing vast dense clouds of smoke into atmosphere. Limited long-term damage. (More pollution occurs in the normal discharge of tankers into Gulf than through the Iraqis' sabotage!)

Sadly, more will follow.

▶ Deserts developing in Africa and elsewhere as rain is reduced there while rainfall increases elsewhere

Acid rain

This was first identified in 1852 following a study 'On the air and rain of Manchester'. Until recently it was thought that this was particularly due to the gases released by power stations, vehicles and other industrial processes involving the burning of fossil fuels.

New research has cast doubt on the significance of this cause—as vast amounts of these gases occur naturally in the atmosphere probably from the result of plankton in the oceans. It is not clear at present if this is an issue that we can do much about.

On all these subjects our knowledge is incomplete. Some of the world's most powerful governments have used this as a reason or excuse for doing little or nothing.

Often short-term interests—financial, increased unemployment, disruption of lifestyle, business interests and electoral prospects—have prevailed over longer-term concerns.

continued on page 20

Environmental problems of Two-Thirds World nations

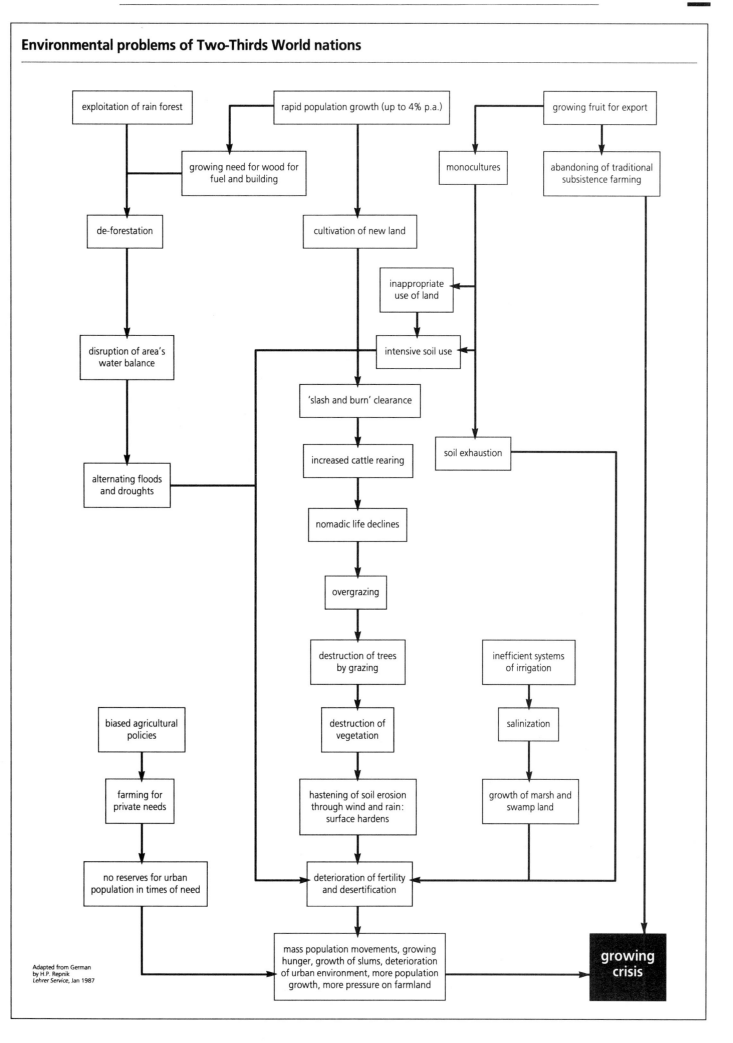

Adapted from German
by H.P. Repnik
Lehrer Service, Jan 1987

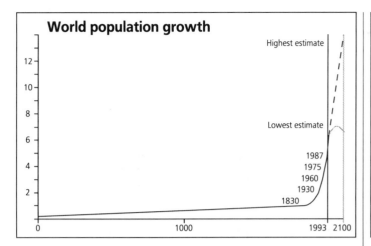

World population growth

Highest estimate

Lowest estimate

1987
1975
1960
1930
1830

World population estimates by continent

	1900	2000
Africa	661,000,000	884,000,000
Asia	3,116,000,000	3,718,000,000
N America	278,000,000	298,000,000
S & C America	447,000,000	535,000,000
Europe & CIS	792,000,000	827,000,000
Oceania	27,000,000	31,000,000
Total World	5,321,000,000	6,293,000,000

Adapted from *1990 World Population Data Sheet*, PRB, Washington DC

Population Growth

No one knows how many people our planet can sustain at a reasonable standard of life. Until now there has not been a serious problem.

Figures for world population look like this:

▶ At the time of Christ it is estimated to have been 169 million

▶ It took until 1830 before it rose to 1 billion

▶ By the 1930s it had risen to 2 billion

▶ By the 1960s 3 billion

▶ By 1975 4 billion

▶ By 1987 5 billion

▶ It is currently estimated at around 5.4 billion which may rise to 6.3 billion by the end of the century

From this point estimates vary dramatically. The lowest estimate suggests a ceiling of around 7 billion around 2050 from whence it falls, and the highest suggests around 14 billion in 2100.

Whether the planet can produce enough food to feed these higher estimates is questionable. At present many are starving because of the inequitable distribution of the food produced.

However, even if both production and distribution were totally just and according to need, it is self-evident that a limited land area suitable for food production must have a theoretical maximum number of people it can sustain in good health.

No one knows what this figure is, nor given the existing inequality in the world how many people can be sustained now. The equation is a complex one. More people implies greater productivity as well as greater need of food and other commodities.

Western Europe population levels are evening out and are projected to fall.

KEY POINT

The dramatic growth in population has been in the poorer nations of the Two-Thirds World.

The rapidly increasing population in the Two-Thirds World is subject to some highly political debate. Is unrestricted growth a cause of the economic problems and food shortages in these countries, as Dr George Carey, Archbishop of Canterbury has argued or an effect of poverty as Pope John Paul II responded?

Some right-wing environmentalists put the prime responsibility for the growing environment crisis down to this rapid growth. They suggest that disease and famine be allowed to control population growth in those countries rather than encourage its growth through better health, food and welfare provision!

Controversy even rages over why poor people have big families. Is it because:

▶ They don't know any better

▶ No one gave them contraceptives

▶ They need security in their old age from their family as the state cannot provide it

▶ Those in their culture like big families

▶ It takes a generation of reduced infant mortality before social attitudes catch up with improved conditions of health

It is a complex problem with profound consequences:

▶ The poor will constantly seek to migrate to those nations which are richer

▶ The poor will continually flock to major cities

The Two-Thirds World is now home to most of the world's 'mega-cities' (see box below). As the rural areas are saturated the masses move to the glamorous urban jungles seeking work and wealth. Vast shanty-towns have sprung up as housing for the urban poor. They are distinguished by:

▶ poor housing

▶ overcrowding

World's top 10 cities (population in millions)

1900	1990	2000 (estimated)
London 6.4	Tokyo/Yokohama 23.0	Mexico City 27.6
New York 4.2	Mexico City 21.8	São Paulo 26.0
Paris 3.9	Shanghai 20.1	Tokyo/Yokohama 24.0
Berlin 2.4	New York/N Jersey 18.8	New York 23.0
Chicago 1.7	São Paulo 17.5	Shanghai 23.0
Vienna 1.6	Beijing 17.4	Beijing 20.0
Tokyo 1.4	Bombay 11.8	Rio de Janeiro 19.0
St Petersberg 1.4	Rio de Janeiro 11.7	Bombay 17.0
Philadelphia 1.4	Calcutta 11.7	Calcutta 17.0
Manchester 1.2	Seoul 11.6	Jakarta 17.0

At the start of the twentieth century, six of the world's largest cities were in Europe. Today, there are none. London is now only the eighteenth largest city in the world.

▶ poor nutrition

▶ poor health care

▶ poor sanitation

▶ epidemics of disease

▶ social disruption

▶ high unemployment

▶ political unrest and extremism of left or right

▶ breakdown of traditional patterns of life and families

▶ exploitation—especially of children

▶ drugs

▶ prostitution

▶ AIDS

▶ breakdown of law and order

▶ violence

▶ criminal gangs

All this within eyesight of the office blocks and neon lights of the rich city centres of the world.

The Depletion of Resources

KEY POINT

Such is the insatiable demand for energy and raw materials, that the resources of the earth are fast disappearing.

▶ In Cornwall the tin mines were exhausted a hundred years ago

▶ In South Wales coal mines were closing on the grounds of exhaustion before the 'economic' closures of the 1980s and 90s

▶ North Sea oil has a strictly limited lifespan

▶ Europe has long lost its old forests

Many scientists are worried that we may be at the point where we have taken so much of the earth's resources that the natural process of renewal may in many cases cease to happen.

In the past we have paid little or no attention to the needs of future generations. We have not restrained our exploitation of the earth. The main hopes for the future are:

▶ Fresh discovery of exploitable fuels and minerals in the earth

▶ New technology-based sources of energy not dependent on fossil fuels

▶ Dramatic reduction of demand for energy due to new, more efficient consumption

KEY POINT
It is the rich, developed nations that have consumed so much of the world's resources.

However, much of the world's remaining energy and mineral assets are located in the underdeveloped world.

Two-Thirds World nations have been limited in their ability to develop their own resources—due to their debt to Western governments. The truth is that the developed world and the Two-Thirds World now need each other to survive.

Meanwhile, renewable energy sources seem limited. This means that, for the foreseeable future, new supplies of traditional energy must be found.

Many saw nuclear power as the answer. It has always been expensive but after the Three Mile Island and Chernobyl accidents it is also seen as too dangerous by many. The early nuclear plants were really built for military reasons—commercial energy production was never possible. Newer reactors can provide economic amounts of electricity if the world wants to accept the potential risk to the environment.

At present 31 nations operate 428 nuclear reactors. The future of the industry is in some doubt.

France operates more nuclear power stations than any other European nation, without much national controversy. Proponents and opponents produce vastly different assessments of the risk posed by nuclear power.

Even in the tragic aftermath of Chernobyl, scientists form different conclusions both of the damage actually done and of the possibility of the same thing happening in a modern Western-designed plant.

It is much easier to oppose the nuclear bomb, which can only be destructive, than civil nuclear power. Many environmentalists have mixed feelings. Nuclear power can:

▶ Significantly reduce regular pollution from gas emissions and does not use up fossil fuels but runs the risk of a calamitous accident.

▶ Have an effect on its workforce through exposure to radiation.

▶ Produce large amounts of contaminated material which must be disposed of by reprocessing to make it relatively safe, as at Sellafield in Cumbria, and disposed of in land-fill sites rendering the land unusable for other purposes.

Green facts

A quarter of the world's population live in the developed world and consume:

■ 80% of all energy supplies

■ 86% of metals

■ 34% of food

950 million people are permanently hungry.

An estimated 80,000 people in the Two-Thirds World die unnecessarily every day.

What Must We Do?

Politicians at the Earth Summit in Rio (June 1992) made their own attempts to face the issues of the environment. However, Christians have a unique responsibility to respond and a unique contribution to make.

The Christians' response must include a prophetic call to justice, mutual concern, concerted action and anticipation of the future. The voice of God is needed.

It is easy to feel overwhelmed and powerless in the face of the deluge of information, the scale of the task and the distance from the geographical location of many of the problems.

The writer, Edmund Burke (1729–97) used the

'It is better to light a candle than to curse the darkness.'
CHINESE PROVERB

expression 'little platoons'. This referred to groups doing the little that they can—often making a significant difference, bringing together individuals who want to make a difference who cannot do so alone.

KEY POINT

Acting together, Christians can effect change.

These are just some of the things we ought to be doing:

Getting the Foundations Right

The failure of evangelicals to fully appreciate what the Bible teaches about creation has limited our own response.

In contrast, liberal churchmen, who share many of the same concerns but without the same commitment to scripture, have spoken out with prophetic resonance.

Our understanding of the Bible and knowledge of the creator should be the basis for our actions.

Whose Earth?

'Whose Earth?' was the project of the youth programme of Spring Harvest 1992 in association with Tear Fund. A startling amount was achieved in only six months.

- Over 650 groups registered to be part of the project, receiving a resource pack giving both teaching and ideas for action.

- Tens of thousands of pounds were raised through these activities for Tear Fund's projects in the Two-Thirds World.

- Three thousand people came to 'Join the World in Hyde Park'—the largest ever expression of concern for creation by Christians in Britain.

- A paper on the 'Whose Earth?' project was read to the international WEF/Au Sable Forum in Michigan, USA.

- Christian environmentalists and leaders from five continents were present. Many have written for the resource pack and see 'Whose Earth?' as a pace-setting initiative.

Listening and Learning

Too many Christians have regarded the environment as an issue of minor significance—and failed to make any serious study of the subject.

We must know the facts if we are to respond appropriately and to apply our faith to this area of life.

Churches can appoint someone with a brief to keep the whole church up-to-date and bring the issue before the congregation for prayer, support and action.

Individuals can discover more by reading one or more of the books—amongst the vast number currently available—in the booklist appended. There are also a great many Green magazines on the market—many reflecting specific viewpoints and many by subscription only. There are also many Green organizations to join.

Small Things First

Good habits begin young. Some of the basic social habits we teach children are the same principles that world governments need to practise to address our current problems.

- ▶ 'Pick up your litter'
- ▶ 'Don't waste your food/energy/time'
- ▶ 'Share your sweets'
- ▶ 'Don't pick on those smaller than you'
- ▶ 'Don't be selfish'
- ▶ 'Don't be greedy'
- ▶ 'Tidy up your room'

Apply each of these principles to the planet and it is obvious that they are vital at both the micro-level of our own homes and the macro-level of the world.

If every individual—and group of people—lived consistently by this code there would be a greatly diminished environmental problem!

The role of the church must be to lead by example.

Ethics and the Environment

An understanding of God's creation must go hand in hand with an understanding of God's view of justice.

KEY POINT

This means that a concern for the environment and concern for justice for the poor must go hand in hand. Management of the environment needs an ethical framework to guide it, to regulate our dealings with each other as well as with the animal kingdom and use of natural resources.

Profit is the main motive for business, while power is the motive for governments. Both of these can work against the weak.

The Soviet government in its desire to compete with the Americans during the Cold War exposed many of its citizens to large amounts of radiation through grossly inadequate safety measures to cut costs. In Marxism, as practised, the individual was considered expendable.

The Western World is demanding that Brazil should halt its rapid destruction of the rain forest. Brazil responds that it is being asked to curtail its industrialization and prospect of economic growth—the West must compensate Brazil by a massive aid programme. The West denies responsibility.

'The love of money is the root of all evil' (1 Timothy 6:10, AV)—and a major cause of our current environmental crisis. Responsibility can be traced to selfish Western consumers—who buy without thinking about the origins of the product and its effect on the environment—as well as the governments they elect.

Environmental Concern and Evangelism

In terms of scripture, action for the environment, social concern and preaching the gospel all stem from the same problem—the fall. The remedy for all is in the work of Christ on the cross. The three areas belong together.

God is one. He is creator, redeemer and God of justice all at the same time. This should show through his ambassadors on earth.

Practical involvement in ecology will generate opportunities to speak of what we know about Jesus. Our motivation in working for creation is a response to its creator. But our actions will speak volumes and provoke questions.

At a Spring Harvest 'High Risk' week in Minehead in 1992 a reluctant group of guests were engaged in a 'trash bash' of the local streets as part of an exercise.

An elderly resident confronted two young people with black plastic rubbish sacks picking up discarded cigarette-ends and other unpleasant refuse from outside his front gate. 'What are you doing?' he asked quizzically.

'Well, we're from Spring Harvest,' they replied and went on to explain that as Christians they wanted to do something practical to say 'thank you' to the town that has hosted the event for many years.

Later, over a cup of tea he recounted the incident to a Christian neighbour and confessed, 'It makes you think, doesn't it?'

Green action

A youth group, 'Nutty 200', decided to set up a can collection scheme. They are collecting 2,000 aluminium cans from around the streets and public places of Chichester and will sell them on to a recycler. The proceeds are being passed on to 'Whose Earth?'

Nutty also organized a sponsored clean-up of the local River Lavant. Funds were raised by the number of sacks filled and a press release was sent to the local media.

Members of Nutty involved those outside the church to help. The youth group is part of the Revelation Christian Fellowship which now has a 'Green Task Group'. This prepared and presented teaching materials to all six church congregations. The group has prepared a Green Audit for church members and the church office. And it is helping to organize a major evangelistic 'Creation Celebration' to be held in Chichester.

Green action

Chawn Hill Christian Centre, in partnership with eight other local churches adopted the 'Whose Earth?' initiative.

■ Local churches were encouraged to explore environmental issues and hold an educational 'Environment Day'.

■ Church members were invited to sign the letter of concern to the Prime Minister prior to UNCED.

■ Schools were contacted and a number of assemblies taken using the 'Whose Earth?' theme.

■ Apart from holding an educational 'Green Show', the main activity has been involvement in the local town carnival.

A Green Audit

The best way to begin is to examine how we behave at home, at work and in church. Do we:

▶ conserve energy

▶ recycle waste

▶ buy 'green' products such as lead-free petrol, CFC-free aerosols, cleaning material without bleach, recycled writing paper and so on

▶ share resources with our neighbours

▶ eat modestly

See the special 'Spring Harvest Green Audit for Churches' on page 24. Arrange to use this one Sunday as part of a 'Green emphasis Sunday', complete with Bible teaching, Sunday School activities, bring-and-share lunch with a Two-Thirds World theme, young people's sponsored car-wash for 'Whose Earth?' or similar project and even a 'trash bash' around the church!

Part of the problem is that we all want to be green until there is a price to pay. An audit will help see where we can change our practices. A lot of this is pretty painless, we just need to get on with it.

Taking Political Action

Many of the environmental problems seem so vast we are tempted to opt out as we feel so powerless. Governments, local as well as national, and multinational companies are all conscious of public opinion. Next time there is an environmental issue in the news which you feel strongly about:

▶ Inform the church leadership and ask them to draw it to the attention of the whole church, for both prayer and action.

▶ Write letters to: MPs; local councillors; the Department of the Environment; the Prime Minister; the head of a foreign government concerned (if any); the United Nations (where appropriate); the Archbishop of Canterbury; other religious leaders; the directors of the commercial companies involved; your local newspapers; national newspapers.

▶ Phone your local radio station especially if there is a suitable phone-in programme.

▶ If it is a major long-term issue involving a public company arrange for a group of concerned Christians each to buy a few shares in that company. Together attend the next AGM of the company. Ask through the due processes for a motion discussing your concerns to be put on the agenda. You will be unlikely to win the motion, as the company will probably be able to rely on its institutional investors to crush your initiative. But you may succeed in embarrassing the directors into action. They *hate* bad publicity— the share price could go down!

▶ At election time ask all the candidates for their views on selected ethical and environmental issues. General questions will get general and often meaningless answers. Ask specific questions—preferably publicly—and get specific answers. If elected they will have to stand by any commitment they have made.

▶ If there is a local environmental problem, offer, as a church or youth group, to arrange a clean-up. Talk to the responsible authorities. Contact the local press and radio. Mobilize any professional assistance needed—preferably for free as their contribution to a project for the good of the whole community.

Spring Harvest Green Audit for Churches

Adapted from an original by Peter Stanbridge of Stopsley Baptist Church, Luton

Please answer all questions honestly and anonymously, once per household.

1. Are you a committed Christian?   Yes/No

2. Do you attend church most Sundays (more than half the Sundays in a month)?   Yes/No

3. Please tick **one** of the statements below that best represents your attitude towards the Green issue.

- ☐ I am confused by the Green issue
- ☐ I do not believe everything that scientists tell me
- ☐ I believe it is a front for the 'New Age' movement
- ☐ I believe the issue has been hyped-up by the media
- ☐ There are more important things in life to worry about
- ☐ I believe it distracts Christians from their true priorities in life
- ☐ I am concerned about this issue
- ☐ I believe strongly that we should save the environment
- ☐ The environment is one of my highest priorities

4. Please tick **one** of the statements below that best represents what you think the church's attitude should be with respect to the Green issue:

- ☐ It should not be concerned, because Christ is returning soon anyway
- ☐ It should not waste time and money being 'Green' when there is a world to save and a gospel to preach
- ☐ God is in control and the church should trust in him to look after his earth
- ☐ It should respond to the green issue, but we do not need to worry like non-Christians, because we have a God who will take care of us
- ☐ It should act as much as non-Christians because the environment affects us all
- ☐ It should act positively, because we need to save our environment, and because we have a moral duty to look after God's creation
- ☐ It should see looking after the environment as a very high priority, second only to preaching the gospel and looking after the poor

5. If a particular product is more 'environmentally friendly' than another similar product, how likely would you be to buy the 'environmentally friendly' product? If the product is:

	Always	Most Times	Sometimes	Never
Made from recycled material	☐	☐	☐	☐
Able to be recycled after use	☐	☐	☐	☐
Biodegradable (will rot after use)	☐	☐	☐	☐
Contains no CFCs	☐	☐	☐	☐
Pollutes the atmosphere less	☐	☐	☐	☐
Uses less energy	☐	☐	☐	☐
Contains less packaging	☐	☐	☐	☐
Costs only a little more	☐	☐	☐	☐

Other (please state)

6. Do you recycle any of the following materials?

	Always	Most Times	Sometimes	Never
Paper	☐	☐	☐	☐
Glass	☐	☐	☐	☐
Aluminium	☐	☐	☐	☐
Other metals	☐	☐	☐	☐
Plastics	☐	☐	☐	☐
Motor oil	☐	☐	☐	☐

Other (please state)

7. Why do you not recycle your waste more? (Please tick a maximum of **two** answers.)

- ☐ Too much hassle
- ☐ Always forget
- ☐ Do not know where recycling points are
- ☐ Recycling points too far away
- ☐ Too much waste to recycle
- ☐ Do not believe in it
- ☐ Other reasons (please state)

8. How many cars does your household have?
(Please circle number of private cars.)   0   1   2   3   4   5   Above 5

9. How many cars within your household:

a. Regularly use lead-free petrol?   0   1   2   3   4   5   Above 5
b. Have catalytic converters?   0   1   2   3   4   5   Above 5

10. If a journey can be made on *foot* or by car, when—assuming it is a fine day—would you not use your car?

Length of time of walk	Always	Most Times	Sometimes	Never
0–2 mins	☐	☐	☐	☐
3–4 mins	☐	☐	☐	☐
5–6 mins	☐	☐	☐	☐
7–8 mins	☐	☐	☐	☐
9–10 mins	☐	☐	☐	☐
10 mins +	☐	☐	☐	☐

11. If a journey can be made by bicycle (assuming you own one) or by car, when would you not use your car—assuming it is a fine summer's day?

Length of time by bicycle	Always	Most Times	Sometimes	Never
0–2 mins	☐	☐	☐	☐
3–4 mins	☐	☐	☐	☐
5–9 mins	☐	☐	☐	☐
10–14 mins	☐	☐	☐	☐
15–19 mins	☐	☐	☐	☐
20–29 mins	☐	☐	☐	☐
30 mins +	☐	☐	☐	☐

12. Do you own a bicycle?   Yes/No

13. If you do own a bicycle, have you used it more than once in the last six months?   Yes/No

Other ideas with an environmental dimension:

▶ Redecoration of elderly and disabled people's homes.

▶ Gardening of elderly and disabled people's homes.

▶ A green audit of the shops in the high street. Contact the manager and arrange for two people only to conduct the survey. Publish the results in the local press.

▶ Organize a neighbourhood watch scheme not just for crime but also environmental pollution. In a strong community you can consider sharing DIY and gardening equipment—avoiding unnecessary duplication of rarely-used items.

▶ Ask the local council to declare a 'car-free' day in the town centre. All private cars (except for the infirm and so on) normally used for commuting to work are to be voluntarily left at home. Everyone must walk, cycle or use public transport to get to work and the money saved donated to a charitable project. The 'ban' is only until 9.30am so shoppers are not affected. If well-publicized and portrayed as fun, a significant reduction in traffic can be achieved.

Ideas for Households

A 'green' day in the garden

Set aside a day not just to do the ordinary gardening chores but as a time of discovery and enjoyment.

▶ If the household has children make it a fun time

▶ Invite friends who do not have their own garden to join in

▶ Everyone is to discover something new to them and report back

▶ Talk about what you most enjoy in the garden

▶ Make your own fire for cooking from garden refuse, relegating the barbecue to the shed

▶ Plant some new seeds/plants/shrubs and monitor their growth through the summer

▶ Plan a major project for the day—new rockery, clear an uncultivated plot, build a bird table or fish pond and so on

▶ Teach the less experienced good garden practice

▶ For a week before or after monitor the weather measuring temperature, air pressure, rainfall and hours of sunshine

A 'green' spring clean

Everybody has a good clear out starting with their own room. All unwanted possessions should be sorted into piles:

▶ in good condition

▶ to sell or give away

▶ in average condition

▶ for repair, cleaning, painting and so on

▶ for recycling

▶ for the bin

If you have enough goods in the first two categories you can hold a car-boot sale for your favourite charity or church. If not give it to a local charity shop.

Husbands and wives or brothers and sisters or children and parents should allow each other to inspect the clothes they intend to keep. Objections are encouraged but everyone has the right to defend their choice. It may seem threatening but it is *very* illuminating.

Hold a household 'green' audit. Use the 'Spring Harvest' questionnaire. Examine all food and cleaning materials to see how many are 'green' and what could be replaced next time with a 'greener' product.

A 'green' holiday

One day of your next holiday together attempt a 'technology-free' day.

▶ Walk somewhere leaving the car behind.

▶ Pack a picnic made from raw materials—no packaged foods or drinks—bought fresh not preserved (this is difficult if not impossible, so try hard)

▶ Visit somewhere of natural beauty, not artificially created

▶ Enjoy home-made games and entertainment which do not need expensive equipment

▶ No radios, cassette players or personal stereos, but music with your own instruments is encouraged

▶ Parents and children can tell a story to each other which is made up as you go along

▶ At a suitable time (lunchtime?) have a time of prayer together using the sights and sounds around to worship God and thank him for his creation

Taking Personal Action

All of us can do some, if not all, of the following:

▶ Study the theme of creation in scripture.

▶ Pray about the environmental issues.

▶ Financially support those active in combating the problems, particularly Christian groups such as World Vision and Tear Fund.

▶ Regularly practise recycling—if your local council does not already operate this service, lobby your councillors to get them to copy other towns which do.

▶ Share possessions especially those items which are irregularly used—gardening equipment, motor tools and so on.

▶ Support Two-Thirds World producers by choosing to buy their products, especially where there is an assurance of the producers receiving a fair price.

▶ Eat less meat—animals consume vast amounts of grain which would otherwise feed humans.

▶ Make the most of your garden—use it productively and with the minimum of artificial fertilizers or pesticides: have a compost heap.

▶ Use recycled stationery, conserve paper supplies, recycle newspapers.

▶ Look after your church building and grounds. Make it an example not an eye-sore.

► Shop with ethical and environmental considerations in mind—waste of money and waste of resources go together.

► Use public transport, and walk or cycle where possible.

► Develop concern for those from other countries or cultures; get to know those resident in your area; when abroad explore the local culture.

► Start a local 'Green' group to tackle environmental issues in your neighbourhood. Organize work parties for clean-ups, decorating, gardening and so on.

► Enjoy the beauty of creation—use it to meditate on God and as an occasion to commune with him. Look at the sky at night—try counting the stars!

FOUNDATIONAL READING

Ron Elsdon, *Green House Theology*, Monarch, 1992

Lawrence Osborn, *Guardians of Creation*, Apollos, 1993

Chris Park, *Caring for Creation*, Marshall Pickering, 1991

Chris Seaton, *Whose Earth?*, Crossway, 1992

FURTHER READING

Michael Allaby, *Green Facts*, Hamlyn, 1986

Rex Ambler, *Global Theology*, SCM Press/Trinity Press Int, 1990

R.J. Berry, editor, *Real Science, Real Faith*, Monarch, 1991

Thomas Berry and Thomas Clarke, *Befriending the Earth*, Twenty-Third Publications, 1991

Steve Bishop and Christopher Droop, *The Earth is the Lord's*, Regius, 1990

Henri Blocher, *In the Beginning*, Inter-Varsity Press, 1984

Ian Bradley, *God is Green*, Darton, Longman and Todd, 1990

Derek Burke, editor, *Creation and Evolution*, Inter-Varsity Press, 1985

Tony Campolo, *How to Rescue the Earth Without Worshipping Nature*, Word, 1992

Tony Campolo and Gordon Aeschliman, *Fifty Ways You Can Feed a Hungry World*, Kingsway, 1992

William A. Charland, Jnr, *The Heart of the Global Village*, SCM Press/Trinity Press Int, 1990

Tim Cooper, *Green Christianity*, Spire, 1990

Paul Davies, *The Mind of God*, Simon and Schluter, 1992

Vincent Donovan, *The Church in the Midst of Creation*, SCM Press, 1991

Donal Dorr, *The Social Justice Agenda*, Gill & Macmillan, 1991

Ulrich Duchrow and Gerhard Liedke, *Shalom—Biblical Perspectives on Creation, Justice and Peace*, WCC, 1987

Ron Elsdon, *Bent World*, Inter-Varsity Press, 1981

Kenneth Hamilton, *Earthly Good*, Eerdmans, 1991

Stephen W. Hawking, *A Brief History of Time*, Transworld Publishing, 1988

Tim Hawthorne, *Windows on Science and Faith*, Inter-Varsity Press, 1986

James Houston, *I Believe in the Creator*, Hodder & Stoughton, 1979

Ben Jackson, *Poverty and the Planet*, Penguin Books, 1990

Hans Küng, *Global Responsibility*, SCM Press, 1991

Katie McBratney, editor, *You and the Environment*, Hodder & Stoughton, 1990

Paul Miller, *Into the Arena*, Kingsway, 1992 Henry M. Morris, *Science and the Bible*, Scripture Press, 1988

Roy E. Peacock, *A Brief History of Eternity*, Monarch, 1989

Lewis G. Regenstein, *Replenish the Earth*, SCM Press, 1991

C. von Ruhland, *Going Green*, Marshall Pickering, 1991

Francis Schaeffer, *Genesis in Space and Time*, Hodder & Stoughton, 1972

John Stott, *Issues Facing Christians Today*, revised, Marshall Pickering, 1990

Robert Van de Weyer, *Wickwyn—A Vision of the Future*, SPCK, 1986

Robert Van de Weyer, *The Health of Nations*, Green Books, 1991

James Wilkinson, *Green or Bust*, BBC Books, 1990

Loren Wilkinson, editor, *Earth Keeping in the 90s*, revised, Eerdmans, 1991

Albert Wolters, *Creation Regained*, Inter-Varsity Press, 1985

Not all of these books may be available at the event.

Ethics
Living in the Moral World

CONTENTS

Book of the seminar day:
David Watson, *I Believe in Evangelism*, Hodder & Stoughton

Introduction

'Live fast, die young and leave a good-looking corpse.'
JAMES DEAN

Welcome to a world of big questions on the issue of right and wrong—and how you decide which is which.

▶ How do you make up your mind what is morally right or wrong?

▶ Does right and wrong ever change—due to the situation or circumstances?

▶ On what basis should we make decisions on issues like: the death penalty; experiments on animals; embryo transplants; abortion; war; contraception, and the like?

Far from being boring, academic and of little practical value, ethics deal with the issues of:

▶ What is right and good
▶ How we ought to behave
▶ The standards we set ourselves
▶ What behaviour society expects of its members

KEY POINT

It is our ethics—our basis of what is right and wrong—that largely determine the way we live and behave.

For the Christian, ethics is not a matter of abstract thought. It carries a practical challenge for us to answer the profound question: 'How shall we then live?'

A few definitions

▶ **Ethics.** The science of morals, that branch of philosophy which is concerned with human character and conduct: a system of morals, rules of behaviour: a treatise on morals.
CHAMBERS ENGLISH DICTIONARY, 1988

Other uses of the word 'ethics':

▶ **Situational ethics.** The insistence that the right solution of any moral problem depends primarily on the prevailing circumstances, rather than on any fixed external code.

▶ **Ethical.** Relating to morals, conforming to approved moral behaviour.

▶ **Unethical.** Contrary to an accepted system of morals.

▶ **Ethics Committee.** A group responsible for supervision of a professional code of conduct especially in law and medicine.

▶ **Ethical Fund.** Money, often for investment, which is subject to certain restraints based on the moral convictions of those responsible.

Note that 'ethics' and 'morality' are not the same.

> *'A moral problem is first and foremost a practical problem, although not all practical problems are moral problems. A moral problem is concerned with right and wrong. Ethics may conveniently be defined as the study of morality. Ethics, is a reflective, or theoretical business . . . it steps back from the immediately practical and attempts to discover some underlying pattern or order in the immense variety of moral decisions and practices of both individuals and of societies.'*
> P. BAELZ, *ETHICS AND BELIEF*, SHELDON PRESS, 1977

Our Typical Response

For the Christian some issues of ethics—what is right and wrong and how we decide—are easy. A quick glance at the Ten Commandments answers all about murder, dishonesty, and so on.

However, the world is often more complicated than that.

Many seemingly 'grey' issues face us—demanding study, clear thinking and, sometimes, brave action.

As a result Christians face three temptations:

We major on worship and fellowship and not also on living effective lives in the real world.

Our church business meeting or PCC, is a good way to measure this truth. What gets the greatest attention—the style and content of Sunday morning music or the plight of the local homeless?

We concentrate on personal piety and not also on the way that society behaves as a whole.

Sometimes we feel the pressure of living as a Christian in a secular society and we are tempted to withdraw from involvement. It is easier to moralize at home and mourn 'these last days' than to speak up or act in a way that may be costly to us.

We select issues mainly of significance to Christians and not also those of concern to the world at large.

This is seen by the way we emphasize matters of sexual morality rather than also those of social concern.

As a result, Christians have been viewed as being backward concerning social change— bothered only by legislation relating to matters like abortion and homosexuality, and seemingly less concerned about overseas aid or education.

In effect, Christians—particularly evangelicals—have tended to be detached from the real world. We have majored on the spiritual—often as though this is all that matters.

The Example of Jesus

In John's Gospel, Jesus is described as beginning his public ministry at a party. This action is a vivid demonstration of the way in which Jesus never distinguished between the 'spiritual' and 'secular' world.

Jesus did not found a monastic order to withdraw from society. Rather, he called his disciples to live 'in the world'—as transforming agents. They were to be 'salt of the earth', and 'light of the world' (Matthew 5:13–14).

Far from concentrating exclusively on individual moral issues, the teaching of Jesus spanned the whole range of social, economic, religious and moral matters.

▶ Love your enemies (Matthew 5:44)
▶ Against materialism (Matthew 6:19–21)
▶ About anxiety (Matthew 6:25–34)
▶ Right thinking (Matthew 15:16–20)
▶ Esteeming children (Matthew 18:10)
▶ Divorce and singleness (Matthew 19:1–12)

Are we more afraid of upsetting our neighbour than we are of upsetting God?

KEY POINT

KEY POINT

KEY POINT

KEY POINT

What is more important, the scandal of youth homelessness or learning the words of a new worship song? On which do we spend more time?

KEY POINT

▶ Taxes (Matthew 22:15–22)

Over the centuries, the Christian church has responded in a variety of ways to the ethical message of Jesus.

▶ When the church and ruling authorities have been closely related, there have been attempts to impose Christian standards on society—for example, the Holy Roman Empire in Central Europe in the Middle Ages.

▶ Sometimes Christian communities have been formed to demonstrate standards which are an alternative to those of secular society—for example, Jean Calvin's 'City of God' in Geneva in 1541.

▶ At other times secular standards have infiltrated the church and been accepted—for example, the Lutheran church in Germany in the 1930s, which attempted to accommodate rather than oppose Nazism.

If the church is to be faithful to its role as a conveyor of truth, it must get the basics right.

This involves a need to:

▶ Look at the way the world at large makes up its mind about what is morally right and wrong.

▶ Examine what the Bible says about the basis for moral decisions.

▶ Work at the way the teaching of scripture confronts the way our world thinks and behaves.

KEY POINT

'*T*he Christian ideal has not been tried and found wanting. It has been found difficult; and left untried.'
G.K. CHESTERTON

The Ethics of Our World

KEY POINT

Even before the earliest law-codes were written down, human society developed its own understanding of how its people should behave towards each other.

Throughout history, societies and cultural groups have developed their own code as to what was right and wrong.

These views of right and wrong have been influenced by the beliefs of the particular society. For example:

▶ If God is all-powerful and all of life pre-determined, there is no point in trying to change any set of circumstances, no matter how awful, as it is his will.

▶ If reincarnation is true, it is wrong to kill any animal.

▶ If black people have no souls then enslaving them is not wrong.

▶ If God is displeased with a society and withholds the rain, then offering a human sacrifice to appease his wrath is a good thing.

We live in a society where thinking and actions are totally dominated by secular thinking.

Despite the richness of our Christian heritage, it is secular ethics that dominate the way people set standards of right and wrong. This has an impact on us as Christians because:

▶ We need to understand what lies behind the thinking of the world in which we live.

▶ We need to understand the impact that this has on our own thoughts, beliefs and actions.

During the eighteenth century, the church was at the centre of life in Europe—and it set the standards for what was 'normal' behaviour. The impact of almost universal church attendance—and later Sunday Schools—created a population that at least understood who God was and what he expected. This created a Christianized society which resulted in:

▶ A belief that there were fixed standards of right and wrong—established by a creator God—even though they were often broken.

▶ Dissent from Christian standards was confined to a small minority.

▶ Christianity—including its ethics—was believed to be superior to all other religions.

Such clear convictions are no longer held by the majority of people in the United Kingdom today.

KEY POINT

Such beliefs have been affected by the experiences and philosophy of the past generations.

In Europe in the eighteenth century some people known as 'deists' began to see God as:

▶ An impersonal force

▶ The creator of a huge clockwork universe

▶ An absentee landlord having left this world, which was seen as a huge mechanism, to operate in the way that it was designed

▶ An impersonal source of energy

▶ Not involved with the people in the world, or the operation of the universe

In the seventeenth and eighteenth centuries, the great debate amongst philosophers was between the 'empiricists' who believed all helpful knowledge came from experience and 'rationalists' who believed reason was the source of all knowledge. While followers of the Enlightenment—who stressed tolerance, common sense and reasonableness—saw human reason as the ultimate standard for determining truth and morals. To them, something could only be true if it could be demonstrated that it was reasonable—whether God said it or not.

As a result, the traditional ethics of Western society based on the Bible were opened to challenge. Man was to be the judge of right and wrong.

KEY POINT

This self-confidence in human reason was shattered by the horrors of modern warfare on the battlefields of the Somme. Such violence—and the scale of human destruction—was clearly not rational, even though it was human in its origin. So another basis for ethical judgments was needed.

The solution was to conclude that it could not be our fault. Flawed human actions must be:

▶ Influenced by our genetic make-up

▶ The effects of our environment

This means that human beings were purely the result of external forces in the past—over which they have no control. Even the concept of human freedom was an illusion.

This meant that:

'*D*oes morality in any significant sense exist any more? We speak of right and wrong, good and bad, justice and rights. But these are all words which were once thought to refer to objective principles, and it is these that we now believe do not exist.'
JONATHAN SACK, 1990 REITH LECTURE

▶ No one could be held responsible for their own actions.

▶ Life became purposeless, Godless, meaningless and absurd.

These views existed before the First World War. But they gained momentum through the nightmare of the trenches, the economic depression and unemployment which followed, and the rise of Nazism in the 1930s.

The awful scenes of war, depression and unemployment painted a vivid picture of the absurdity of life. They provoked the suggestion that perhaps human life was meaningless.

As a result:

▶ Some people turned to political anarchism—rejecting all law and order.

▶ Others turned to the unrestrained pursuit of pleasure.

▶ A few took this view of life to its logical conclusion—and committed suicide.

Existentialism

Into this area stepped existentialism—a down-to-earth belief which claims that:

▶ Reason is not able to solve the world's problems.

▶ Reason can only define what we already know through our experience.

Existentialism offers:

▶ Meaning in the midst of meaninglessness

▶ Hope to apparent hopelessness

▶ Light into what appeared to be universal darkness

KEY POINT

Existentialism is a belief that the only valid truth is what each person experiences. And what one person may experience as truth may not be true for someone else.

Existentialism proclaimed that while the world might be absurd, an individual can possess meaning and personal significance—because in contrast to inanimate objects they have both consciousness and a will.

The existentialist believes that:

▶ Our personal choices and decisions determine the individuals we are today. We were born as a blank sheet of paper; and today we are the sum of our own past actions. Everything derives from that alone.

▶ The experiences we have of life combine to make our knowledge of the truth.

▶ Truth entirely depends on our own personal experience.

▶ There is no ultimate truth—only what we discover works for us.

This means that while there is a universal agreement as to how heavy a ton is, or how long a day is, there can be no universal agreement as to what is right and wrong.

▶ One individual may choose to engage in a promiscuous heterosexual lifestyle.

▶ Another can develop a homosexual relationship.

KEY POINT

Case study

'In his famous lecture on existentialism, Jean-Paul Sartre, the last existentialist to avow the title, tells of his refusal to advise a young man facing an ethical dilemma. In the subsequent discussion with the philosophers who heard the lecture, two people criticized him. "You should have told him what to do," they said. One of these was a Christian, the other a Communist.

'Existentialists make a virtue of not knowing what to do.'

Carl Michalson, 'Existentialist Ethics' in J. Macquarrie and J. Childress, editors, *A New Dictionary of Christian Ethics*, SCM Press, 1986

▶ Others may choose to marry and remain faithful to one partner.

In each case, the existentialist argues, it is an appropriate and valid choice for the person concerned. But it may not be so for someone with a different set of experiences.

The philosophy of existentialism began with Søren Kierkegaard (1813–55), the Danish theologian who taught that there was a great gulf between God and man. Only God can bridge it. What is therefore important is what faith means to me—not whether it is absolutely true.

Kierkegaard was the father of both atheistic existentialism, for example, Jean-Paul Sartre (1905–80), and of the attempt by the radical twentieth-century theologians such as Rudolph Bultmann and Paul Tillich to reconcile this philosophy to scripture.

In its popular rather than academic form, existentialism quickly spread through the educators to the masses who are now existentialists without realizing it.

For example, such expressions as 'If it feels good, do it' and 'I did it my way' are pure existentialism.

In effect, the impact of existentialism has touched all of Western society. It has led to a system of ethics where:

▶ There is no longer any moral issue where right or wrong is true for everyone.

▶ Right and wrong depend on what we believe to be right or wrong—and the circumstances at the time.

There is no 'true truth', only truth for me. And my truth can never be yours unless it is embraced by your own experience.

For the existentialist it is unthinkable for anyone to claim any religion to be superior to another; any moral or ethical code to be the final word; that their faith is valid for anyone other than themselves.

Today Christian ethics and the secular ethics of existentialism operate side by side. Both can face the same specific situation and find that their conclusions are:

▶ completely different

or

▶ almost the same

They have reached their conclusions by different routes. And, when agreeing on certain ethical issues, their reasons for doing so will vary.

The following case studies illustrate that point:

KEY POINT

KEY POINT

Case Study: An Unwanted Pregnancy

Jenny was eighteen—and was shocked to be pregnant. Friends sympathized: 'Rotten luck, and from only a one-night stand.' David promised to stand by her—then didn't seem to be around any more. She was now two months away from going to college and six months short of motherhood.

Her parents were not troubled about her loss of virginity. But they faced the news of her pregnancy with visible horror. As a result, Jenny found herself in the doctor's surgery pouring out her story.

Her situation was accepted as both normal and straightforward. No advice was given. But Jenny was told that she was in danger of ruining her career.

▶ Abortion was a simple operation, with little risk to her subsequent fertility.

▶ Counselling was available to assist her.

▶ The difficulty lay in hospital waiting lists.

The operation had to be within the next 13 weeks. The NHS may not be able to cope—but a local private clinic could—for just over £200.

Jenny, an occasional churchgoer, asked for time to think. Perhaps the vicar might be able to give an opinion. Indeed, his advice was simple and to the point.

▶ Sex outside marriage was never God's intention, but we are human and do make mistakes.

▶ Within her womb was an embryonic child. She had no right to take that life away.

▶ In his love God would freely forgive her—but she should have the baby and either keep it or have it adopted.

▶ The operation could lead to the emotional trauma of post-abortion syndrome.

▶ She should visit the local social services for details of how an adoption could be arranged.

Then he prayed for her and Jenny sensed the warmth of God's love and forgiveness.

The advice from her mum was very different.

▶ Although she could put off college for a year it could hamper her future.

▶ Adoption was a clear possibility but motherhood produced its own traumas.

▶ An abortion could be swiftly arranged and without financial cost to her. In a few weeks the whole matter would be over.

▶ As a woman she had the rights over her own body and should decide what was best for her.

▶ The life within her womb was barely considered.

Jenny chose the abortion—sanctioned on the grounds that 'There was risk of injury to physical or mental health of the woman.'

Christian and secular ethics had collided.

▶ The church had offered forgiveness and care.

▶ Secular ethics had demanded an immediate solution to what was little more than 'a problem'.

The two views could not be reconciled and a choice had to be made.

Case Study: Sunday Trading

Steve was a shop steward. As the local representative of USDAW, the Union of Shop, Distributive and Allied Workers, he was there to serve his members, the workers on the shop floor.

This new attempt to reform the laws on Sunday trading was a real concern for him. He was committed to gain the full protection of employees who faced the threat of compulsion to work late hours and weekends—especially Sundays. Sunday represented, for many employees, the only opportunity to spend quality time with their families.

Steve knew that some were willing to work—but with what financial reward? And how could their right to refuse to work on a family day be protected?

That was why Steve, a convinced atheist, found himself sitting at a table alongside the local Baptist pastor. The Keep Sunday Special Campaign had called a local meeting of retailers, union representatives, clergy and interested activists on this issue. They were there to discuss the new parliamentary bill and to coordinate their opposition to it.

Steve was uncomfortable being so close to a 'man of the cloth'. How on earth could they both be on the same side? He made the point that the United Kingdom was out of step with the rest of Europe in terms of legal protection for workers.

To Steve's amazement the pastor voiced strong agreement. Then the pastor turned to religious issues. He spoke of:

▶ The need to respect Sunday as a day of worship.

▶ The Bible's insistence that the sabbath day was holy.

▶ People having no right to destroy the integrity of Sunday as a special and different day to the rest of the week.

Steve's eyes closed—but he was not praying. He simply wondered why religion had to get in everywhere. He knew the score—the pastor was just protecting the size of his congregation, and their use of the municipal car park.

Then Steve could hardly believe his ears. The pastor was speaking of:

▶ The uniqueness of the individual in the sight of God.

▶ 'Relationist ethics' and the need to protect the weak and the vulnerable.

▶ The way Jesus and the Old Testament prophets had spoken of the priority of justice and compassion for the poor.

▶ The rest principle—with the need to recognize the biblical pattern of work and rest.

▶ Those who tried to buck God's system being motivated by personal greed—using the workers to multiply financial gain for the rich and the powerful.

▶ The need to resist the pressure of big business and political lobbies, for the sake of the family.

Steve wished the Bible was not being quoted in support of his own ideals. But he fully agreed with the message!

(continued on following page)

'All nature is but art, unknown to thee; All chance, direction which thou canst not see; All discord, harmony not understood; All partial evil, universal good; And, spite of pride, in erring reason's spite, One truth is clear; WHATEVER IS, IS RIGHT.'
ALEXANDER POPE

'I give my body to the heat of the night, And let no man judge if it's wrong or right.'
SAMANTHA FOX

'Christianity is not just a series of truths but TRUTH—truth about all of reality.'
FRANCIS SCHAEFFER

'An ethical man is a Christian holding four aces.'
MARK TWAIN

CASE STUDY – SUNDAY TRADING – continued

Afterwards he spoke to the pastor. They adjourned for a friendly drink and further conversation. A bond was formed—without prejudice on either side.

KEY POINT

However, Christian and secular ethics possess completely different foundations.

▶ Secular ethics draw their context from current philosophical opinions, and deny the validity of any appeal to God as a basis for their position.

▶ Christian ethics are firmly rooted in the teaching of the Bible.

Although these foundations are different, the results will not always be different. One reason is that our society has, for centuries, established much of its thinking upon a Judaeo-Christian foundation.

KEY POINT

This has so infiltrated the subconscious mind that non-Christians often take on a Christian ethical position without realizing that their perspective is Christian in its origin.

But if scripture is God's revelation for humankind and, therefore, truth for everyone without exception, we should not be surprised when non-Christians sometimes agree with us.

These case studies help us to recognize how important our ethical position really is.

KEY POINT

We are not merely dealing with abstract thought, but the practical results of our beliefs when brought into the reality of everyday life.

Other Influences on Popular Thinking

KEY POINT

Existentialism is not the only modern influence that shapes the way people think regarding moral choices.

The following are adapted from David Cook's book, *The Moral Maze*, SPCK, 1983:

Alienation. The experience of feeling lost and alone. It comes from:

▶ The sense that we are merely cogs in a vast machine

▶ Decisions which affect our lives are taken without our consultation or consent

▶ Seeing ourselves as the disposable people manipulated by the world of big business, politics and finance

▶ Feeling removed from reality, depersonalized and less than human

As a result, we feel of little value or importance—lost and/or bewildered.

Futurity. The experience of feeling powerless and unable to make a difference. It comes from:

▶ Concern over current ecological problems and the threat of nuclear disaster

▶ Believing that improvement is possible—but that we are powerless to bring it about

This can lead to seeking the escape-route from our situation offered by an anticipation of what the future can bring. Popular interest in science fiction, astrology and occultism offer escapism from the

---

Christian and secular ethics had combined in their conclusion. Both the motivation and the route travelled were different. But a shared concern for the vulnerable united the two perspectives.

current dilemma.

Individualism. A sense of hopelessness and despair which leads to a concentration on the world of the individual.

Popular existentialism maintains that what is important is what happens in the individual. This emphasizes that reality lies in the inner world of the individual who chooses whatever he or she wants; the rest is dismissed as meaninglessness.

Liberation. The emphasis on minority movements looking for the freedom to do their own thing, on their own terms, and without outside interference or control.

Reductionism. The attempt to reduce complex situations to simple elements. It is a result of a world where the emphasis is on being a specialist. Modern experts know more and more about less and less.

As a result, attempts are made to retreat from generalizations into simple and more understandable specifics:

▶ Thought becomes a series of physical processes in the brain. There is no real inner world of the mind, it is an illusion which stems from automatic electro-chemical reactions shaped by our behaviour.

▶ Our complex behaviour can be understood by considering a series of simple responses which combine together. One simple response mechanism is thought to lie behind all decisions and actions—just as a computer programme is built on an immense series of yes/no choices.

Privatization. A lack of interest in the macro-world which we cannot change, to the micro-world of home and personal fulfilment. The argument is:

▶ We should avoid trying to change the larger world. The only world we can change is our own.

Pluralism. An awareness that ours is not the only viewpoint or the only religion.

It is the result of:

▶ The mass media

▶ Popular travel

▶ The increased pressure of ethnic population

The result is to recognize that there is no reason why we should be correct and others wrong. We are not to judge anything but to tolerate everything as equally valid and right.

'I am not promiscuous. I can count the lovers I have had on the fingers of two hands.'
JAMIE LEE CURTIS

Jeremy Bentham's seven tests of the Greatest Happiness Principle (GHP)

Duration	How long it lasts
Intensity	How strong it is
Propinquity	How close it is
Extent	How wide it goes
Certainty	How sure we are of it
Purity	How free it is from pain
Fecundity	How much more pleasure will stem from it

Secularization. The process by which religious thinking, practice and institutions have lost their social significance.

We live in a secular society where:

▶ All authority, the church included, is open to question.

▶ Scientific discovery has been understood to reinforce popular scepticism about religion.

Relativism. A philosophical position maintaining that things can only be judged to be right or wrong according to:

▶ The specific situation

▶ The particular individuals involved

There are no longer any absolutes (unchanging standards) which apply to everybody. Everything is relative (dependent on the situation).

KEY POINT

All these influences affect society as a whole. This can be seen in a number of attitudes which underline the way people think and behave. For example:

Hedonism. The pursuit of personal pleasure above all else. 'What does it matter so long as I enjoy myself?'

Materialism. The quest for possessions and wealth. 'I want it—all of it—and I want it *now!*'

Utilitarianism. The creation of laws designed to make people happy. At its heart lies the GHP—the Greatest Happiness Principle. This insists that morality is about the creation of the greatest happiness for the greatest number of people. It is a prime motivation behind much contemporary political decision-making of all political parties.

Evolutionism. A belief that the evolutionists' principle of 'the survival of the fittest' affects every aspect of life—from business to education.

Subjectivism. The desire to be involved in 'doing my own thing'.

These concepts, and many others, arise from a climate of opinion which insists that each of us:

▶ Decides our own destiny

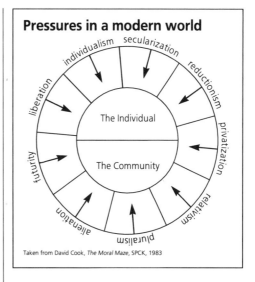

Pressures in a modern world

Taken from David Cook, *The Moral Maze*, SPCK, 1983

▶ Chooses what is 'right' for us as individuals

This contemporary ethic is neither Christian, nor is it biblical. It is not new. It has appeared in different forms throughout history—with devastating results.

In the Old Testament, Israel experienced times of social breakdown—'everyone did just as he pleased' (Judges 21:25 GNB).

In England prior to the Wesleyan/Whitefield revival, sexual immorality, gambling and public disorder were common.

In America's 'Wild West' many frontier towns lived in a virtual state of anarchy until the church and rule of law brought a degree of order.

Existentialism—and its attendant secular world-view 'isms'—is in stark contrast to the world-view of the Bible—or, as it is called, the Judaeo-Christian view.

Four contemporary examples illustrate the point perfectly:

▶ **Abortion.** If having a child might damage the physical or emotional health of the mother she can choose whether to continue with the pregnancy. It's her choice. There are no rules to determine such a decision. Each individual is to have their own view respected—unless, of course, it is a pro-life view. It is then that existentialist tolerance often runs out.

▶ **Sexuality.** Choice is the ultimate. No one person can enforce their sexual values and morality on another. Each must do what is 'right for themselves'. The only responsibility lies in seeking to shield them from the results of their actions. Consequently condoms are the 'answer', not chastity.

▶ **Honesty.** Stealing from an individual is frowned on. But stealing from the collective or the system is viewed differently. So it is bad to steal a woman's purse. But fine to 'mug' an insurance company or ride the tube for free.

▶ **Censorship.** If no individual can ever dictate to another then all censorship is invalid. The argument is simple: 'If you don't like it, then don't buy it, or switch it off.' The idea of protecting people from themselves must be lost forever.

Similarly **voluntary euthanasia** and **suicide** are ethically acceptable when viewed from an

KEY POINT

The minefield of modern belief

Christians beware. The beliefs of our secularist society have made the ground unsafe to walk on.

■ If ethics depend on experience then, just as one man's meat is another's poison, so one person's ethical standards may not apply to the next person. After all, our experiences differ.

■ If God is in everything, then we cannot make laws forbidding our involvement in one sphere of life or another. Whatever *is*, is good. If it exists it is acceptable and should not be banned or limited as there are no external absolutes.

■ If truth can never be 'true truth' or absolute (unchanging) truth, and if what is true for one may not be true for another, then all truth depends on circumstances—absolute commands are out. There is nothing that is always right or always wrong.

■ If each person is the combined product of their own experience, each person can choose their own path through life.

■ If ethics are a matter of each person's belief, it doesn't matter what you do, or do not do. Sincerity is enough.

existentialist perspective. Those involved can be applauded for resisting collective dictatorship and extolling the freedom of the individual.

It is wrong to suggest that these changes in moral attitude are the result of a conspiracy aimed at undermining Christianity.

The truth is that human beings without Christ will design their own world-view and ideas.

However, the danger is that Christians will absorb these non-biblical concepts and fail to respond to the challenge which they offer.

The Exclusive Claims of Christianity

Popular opinion has been conditioned to believe that tolerance is the highest of all virtues.

That it must be good and right to accept each person, attitude or belief as equally valid and true.

Many would see this as a proper 'Christian' way to behave. Yet this concept is totally anti-Christian and defies the Christian gospel at its very roots.

Christianity has always made exclusive claims for itself.

It affirms that:

▶ Jesus is uniquely the Son of God (John 1:14).
▶ Truth can only be found in Jesus (John 14:6).
▶ Jesus is the only means for personal forgiveness (Acts 4:12; 1 Timothy 2:5–6).
▶ Jesus alone will ultimately inherit all things (Hebrews 1:2).
▶ Jesus alone will return one day as Lord and King (John 14:3; 1 Thessalonians 4:16; Matthew 26:64).
▶ Jesus alone will judge all people (Acts 10:42).
▶ Every knee will bow before Jesus (Philippians 2:10).
▶ God's commands are unchanging, binding and do not depend on the situation at the time (Matthew 5:17–20).

Christianity claims to be *the* truth for humankind. Only through Jesus are forgiveness, friendship with God and salvation obtainable.

The Bible does not portray Jesus as one Messiah among many. It affirms that he is *the* Christ—the one and only (Mark 8:29; Matthew 16:16; Luke 9:20).

The heart of Christianity does not lie in being tolerant of other views but in recognizing what is true.

Likewise, human freedom does not lie in equal acceptance of all viewpoints but in embracing the truth of Jesus Christ (John 8:32, 36).

Christianity claims that:

▶ Jesus alone is the truth (John 14:6).
▶ Scripture is unique truth which is God-breathed (2 Timothy 3:15, 16).

There is nothing else which even bears comparison.

This means that:

▶ It is not biblical to place the teaching of Jesus alongside that of other great moral teachers.
▶ It is not Christian to worship 'God' in a Buddhist shrine.
▶ We are not permitted the luxury of placing the instructions of the Bible at the same level as the ethical teaching contained in the Qur'an or the Bhagavad Gita.

The Place of Tolerance

This history of the church is littered with examples of intolerance that should not have been.

Persecutions and the horrors of the Inquisition are not the basis for maintaining the truth.

Christians are:

▶ Not commanded to force their standards upon a reluctant society.
▶ Called to proclaim and spread the truth of scripture, so that everyone may know and understand what God expected and why it is good news.

Unlike Islam, Christianity has no place for the sword in spreading its rule or maintaining orthodoxy.

If we are convinced that Jesus is the truth:

▶ We should play our part in making sure that all can hear the message and respond.
▶ Our own lives must match up to the message we share.
▶ We must have confidence to enter into debate with other viewpoints.

It has been common for Christians to be frightened at the thought of confrontation. This is especially true when we are faced with challenging beliefs that most people consider to be normal.

However, tolerance is not enough. We must also help people face the fact that it is possible to be sincerely wrong. The assumptions of tolerance must be challenged.

Christian Ethics

The God of the Bible makes unique claims for himself. It is from this starting point that Christians establish their view of ethics.

Christian ethics is not based on human reason but on what God has said. As creator, God is concerned for all of his creation and is uniquely positioned to help us live our lives to the full.

The Foundations

There are simple basic principles on which a Christian view of ethics is built.

1. God's moral character never changes (Malachi 3:6; James 1:17). So moral codes which are based on his character can never change.

2. These moral codes which God has established apply to all humankind—because each person has

The British church has not spoken with one voice on many ethical issues in recent years. How much is this the result of the lack of confidence of many prominent leaders in the authority of scripture? What have been the consequences?

been created in the 'image of God' (Genesis 1:27; James 3:9).

▶ Commandments like 'do not commit adultery', for example, are linked to the nature of a God who never changes—not to the changing circumstances of those involved. In effect, ethics based on the situation of the moment deny the very character of God.

However:

▶ Instructions that God has given which relate to a particular time and place must be viewed differently. For example, the dietary laws of the Old Testament did not usually relate to God's moral character but often to the health needs of the people in that situation.

3. God has made himself known.

Even those who are unaware of the gospel, still have the revelation of God contained in conscience, nature and creation (Psalm 19:1–6; Romans 1:19–20).

Failure to see that God is the one to whom we must answer does not excuse anyone (Romans 2:14–15).

Because God has made his will known in scripture (Psalm 19:7–14), Christians have a double obligation to submit to God's standards, both general and special (Romans 2:18; 3:2). We are uniquely his people and responsible to obey his directions (Luke 11:28; Acts 5:29; Hebrews 5:9; 1 John 5:3; Revelation 14:12).

4. God's will is the basis for our conclusions.

God has issued divine commands and, because he is perfect, his commands cannot be other than perfectly correct. This means that every command of God is always for our good—to protect us and provide for us.

5. The basis is what ought to be, not on the measure we actually achieve.

God demands:

▶ That we love our neighbours as ourselves (Matthew 22:39)

▶ That we turn the other cheek (Matthew 5:39; Luke 6:29)

▶ That we should 'love our enemies' (Luke 6:27)

Because these standards are beyond our ability to fulfil, God gives us his Holy Spirit so that we can have his help to match his standards (John 14:17).

Even then we still fail (Romans 7:19–20). But, when we do, God is still willing to forgive us because of the work of Jesus (1 John 1:9—2:2). This should encourage us to continue to keep his commandments (1 John 2:3).

Private Morality?

Dealing with public morality is one thing. But what about private morals? For example:

▶ Does it really matter what a consenting adult does in the privacy of their own room. Is their morality the business of anyone else?

▶ Is the private life of a public figure any business of the public at large?

The answer on both counts is 'yes' because—the

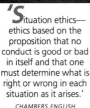
KEY POINT

KEY POINT

KEY POINT

KEY POINT

KEY POINT

What is right?

How do you define what is right?

1. Right is the greatest good for the greatest number.

2. Right is the moderate viewpoint in all things.

3. Right is what is desirable for its own sake.

4. Right is beyond definition!

5. Right is what is best for the whole human race.

6. Right is on the side of the biggest battalions!

7. Right is determined by each individual.

8. Right is that which is best for the community.

9. Right is what brings the most pleasure to the individual.

10. Right is what God calls 'good' from his own perspective.

---

way we behave in private affects both our relationship with God and our relationship with others.

▶ Actions towards others are acts towards God (Matthew 25:45).

▶ What is in a person's heart corrupts them and is shown through speech in particular (Matthew 15:17–20).

Private behaviour that breaks God's laws and tarnishes a person's moral character makes them a less valuable member of society. In effect, the world is a poorer place because of the way they have behaved in private.

Politicians are particularly prone to insisting that their private morality has nothing to do with their public service. However, why should we be prepared to believe anything that a politician says if they are prepared to lie to their wife? Private morality is surely an essential requirement for public trust.

KEY POINT

The Bible and Ethics

Scripture insists that it is God and his requirements which must determine our expected behaviour—not humankind and their habits.

To take the Bible seriously on specific ethical issues we need to understand the emphasis that is in different parts of scripture.

KEY POINT

Creation

Natural law. Genesis presents the picture of a perfect garden where harmony reigned. This expressed the unbroken relationship with God that was enjoyed by nature, animals and human beings.

God had built morality into this world and into human nature. What is good helps us. What is bad harms us. For example, we instinctively recognize harmony with other people is good but conflict is bad. This natural law is God's law expressed in us and our environment.

KEY POINT

Image of God. Because men and women are made in God's image they are morally responsible beings, answerable to God. In scripture God is not first explained or described.

In Genesis 1, God is recorded as acting. He is understood to be both good and all-powerful but this is only demonstrated as he interacts with his creation. Our understanding of morality comes from this interaction. We have no other external standard to evaluate right and wrong.

Principles from creation. Genesis not only concentrates on the way that creation took place, it also sets out the maker's instructions for the world that he has designed.

These instructions that relate to the whole of God's creation ordinances include instructions as to:

▶ The relationship between human beings and animals

▶ The nature of work

▶ Responsibility for the environment

▶ Accountability to God

▶ The complementary relationship between men and women

These instructions give basic guidelines for those who want their lifestyle to be in line with the ideal set by their creator.

Conscience. Part of being human, created in God's image, is an intuitive sense of right and wrong (Romans 2:12–16). We are aware, because of God's voice within, of the right or wrong of a particular choice to be made. If we choose wrong we feel guilt and remorse.

The fall. Human disobedience resulted in the loss of paradise. It was a disaster resulting in death, destruction, hatred, toil and disorder. It spoilt everything and distorted all that had originally been created in the image of God. Conscience continues to exist but is no longer totally reliable.

Our loss of a proper relationship with God and the tendency within us to serve our own self-interest will constantly distort our judgment over moral issues.

Covenant

After the fall, God created for humanity a series of agreements, by which they should live. Each agreement set out demands and promises, so we would know how we should live.

As time progressed and as the people of God learned more about him and his ways, new covenants were introduced which provided a better way ahead. The two most important are the Law of Moses (including the Ten Commandments) and the 'New Covenant' which Jesus introduced so that we are saved by faith in him, not keeping the Law.

KEY POINT

God had promised to bless his people in response to their obedience.

This relationship, like a contract, was based on the principle of the binding covenant which God made with them (Genesis 17:11–12; Deuteronomy 7:7–8; 30:1–10). The agreements were two-way (although initiated and maintained by God). Israel's part in the arrangement was obedience to the law.

The covenant which God made with Israel

God's ethical instructions

■ **Biblical ethics are always right ethics**—they are rooted in the perfect will of the God who knows and loves his people personally (Romans 12:2).

■ **Biblical ethics demand that we imitate God**— we achieve this as we live in the love of his Son (Leviticus 11:44; Luke 6:36; Ephesians 5:1–2) and by the power of his Holy Spirit (Galatians 5:16–18, 22–23).

■ **Biblical ethics represent the revealed will of God**—the knowledge of right and wrong does not come through philosophical speculation but by simple obedience to what God has declared in his law (1 Samuel 15:22; Romans 2:18).

■ **Biblical ethics and Christian doctrine are inseparable**—the teaching of the law, of Jesus and of Paul's epistles all begin with theological statements and end with ethical conclusions (Exodus 20:2; Matthew 5:43–48; 1 Corinthians 6:12–20).

(Exodus 24) had great ethical significance. It was God's gracious choice which meant that Israel would enjoy a special relationship with himself.

In the same way that God had shown compassion to Israel, he instructed that each individual Israelite should demonstrate similar compassion to others.

KEY POINT

God was specific in his ethical instructions:

▶ Weaker members of society—the widow, the orphan, the stranger and the poor—should receive special protection (Exodus 22 and 23).

The Bible as a source of ethical decisions

Where to find different types of material

Old Testament	New Testament
1. Creation	**6. Jesus**
Natural law	Kingdom
Image of God	Lifestyle
Principles from creation	Love
Conscience	
The fall	
	7. The Epistles
	Law
2. Covenant	Imitation
Binding agreement	Doctrine
3. Law	**8. The Pastoral Epistles**
Commandments	Direct advice
Ritual observances	
4. Wisdom Literature	
Moral teaching	
5. The Prophets	
Justice	
Immorality	
Judgment	

Can a Christian live according to God's highest ethical standards if they have not read the whole of the Old Testament?

- ▶ Slaves should be treated generously because of the way God delivered his people when they were slaves in Egypt (Deuteronomy 15:12).

- ▶ Businessmen should not weight scales unfairly but have 'just balances', like the God of justice (Leviticus 19:36; Amos 8:5).

- ▶ Strangers were to be treated in the same way that God had graciously dealt with his people (Leviticus 19:33–34). The instruction was to 'love him as yourself, for you were aliens in Egypt.'

- ▶ High moral standards were compulsory with specific commandments on religious practices and sabbath observance (Exodus 34:21; Leviticus 6:1–4; 18:6–24).

- ▶ Warnings were given against occult practices and worship of false gods (Exodus 34:17; Leviticus 19:26; 26:1).

- ▶ The Ten Commandments set the same high standard of moral, ethical and spiritual purity for all (Exodus 20:2–17).

- ▶ Israelites were instructed to treat each other fairly (Leviticus 25:17).

- ▶ They had to leave the land fallow every seven years for twelve months (Leviticus 25:4).

- ▶ The Jubilee year occurred every fifty years and was a time of reimbursement and return to family property and territory (Leviticus 25:10). It was also a time for the release of slaves and their families (Leviticus 25:40–41).

- ▶ Community ethics were also extremely important.

- ▶ When an individual fell on hard times everyone felt the obligation to offer help and support (Leviticus 25:35).

- ▶ When one man disobeyed God the whole community felt the consequences (Joshua 7:1).

The covenant between God and the Children of Israel was based on him offering them undeserved love. Israel's response, in seeking to meet the ethical standard that he required, was not to be inspired by fear but to demonstrate their own gratitude for God's favour to them. Nor should it be inspired by fear based on God's warnings of the punishment which would follow their disobedience.

Law

In the Old Testament the first five books are known as 'The Book of the Law'. They describe how God gradually revealed more of himself and the laws necessary for the good of both individual and society.

The climax of this process was Moses' dramatic encounter with God on Mount Sinai, during the Jews' wanderings in the wilderness after their exodus from Egypt.

It was here that God gave Moses the Ten Commandments that formed the basis for the wide ranging system of moral and civil laws which together are known as 'the laws of Moses'. All of Jewish society has been based on the Law and the interpretation of it ever since.

KEY POINT

God's Law was given in the context of his covenant relationship with his people.

It was designed to cement good relationships between the Israelites, and between God and his people.

This explains the positive way in which the law was seen by those who had to keep its precepts (Psalm 19:7; 119:72), before a more rigid legalism began to take hold of Israel.

The law of God was an expression of God's:

- ▶ Nature
- ▶ Character
- ▶ Will

God gave the law in terms of:

- ▶ Statutes
- ▶ Judgments

These proclaimed his moral standards for his people. This covered:

- ▶ Duties to God
- ▶ Duties to fellow citizens
- ▶ A variety of civil, ceremonial and moral requirements

Wisdom Literature

The Wisdom literature of Proverbs, Job, Ecclesiastes and Song of Solomon contains wise ethical instructions which have been called 'guidance from heaven for life on earth'. The teaching is both practical and down-to-earth.

However, it is important to note that proverbs are expressions of what *usually* happens rather than specific promises that the outcome is guaranteed.

The Prophets

The prophets reflected the concern of the covenant for social justice and compassion. Writing during a period of spiritual decay and moral decline, they:

- ▶ Denounced injustice and abuse towards the powerless in society (Amos 2:6; 5:12; Micah 6:11).

- ▶ Insisted that routine religious observance without a matching lifestyle was a mockery to God (Isaiah 1:11; Hosea 6:6; Amos 5:21).

- ▶ Stressed that true religion and a proper moral lifestyle go hand-in-hand (Micah 6:6–8; Jeremiah 6:19–20).

- ▶ Denounced the sense of narrow nationalism which caused Israelites to despise foreigners (Amos 9:7).

- ▶ Argued that Israel's privileged position should not be a basis for complacency but brought with it greater responsibilities (Isaiah 42:8–17).

- ▶ Were powerful critics of dishonesty and the abuse of wealth and power in Israel and Judah (Isaiah 5:7, 23; Micah 2:8–9; Zephaniah 3:3).

- ▶ Attacked personal immorality (Hosea 4:10–14; 6:8–10; Jeremiah 7:9; 9:3–6).

- ▶ Stressed that God's judgment was intended as a sign of his desire to forgive and restore his people (Amos 9:11–15; Zephaniah 3:11–20).

Jesus

In searching for a New Testament source of moral principle you need go no further than Jesus himself.

His life and words were a living demonstration of all that God wanted from his people.

Jesus did not just explain how people should act. He also provided a perfect illustration of life as God intended it to be lived.

Jesus introduced principles which demanded radical change and transformation. By his salvation, healing and restoration he made it possible for people to be revolutionized so they could live the life that God intended.

The ethical teaching of Jesus was unlike any that had been heard previously.

While the Law had dealt with actions, Jesus dealt with the character of the individual and the motives which inspired their actions.

Supremely in the Sermon on the Mount, but also in the rest of his recorded words, Jesus challenged people to the very heart of their being.

▶ He condemned moral blindness, callousness and pride (Matthew 7:3; Mark 3:5; Luke 18:9).

▶ He denounced those who committed murder and adultery in their hearts—even if it did not surface in their actions (Matthew 5:21–22, 28).

▶ He cut across the racial convictions of many of his contemporaries (Luke 10:33; Matthew 8:10–12).

▶ He affirmed both women and children (Matthew 19:14; John 14:21).

▶ He challenged the desire to accumulate wealth and power (Matthew 6:19–33; Mark 4:18–19; Luke 12:15; 21:1–4).

▶ He advocated a neighbour-love which operated with no conditions or requirements on the part of the recipient. It even extended to our enemies (Luke 6:32–36; 14:12–14).

Jesus also called for different standards from his followers on topics like:

▶ Murder (Matthew 5:21–22)

▶ Reconciliation (vv. 23–24)

▶ Legal action (vv. 25–26)

▶ Adultery (vv. 27–30)

▶ Divorce and remarriage (vv. 31–32)

▶ Oaths (vv. 33–37)

▶ Revenge (vv. 38–42)

▶ Hatred of enemies (vv. 43–48)

Religious leaders and their lifestyle also received short shrift from Jesus. He attacked their:

▶ Hypocrisy (Matthew 6:1)

▶ Public giving (vv. 2–4)

▶ Prayer lives (vv. 5–15)

▶ Fasting (vv. 16–18)

The demands of the ethical standards set by Jesus were quite immense. But he also offered supernatural moral power to enable his followers to live up to the challenge.

The Epistles

The Epistles stress that Christian truth and ethics are partners together.

What we believe must work out in the way we live. It is not enough to think right things. We also are required to live right lives.

The epistles were written as practical answers to urgent questions from active churches. While Jesus mainly taught in broad, general principles, the ethical teaching in the epistles is more specific.

Jesus normally left his hearers to arrive at their own conclusions.

However, the epistles spell out the applications of moral teaching in a more straightforward manner. For example, very detailed treatment is given to:

▶ Sins of speech (Romans 1:29–32; Ephesians 4:29; James 3:5–6)

▶ Sexual sins (1 Corinthians 6:9; 2 Corinthians 12:21)

The church functioned in the context of the strained relationship which existed between the small Christian communities and powerful secular authorities. This demanded clear ethical teaching.

▶ Believers felt they were called to martyrdom rather than revolution—as reinforced by the conservative teaching of the epistles on this issue (Romans 13:1–7; 1 Peter 2:13–21).

▶ Paul strongly emphasized that Christ's life is one of love (1 Corinthians 13), which fulfils the Law (Galatians 5:14; Romans 13:8). He calls believers to follow Christ's example and where appropriate, to imitate Paul himself.

The Pastoral Epistles

The Pastoral Epistles—1 and 2 Timothy and Titus—are vivid examples of Paul's response to the specific problems of those to whom he is writing. Here he sets out the ethical standards that should apply to Christian leaders.

Significant sections of these epistles emphasize right relationships in family life and in society (1 Timothy 2:8–15; Titus 2:2–8). These 'household codes' are also paralleled in Ephesians, Colossians and 1 Peter.

These epistles are written to individuals as well as to whole churches, and thus, include valuable insights about personal moral values.

Biblical teaching on ethical issues is essential for Christians seeking direction for their lives. Even though its material is at least 1900 years old—what the Bible has to say is still powerfully relevant. After all, the Bible affirms that: 'All Scripture is God-breathed and is useful for teaching, rebuking, correcting and training in righteousness, so that the man of God may be thoroughly equipped for every good work' (2 Timothy 3:16–17).

The issue is what is expected of us rather than what we manage to achieve.

God has called us to be faithful, but that does not mean we will always be successful. At least not within our own terms of reference.

KEY POINT

'Jesus Christ is the essence of Christian morality . . . Jesus is God incarnate. The previous revelations of moral standards have been abstract. Now they are personified in the God who becomes human.'
DAVID COOK

KEY POINT

'All moral obligation resolves itself into the obligation of conformity to the will of God.'
CHARLES HODGE

It is popular to believe that Jesus was a great moral teacher. Would this view be so popular if people knew what he really taught?

'There are no pastel shades in the Christian ethic.'
ARNOLD LOWE

'Here is a Christian value system, ethical standard, religious devotion, attitude to money, ambition, lifestyle and network of relationships—all of which are totally at variance with those of the non-Christian world. And this Christian counter-culture is the life of the Kingdom of God, a fully human life indeed but lived out under the divine rule.'
JOHN STOTT

KEY POINT

'Strive we then to think aright; that is the first principle of moral life.'
BLAISE PASCAL

'Jesus not only proclaimed that the Kingdom of God had come with himself and his work; he also set before his disciples the moral ideal of that kingdom . . . in the Sermon on the Mount.'
A.M. HUNTER

Do you and I share the same personal ethics? If not, why not?

'Ethics deals with what ought to be, not with what is. Christians do not find their ethical duties in the standard of Christians but in the standard for Christians—the Bible.'
NORMAN GEISLER

KEY POINT

What comes first in our thinking

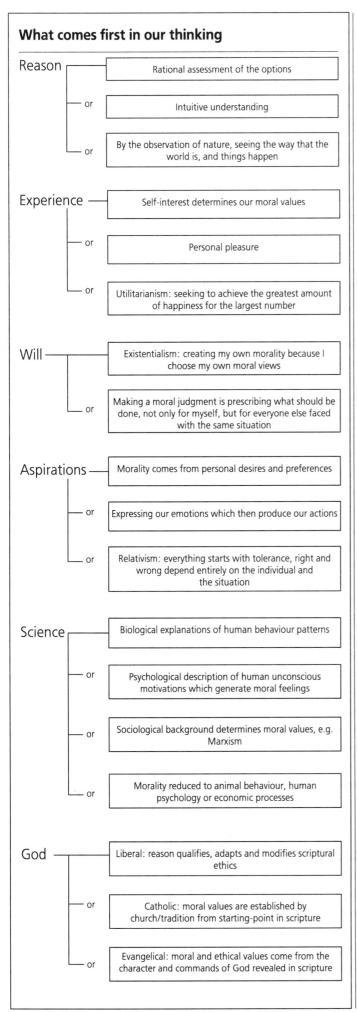

Reason
- Rational assessment of the options
- or Intuitive understanding
- or By the observation of nature, seeing the way that the world is, and things happen

Experience
- Self-interest determines our moral values
- or Personal pleasure
- or Utilitarianism: seeking to achieve the greatest amount of happiness for the largest number

Will
- Existentialism: creating my own morality because I choose my own moral views
- or Making a moral judgment is prescribing what should be done, not only for myself, but for everyone else faced with the same situation

Aspirations
- Morality comes from personal desires and preferences
- or Expressing our emotions which then produce our actions
- or Relativism: everything starts with tolerance, right and wrong depend entirely on the individual and the situation

Science
- Biological explanations of human behaviour patterns
- or Psychological description of human unconscious motivations which generate moral feelings
- or Sociological background determines moral values, e.g. Marxism
- or Morality reduced to animal behaviour, human psychology or economic processes

God
- Liberal: reason qualifies, adapts and modifies scriptural ethics
- or Catholic: moral values are established by church/tradition from starting-point in scripture
- or Evangelical: moral and ethical values come from the character and commands of God revealed in scripture

KEY POINT

We are called to attempt that which God has laid down for us, whatever the result proves to be.

To sum up, there is a stark contrast between Christian and non-Christian ethics. One looks to what God has said. The other to the situation and standards of the time.

Non-Christian ethics are based on:
▶ Human reason
▶ Personal experience
▶ Feelings
▶ Human aspirations

Christian ethics are based on:
▶ God's character
▶ What God has said in scripture

However, it is not that simple. In truth:
▶ The secular world is still influenced by Christian principles—often without realizing it.
▶ Christians, increasingly, are influenced by secular thinking—without realizing it.

Christian Influence on Secular Ethics

The Christian heritage of past generations still influences thinking today.

▶ Existentialist thinking and situational ethics still confront a world where many still hold onto values that they hold dear—even if they fail to realize where they come from.

If it were not for the influence of Christian thought there would be no basis to say:

▶ Tell the truth
▶ Always keep your word
▶ Love your neighbour
▶ Value all human life
▶ Respect other people's property

It is the remnants of past Christian ethics that hold our society together. For example, no business deal could work if both parties interpreted it in terms of how they felt at the time.

Sir Fred Catherwood has described this effect as the invisible cement that holds the bricks of society together. But the cement is crumbling and the wall is beginning to fall apart.

However, many in society have a concern that certain things are right and wrong—but are unable to point to why they feel that way. They will either eventually cave in under the existentialist barrage—or discover that the 'unknown God' is the basis of ethics that are the most sound foundation for life that there is.

Secular Influence on Christian Ethics

It is also true that the views that Christians hold regarding what is right and wrong are often shaped by secular ethics. For example, in the way some Christians view sex outside of marriage.

Few non-Christian couples feel guilty about sleeping together before marriage, especially when in 'a stable relationship'. But they do *feel* that adultery is a betrayal of their partner.

▶ Many young Christians echo this view saying 'It feels so right it can't be wrong'. This becomes an excuse for pre-marital intercourse.

▶ Love and lack of guilt feelings are used to support their argument.

▶ Some Christians believe that although such behaviour is wrong for them personally, it is not wrong for non-Christians whose lives are based on other philosophies.

However, scripture teaches:

▶ God's moral law is universal (Romans 2:1, 12, 13, 23).

▶ The consequences of sin, both social and spiritual, are inevitable and bad (Romans 1:18–32; 2:5–6; Galatians 6:7–8).

▶ A non-Christian's conscience is unreliable (Titus 1:15).

▶ Feelings are often misleading (Ecclesiastes 11:9).

▶ Purity is a great virtue (1 Thessalonians 4:7).

▶ Immorality and Christianity are incompatible (1 Corinthians 6:9).

▶ Immorality is unnatural (1 Corinthians 6:13).

▶ Sex was intended to be a unique form of union between two people (1 Corinthians 6:16).

▶ Sexual sin can harm the body—AIDS, syphilis, gonorrhoea (1 Corinthians 6:18).

'*S*ome Christians have failed to notice the division between Christian values and secular values. Their situation is rather like the man sleeping in his tent, who is disturbed by his camel asking if he might put his head in the tent. Gradually there is more and more camel and less and less room for the man in the tent. Secular values have imperceptibly eroded and replaced Christian values and some people have not even noticed the difference.'

DAVID COOK, *THE MORAL MAZE*, SPCK, 1983

Other Ethical Systems

Christianity is not the only faith or philosophy to have its own system of ethics. Every belief system—whether it is a God-made or a man-made principle—creates its own basis on which moral decisions and views are made.

When considering the following examples, it is helpful to examine Christian ethics alongside them in order to understand how different our faith really is.

Islamic Ethics

Islam places great stress on the education of its young people. They are taught two main elements:

▶ Theology—what they should believe

▶ Sacred law—how they should behave

It is the second of these two that receives the most attention. Islam's sacred law, the 'Sharia', is built on:

▶ The Qur'an—their holy book.

▶ The 'sunna'—what the prophet Mohammed did, said and permitted as recorded by tradition.

▶ The 'ijma'—the consensus teaching of the Muslim community.

▶ 'Giyas'—the use of analogy, from the other three sources, to cover situations where there is no clear teaching.

As a result, the scope of the *sacred* law is to cover every area of life, from the prohibition of murder to the use of a toothpick.

The duties and obligations of a Muslim

The major commands on which Muslim ethics are based are:

■ To worship the One God

■ Kindness to others especially parents, orphans and the needy

■ Giving alms

■ Keeping promises and covenants

■ Patient endurance of adversity

■ Just trading

The five major duties of a Muslim are:

■ Profession of faith in the One True God

■ Worship—five times daily

■ Fasting—the month of Ramadan

■ Almsgiving

■ Pilgrimage to Mecca—at least once in a lifetime if possible

To these may be added 'jihad'. This is primarily the struggle against 'evil'. This can be against the evil inclinations of the soul or, as more popularly perceived in the West, a 'holy war' against external enemies.

Loyalty, especially to Islam itself, is also of great importance. It is seen to be of greater importance than allegiance to one's country of residence—especially where there is a conflict of interest.

Islam also teaches that actions are to be judged by the intention. There are both individual and collective duties.

All actions fall into one of five categories:

▶ Obligatory

▶ Recommended

▶ Neutral or permitted

▶ Disapproved or forbidden

▶ Forbidden

Islamic lawyers and spiritual advisers will instruct enquirers which category any action belongs in and its merit before God is attached to it.

Thus, for each Muslim, the basis for taking a moral decision on any issue is quite clear. Fixed rules have been established—with no room for debate.

However, the Islamic world is divided into nations where 'Sharia' is a part of the national law and nations where it isn't. This second category:

▶ Respect and reflect Islamic principles.

▶ Also introduce Western, or other notions of jurisprudence.

To many Muslims this is considered to be a betrayal of the faith. But many governments see it as the only way to live in a world which is totally different to that of the nomadic desert society in which Islam was founded.

The relationship between Islamic law and national law provides problems for Muslims:

▶ Countries such as Iran, Pakistan, Egypt and Sudan have been seeing serious conflict over this issue.

▶ Muslims living in Western societies are caught between a national law with Christian roots and contemporary liberal ethics and their duty to Islamic law.

This is reflected in the bid by British Muslims to establish their own parliament.

Case study

Pakistan adopted Sharia (Islamic) Law in 1991. Since then religious minority groups report that acts of violence against them have increased. This affects Christians, who form the largest minority group.

Naimet Ahmer, headmaster of a government school in Dashua, a village near Faisalabad, was knifed to death on 6 January 1992. The murderer, Sheikh Ferooq, slit Ahmer's throat and abdomen.

This attack took place in public after an attempt had been made by the teachers at Ahmer's school to have him dismissed for speaking about his Christian belief. They claimed that his statement was an insult to the Prophet Mohammed, making Naimet liable to the death sentence.

This illustrates the collision of two religious ethical standards.

▶ Christian ethics demand a love for enemies, and doing good to opponents.

▶ Islamic ethics include vengeance and even killing.

Revolutionary Ethics

Some people have rejected any system of ethics, whatever its foundation.

Marxism is a good example. Karl Marx viewed morality in economic terms.

Marx wanted to overthrow society because its values were deemed to serve the interests of the ruling classes. He believed that revolution would sweep away the power of the church, along with the other institutions of the state.

Yet, Marx and his followers, in rejecting established morality—even including conventions such as marriage—had such a strong sense of justice that they needed a highly moral framework of their own to replace it.

In liberating the oppressed masses from the yoke of economic and social exploitation it was necessary to impose a system of ethical values on them.

Judaeo-Christian ethics had to be replaced by an alternative system. It was based not on the individual but on a strategy for the liberation of the masses. Power and economic progress were fundamental. All else was secondary. Marx wrote, 'Right can never be higher than the economic structure of society.'

Other revolutionaries have rejected all forms of human government inspired by the concept of anarchism, believing people could live in community without civil authority and laws. Its idealism of the free association of people without any rules to regulate behaviour could not work in practice. The strong inevitably exploit the weak without any constraints imposed on them.

Anarchism was expressed as a coherent philosophy only by Pierre-Joseph Prouden in the French Revolution.

In the Spanish Civil War, anarchists fought with Marxists and socialists against General Franco, the Fascist leader. Although still embraced by a few on the revolutionary left today, it has never been successfully implemented outside a few closed communities.

Another revolutionary movement is the philosophy of 'nihilism'.

Some philosophers in ancient Greece suggested that nothing exists and, if it did, it would be unknowable.

In modern times Friedrich Nietzsche (1844–1900) used the term 'nihilism' about the need to destroy existing ethical systems. He believed these as to have continued long after their roots of belief in God, or gods, had been discredited.

Nietzsche:

▶ Wanted to replace traditional values with an unlimited freedom to be oneself—even if this meant conflict and that weak and disadvantaged suffer.

▶ Believed weakness within must be conquered.

▶ Saw true life as freedom from all rules.

Various nineteenth-century Russian revolutionaries used the term 'nihilism' politically. More popularly it has come to be associated with the notion that existence is both pointless and meaningless.

The path of freedom is therefore seen as one in which:

▶ You follow your personal instincts.

▶ Fleeting pleasure is the only worthwhile pursuit in the light of nothingness.

If the existence of God is denied, nihilism gives a logical and depressing conclusion to that perspective.

Buddhist Ethics

Of all major world religions it is possible to argue that Buddhism is the most ethical.

Compared to Judaism, Christianity and Islam, Buddhism has little worship or teaching about a divine being. Instead, the emphasis is on obeying ethical standards so as to live a way of life which can lead eventually to 'salvation'.

The goal of salvation for a Buddhist is to be set free from that endless cycle of cause and effect, both morally and physically.

Buddhists believe all living animals, including humans, are part of a cycle involving being reincarnated in a higher or lower cycle, according to their good or evil actions. Liberation from this endless cycle of 'karma' comes through teaching involving both spiritual understanding and behaviour.

A Buddhist expects many lifetimes will be necessary to achieve this journey. Buddha's teaching is summarized in 'The Four Noble Truths' and 'The Noble Eightfold Path' (see boxes on page 42). The path is largely a system of ethics. These include:

▶ Morality of the whole group.

▶ Personal discipline through which enlightenment may be found.

The Four Noble Truths

1. Suffering—physical, mental and emotional—is the universal lot of mankind. It is in the very nature of life.

2. The cause of this suffering is desire, craving wrong things or the right things in the wrong way. Humans have a misplaced sense of values and possessions, including a desire for individuality.

3. Suffering will cease when desire ceases. The human dilemma can be solved when selfish passion is renounced and extinguished.

4. The way to achieve this is the Eightfold Path, the Middle Way which avoids the extremes of self-indulgence and self-mortification.

Buddhism's Noble Eightfold Path

1. **Right views.** Accept the Four Truths and the Eightfold Path. Resolutely reject all unworthy attitudes and acts. For example, covetousness, lying and gossip.

2. **Right desires.** Renounce all sensual pleasures, ill-will towards others and cruelty to any living creature.

3. **Right speech.** No lying, slander, abuse or idle talk. Be plain and truthful. Speech must be gentle, timely and to the heart.

4. **Right actions.** All moral behaviour especially: abstaining from all killing, even of a potential life such as breaking an egg, stealing and illicit sex. Be charitable.

5. **Right livelihood.** One's occupation must harm no one. Work must be useful, serve others and harness a person's abilities.

6. **Right effort.** Keep striving to:

- Prevent evil arising within

- Overcome evil

- Develop good qualities such as detachment, understanding and concentration

- Maintain these meritorious conditions and allow them to mature and perfect. Universal love is the ultimate climax of this process

7. **Right awareness.** Giving careful consideration without the distortion of desire in thought, speech, action and emotion.

8. **Right meditation.** Intense concentration frees the follower from all hindrances to attain a higher state of consciousness resulting ultimately in full enlightenment and the state of perfection.

Buddhists teach that:

▶ Wisdom comes through morality.

▶ Without practising the right things and having the right attitudes there can be no progress. Man must save himself.

In practice the religion is much more complex.

For the Buddhist, the major problem in life is not moral evil but suffering. Moral evil does not exist for Buddhists because they believe that:

▶ Man has no 'eternal soul', nor an independent existence.

▶ There is no creator, devil, fall, redemption, faith, worship, judgment, heaven or hell.

As a result, Buddhism has been called 'a non-theistic ethical discipline'. Or, to put it into English, a disciplined set of rules for life without any reference to a creator God.

Christians can agree with Buddhists on many moral issues—but have reached that point from a very different view of what is true.

Both religions accept a link between behaviour and salvation. However, the contrast is clear:

▶ Christianity teaches that right moral actions are what come as the result of faith in the one true God. And that this only becomes possible when a person receives the power of the Holy Spirit at conversion.

▶ Buddhism teaches that it is right moral actions that are needed to reach the ultimate state of spiritual attainment.

This must be achieved by first doing, and becoming, what is right—something the Bible declares no one can achieve without help from the Holy Spirit.

Greek Philosophical Ethics

KEY POINT

The Gentile—Roman and Greek—world of the New Testament had ethical principles which confronted the first Christians.

This was similar to the way that Jewish society had been forced to face the ideas and morality of the Greeks and Romans. This provoked controversy and division.

▶ Some Jews worked hard to preserve their Jewish purity. The Pharisees belonged to this tradition.

▶ Other Jews took on board much of the Greek culture seeking to work out their faith within it. By the time of Jesus, these Jews were the majority.

There are three bases on which a system of ethics can be built—reason, experience and the will. Many Greek philosophers believed morality stemmed from man's ability to think rationally. Thinking about God, man and the meaning of life—which is what philosophers do—leads on to trying to lay down a prescription of how life ought to be lived—which is ethics.

Each philosopher gathered a group of followers around him whom he taught. In the small circles of the ruling élite their ideas soon became widely known. In Acts 17:18 Paul debated with some of the Epicurean and Stoic philosophers at the Areopagus in Athens, one of the most important meeting places for the intellectuals of his day.

They were also great writers. Many of their works (for example, Plato's *Republic*) are still widely studied today.

The first-century Mediterranean world, to which the gospel came, was part of the Roman empire. It was a world where:

▶ The highly-tuned philosophy and ethics of the Greeks was in decay.

▶ Military discipline was disintegrating.

▶ Sexual infidelity was common.

▶ Life was cheap and slavery normal.

▶ Urbanization destroyed traditional rural social structures.

▶ Infanticide was practised.

▶ Ritual prostitution was not uncommon.

▶ Inequality of wealth was extreme and flaunted.

▶ Cruelty to humans and animals was accepted as normal.

▶ The bloody shows in amphitheatres as men fought to the death were celebrated, not reviled.

▶ Whole populations were brought under control and repressed by force.

Here was a world that needed a moral revolution. But the ethical philosophies of the educated élite were not sufficient for the task. Many of their lofty ideas were too abstract and remote from the uneducated masses. They stimulated thinking without fundamentally changing attitudes and behaviour. They debated amongst themselves and did not present an agreed agenda for change.

Rome was ripe for the gospel and its message of transformation of the individual and radically new norms for society.

What the Philosophers Taught

Greek ethical thought by itself could not prevent the corruption of its society and that of surrounding nations. But it was highly influential within them.

That influence has lasted through the centuries—in particular in Western culture since medieval times. Certainly, Greek philosophers exercised great influence on the Fathers of the early church. Some church Fathers tried to include the insights of the philosophers into their Christian teaching. However, others ardently resisted the trend.

Justin Martyr (d. AD165) had been an earnest student of philosophy before his conversion. Having tried the Stoics, Aristotelians, Pythagorians and Platonists, he met an elderly man who pointed him to the scriptures and to Christ.

As a Christian, Justin proudly wore the pallium, the philosopher's cloak. He taught that Christianity was the fulfilment of the best of philosophy and that God had enlightened philosophers such as Socrates to see the errors of paganism.

Other leaders of the early church such as **Clement of Alexandria** (c. AD150–216) and **Origen** (c. AD185–254) went even further. Origen used Platonism to reinterpret various major doctrines such as God, Jesus and salvation. Though later condemned as a heretic, he remains perhaps the greatest influence on the Eastern (Greek) church.

Major Greek philosophers

Socrates emphasized the value of relentlessly asking questions to discover truth.

Plato stressed order in society; the reality of the unseen; the immortality of the soul; the need to believe in the gods.

Aristotle gave us basic logic. He taught of a 'prime mover' who necessarily initiated all things, because all effects must have a cause. Morality was found in moderation.

Epicurus taught that death was the end and that the pursuit of pleasure was therefore the point of life.

The Stoics emphasized personal self-sufficiency. They held to high moral standards as dictated by conscience—which was the product of reason, the driving force of the universe.

Opposing this view were men like the Latin writer, **Tertullian** (c. AD160–220), the 'father of Western theology'. He regarded Greek philosophy as the parent of false teaching that influenced the church—particularly gnosticism, an early heresy which believed people were saved through knowledge of spiritual secrets. They regarded this material world as evil. They attracted a significant following on the fringes of the church and were regarded as a serious threat to orthodox Christianity.

He faced many questions which struck at the very basis of ethics. For example:

▶ Was only that which is spiritual good and that which is material bad?

▶ Was God so high, pure and above this world that he could have no contact with it?

▶ Is this world only a world of shadows—a copy of the true reality?

▶ Are changeable humans a poor reflection of the divine eternal unchanging idea, like the image made in wax by a seal on a ring?

▶ Could God have feelings?

▶ Was the 'Logos', the Word or reason—which mediated between God and humanity as taught by the Greeks—to be identified with the 'Word made flesh' of John's Gospel?

▶ Was asceticism—the rigid solitary discipline to rise above the corruption of the world—the correct response?

▶ Was creation inherently good or evil?

▶ Was the soul a divine spark imprisoned by the body to be released at death?

▶ Was salvation by reason or faith?

Many of the philosophers were highly moral, turning their backs on the prevailing attitudes of the day. The first Christians sometimes disagreed with what the Greeks taught about life, values and God. But the influence of that Greek teaching has significantly shaped both the beliefs and ethics of the church ever since.

Two of the most enduring examples have been the attitude of Christians towards their own bodies and sex. The body in scripture is good—created by God.

In Greek thought it was evil—in contrast to the spirit which was good. Many Christians have a 'Greek' attitude towards their own physical being. They overemphasize the spirit/soul as something separate from the body, often neglecting or even despising it.

If the flesh is evil it follows that sex, rather than being a wonderful gift of a holy God who is thrilled at the union of a married couple, becomes something dirty and only for the purpose of reproduction.

The Great Decision

It is hard to choose to live out the ethical standards of the Bible when faced with:

▶ Such a choice of ethical views.

▶ The pressure of what is normal practice in our own culture.

However, there are other reasons that complicate the issue:

> *'Ethics ... is concerned primarily with the imperative and with the philosophical premises upon which imperatives are based. Morality is a descriptive science, concerned with "isness" and the indicative. Morals describe what people do; ethics define what people ought to do.'*
> R.C. SPROUL

When looking for answers as to what is right and wrong the Bible does not always offer instant answers.

Check your Bible concordance and a lot of very useful words are not there. Words like:

▶ Abortion

▶ AIDS

▶ Genetic engineering

▶ Nuclear disarmament

▶ Deforestation

What scripture does give us are the principles on which specific moral choices are to be made. It is from these principles that we relate to today's issues of moral choice.

Although scripture does provide principles which can cover these issues, Christians do not always agree as to how these principles should be interpreted in our contemporary society.

KEY POINT

Biblical society was very different from that in which we now live today.

This raises questions as to which biblical standards should still apply today, and which of them is now redundant.

Should we adopt the Levitical cleansing laws? If not, can we also discard what the Bible teaches on adultery?

KEY POINT

The claims of the authority and traditions of the church complicate matters.

For Roman Catholics the statements of the Pope against the use of modern contraceptives is a contemporary example.

Scripture appears silent on the specific issue and many other Christians would interpret the principles that relate to the issue very differently.

KEY POINT

Christians are almost forced to be double-minded.

We move in two very separate worlds. There is the modern world with its secular ideas. And God's world with its defined morality.

This tension between being 'Christian' and 'modern' affects us most in our ethical standards. Christians believe that scripture has the authority to say something to our world. But how people view and use the Bible in our modern world is absolutely vital.

The Bible is full of suggestions, principles, comments, warnings and laws—but how far can these really be applied to our modern society? What is their actual significance?

Faced with this question there are those who will argue that:

▶ A part of the Bible does not actually mean what it appears to say.

▶ The text means what it says but it is sincerely wrong.

▶ The writer's personal prejudices have distorted the overall meaning.

▶ The text means what it says, but is only valid in a particular context.

▶ That the text means what it says—but it means something entirely different to another individual.

*'*Jesus' teaching was intended as a way of life only for those people who subjected their lives to God's rule. This is the point at which Jesus' ethic has most frequently been misunderstood.

'People who claim to be able to accept the Sermon on the Mount but not the claims that Jesus made about his own person have misunderstood the essential character of Jesus' teaching. It is quite impossible to isolate his theology from his ethics, and to do so destroys both.'
JOHN DRANE, *INTRODUCING THE NEW TESTAMENT*, LION, 1986

If our ethics are to be truly biblical we must have a proper procedure for discovering what scripture actually says and means.

Five simple rules help to guide us.

Rule Number 1. Authority has to be placed somewhere. If scripture is what it claims to be—a divine revelation given by divine inspiration—then it has authority over us. God's word carries God's authority. Because of who God is, we have to believe what he says (Numbers 23:19; 1 Samuel 15:29; Titus 1:2; Hebrews 6:18).

Rule Number 2. A text cannot be expected to mean to us what it could never have meant to its author or readers. Therefore fanciful interpretations are out!

Rule Number 3. When the situation being addressed by scripture is the same as our own, God's message to us must be the same to us as it was to his people at that time.

Much Bible interpretation comes down to simple common sense. For example, people would not believe we should obey the system of sacrifice laid out in Leviticus. But most Christians accept that when Paul writes that we should 'give, not reluctantly or under compulsion, for God loves a cheerful giver' (2 Corinthians 9:7), that instruction is valid and applicable to us today.

We must ask whether something that scripture prohibited to a first-century church still has a genuine application in our society today.

▶ Eating meat offered to idols (Romans 14:13–23; 1

KEY POINT

Is there a Christian view of modern ethical subjects or is it possible to have a variety of authentically Christian viewpoints?

*'L*ove and then what you will, do.'
AUGUSTINE

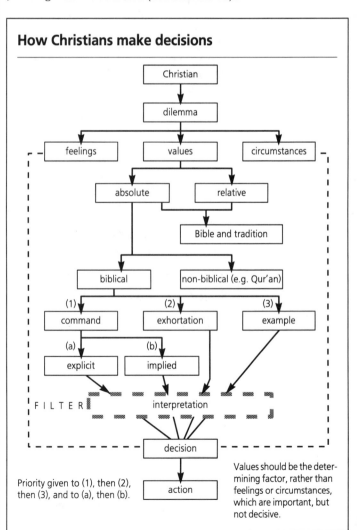

How Christians make decisions

Priority given to (1), then (2), then (3), and to (a), then (b).

Values should be the determining factor, rather than feelings or circumstances, which are important, but not decisive.

Corinthians 8:1–13) might have caused a fellow Christian to stumble in those days. But what is its direct equivalent today?

▶ Ladies wearing head coverings (1 Corinthians 11:4–16) related to Christian women giving the impression through their dress that they were immoral. So what is the equivalent today?

Rule Number 4. We must ensure that scripture determines our response to culture, rather than allow culture to shape our reading of scripture.

Most Christians do translate Bible texts into new settings.

Problems come when a text is not straightforward. The fashion of long hair for men in the 1960s created a clash between culture and the biblical statement: 'Does not the very nature of things teach you that if a man has long hair, it is a disgrace to him' (1 Corinthians 11:14).

This demonstrates that culture affects the common sense we bring to bear on our hermeneutics (what the text says today). But so does our church tradition.

A church will endorse Paul's teaching to Timothy or Titus but deny his policy of establishing plural leadership. Often we will ask how we can get around a text inconvenient to our tradition, rather than enquiring what it actually means.

This practice is sometimes called 'cultural relativity' and we must beware of becoming its unconscious victims.

Instead we need to:

▶ Identify which practices relate only to the culture to which they were written.

▶ Recognize where the New Testament speaks consistently on an issue and where it does not (for example, sexual immorality as opposed to food offered to idols).

▶ Distinguish between principle and specific instruction.

▶ Use Christian charity where we disagree with other Christians.

We should not make concessions to the truth of scripture, but rather express that truth in such a way that it is understood within the culture in which it is being expressed.

Rule Number 5. Begin with a text at its face value. Then examine it in the light of the sense of the whole passage and the whole of scripture.

▶ Examine the obvious and natural meaning of a passage. Too often human cleverness has tried to build vast theories on a passage which completely ignore its simple meaning.

▶ Examine the author's intentions and, using scripture to interpret scripture, we can then arrive at the right conclusion (John 20:31; 2 Timothy 3:15).

▶ Ask that God will speak. Not to say what we want him to say, or necessarily expect him to say. But to communicate whatever is his desire. Our response is not to criticize, or to argue, but to obey.

This may sound a complicated process but it is absolutely vital if we are to adopt biblical attitudes, and think 'Christianly' about these issues which face us today.

How to understand scripture

First we must understand what the passage meant to those it was originally written to. This is called exegesis. Then we must interpret it into our own culture and times so that we can understand its meaning for us. This is hermeneutics.

A few simple rules help us:

1. A text can never be expected to mean to us what it could never have meant to its author or readers.

2. When the situation being addressed by scripture is the same as our own, God's message to us must be the same as it was to his people at that time.

3. We must ensure that scripture determines our response to culture rather than allow culture to shape our reading of scripture.

4. Begin with a text at its face value and then proceed from there to examine it in the light of the sense of the passage and of scripture in its entirety.

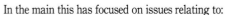

The Wide Agenda

Today's evangelicals have wrongly tended to concentrate on those ethical issues which directly affect them personally. Or where there appears to be a clear response.

In the main this has focused on issues relating to:

▶ Sunday observance

▶ Sexuality

▶ Abortion

However, the concerns of scripture relate ethics to a far wider range of issues.

We must also explore what the Bible has to say about:

▶ Materialism

▶ Infanticide

▶ Poverty

▶ War

▶ Homosexuality

▶ Homelessness

▶ Child abuse

▶ Divorce

▶ Nuclear warfare

▶ Human rights

▶ Unemployment

▶ Genetic engineering

▶ Education

▶ Violence

▶ Pollution

▶ Euthanasia

▶ Slavery

▶ Remarriage

▶ Pornography

▶ Prosperity

▶ Two-Thirds World

▶ Disability

▶ Lesbianism

▶ AIDS

'The infallible rule of interpretation of Scripture is the Scripture itself: therefore, when there is a question about the time and full sense of any Scripture it must be searched and known by other places that speak more clearly.'

THE WESTMINSTER CONFESSION OF FAITH

KEY POINT

KEY POINT

How conscientious are you in using the five principles of understanding scripture in your application of what you read? Do you consistently apply it to your own 'hobby horses'?

What ethical issues are most important to you? Are they the most important for society? Are they the most important to God?

▶ Racism
▶ The elderly
▶ Feminism
▶ Medical ethics
▶ Transvestism

Not that each one of us can play an active part in responding to every ethical issue in scripture. But:

▶ We must support those who are relating scripture to different ethical issues to those on which we are focusing.
▶ We must move beyond theory and speaking about ethical truth in order to respond by means of our gifts, possessions and love.
▶ We must be tolerant of those Christians who after an honest search of an ethical issue have reached a different conclusion to our own.

The Struggle for Answers

KEY POINT

Not all Christians will draw the same conclusions from scripture about each specific ethical issue. But that is no excuse for avoiding the issues.

The following two examples highlight the problems — demonstrating what can be learned, what can not and where we need to disagree with understanding.

What About War?

This is not a subject where all evangelicals agree. During the Second World War some evangelical Christians were:

▶ Fully involved in the fighting
▶ Active in support services
▶ Endured detention as conscientious objectors

It is fifty years since the United Kingdom was engaged in a major war. Yet two minor wars in the last decade should convince us that we do need to consider what our response to this issue should be.

So how do we begin to work out an ethical approach to the subject of war?

How would the secular existentialist respond?

Existentialist thinking is of little help. One person will join one side, his neighbour may join the other, both seeing their own interests differently. A third may take a pacifist's stance and opt out entirely. Jean-Paul Sartre, the most famous of its modern advocates, would refuse to advise his followers faced with an ethical dilemma.

If the guiding principle is 'love'—the problem is how to apply it in a conflict. Who do you love if people hate each other? What does it mean to be free yourself—if this conflicts with another's idea of freedom?

Existentialism alone fails to answer such dilemmas.

How does the biblical Christian respond?

Despite our differences, there is much on which we

agree. We all:

▶ Affirm that the kingdom of God, inaugurated by Jesus, is God's rule of righteousness and peace (Romans 14:17).
▶ Hear the command to love our enemies, forbear revenge, pursue peace and hunger after righteousness (Matthew 5:6, 9, 38–40, 44).

But, at the same time, scripture talks about:

▶ Justice (Micah 6:8; Deuteronomy 32:4).
▶ Living at peace 'as far as you are able'.
▶ Armies sent into battle by God.

So there is a dilemma. As can be seen by highlighting the arguments for each of the three major positions on war held among evangelicals today.

Should Christians Fight?

Scripture describes over thirty occasions in the Old Testament where God commanded the use of armed force (for example, Exodus 17:8–16; Joshua 1:1–9).

Scripture describes God himself as a 'warrior'.

▶ God destroyed the enemies of Israel (Exodus 15:3–4).
▶ More than 200 times in the Old Testament God is called the 'Lord of Hosts' which can mean 'The Commander of Armies'.
▶ The psalmist calls God a warrior (Psalm 35:1–2; Psalm 144:1).
▶ He sanctioned holy war (1 Samuel 15:1–23).

God raised up military commanders and heroes among his people and honoured military leaders.

▶ Gideon
▶ David
▶ Jephthah
▶ Saul

The presence of the Holy Spirit equipped God's people for military conquests or for acts of personal violence.

▶ David (1 Samuel 16:13).
▶ Samson (Judges 15:14–16).

God commanded his people to fight and kill. Examples include:

▶ The conquest of Canaan.
▶ The wars against the Philistines.
▶ The massacre of the prophets of Baal and Asherah by Elijah.
▶ The destruction of Jezebel and her family by Jehu.

Jesus used physical force in cleansing the temple (John 2:13–16).

The New Testament affirms the military:

▶ It avoids the demand that soldiers should leave their employment (Luke 3:14).
▶ A Roman soldier is commended by Jesus (Matthew 8:10; Luke 7:9).
▶ Peter is sent to a Roman centurion (Acts 10).

Jesus predicted:

▶ God would use force in punishing those who

KEY POINT

'For a Christian who believes in Jesus and His gospel, war is an iniquity and a contradiction.'
POPE JOHN XXIII

'A great war leaves the country with three armies—an army of cripples, an army of mourners, and an army of thieves.'
GERMAN PROVERB

'In modern warfare there are no victors; there are only survivors.'
LYNDON B. JOHNSON

'War is sweet to them that know it not.'
ENGLISH PROVERB

'War can only be a desperate remedy in a desperate situation, used in order to spare humanity a still greater evil, when all essentially reasonable and peaceful means have proved ineffective.'
RENÉ COSTE

Why don't we like thinking about war?

'There is nothing that war has ever achieved we could not better achieve without it.'
HAVELOCK ELLIS

'We must have military power to keep mad men from taking over the world.'
BILLY GRAHAM

disobeyed his instructions (Matthew 10:14–15; 18:23–25; Luke 10:10–15).

Paul used the military symbolism, rather than that of the civilian lifestyle, to explain the Christian life (Ephesians 6:10–20; 2 Timothy 2:3–4).

The operation of the death penalty in Israel may indicate that God does not automatically exclude violent death as an act of justice (Genesis 9:6; Exodus 21:12–17; Leviticus 20:2, 27). So if violent death is the price of obtaining justice or liberation, it is therefore permissible.

Jesus never expressed disapproval of those whose occupations indirectly involved military affairs. For example:

▶ Jesus commanded people to pay taxes, even though much of the money raised would support the occupying military forces.

The instruction to be subject to ruling authorities (1 Peter 2:17; Romans 13), implies submission to military forces.

Historically the church has maintained support for the state in military conflicts.

▶ John Calvin stated the classic reformed position: 'The reason for waging war which existed in ancient times, is equally valid in the present age.'

▶ Martin Luther initially supported the bloody suppression of the Peasants' Revolt.

The idea that it is acceptable to take part in a 'just war' predates Christianity. The idea was taken on by the early church leader Augustine. In the Middle Ages the idea was developed by Thomas Aquinas.

Today this view continues to be held by the majority of Protestants and Roman Catholics.

For a war to be regarded as 'just', three factors must be present:

▶ **Its motivation must be a just one.** It should not be caused by a desire for revenge or provoked by hatred and animosity. It is likely to be defensive rather than aggressive; to punish injustice and to prevent greater evils being perpetrated.

▶ **Its means must be controlled.** Violence should be minimized and the intentional killing of civilians outlawed.

▶ **Its message is that evildoers must be punished.** Therefore it is only entered into with the firm expectation of success.

This attitude does not minimize the horrors of war, but it does provide a rationale to distinguish the type of conflict in which Christians might be prepared to be involved.

Those in the armed forces lack any choice as to the ethical basis of the war they are called to fight. They must conform to the demands imposed upon them by the 'ruling authorities' (Romans 13:1).

Should Christians Be Pacifists?

Jesus commended the peacemakers.

▶ This is true in his Sermon on the Mount (Matthew 5:9).

▶ This theme runs throughout the New Testament where the word 'peace' occurs more than 100 times.

The Old Testament principle of holy war shows God fighting for his people, not with them. But when Israel is disobedient God fights against them (Numbers 14:39–45). This is therefore a 'special case', which shows that God is for righteousness not for war.

▶ Military leaders were replaced by God with non-violent prophets.

God told his people not to kill.

▶ This was his word in the Ten Commandments.

▶ He called Abraham to a policy of non-resistance towards the Philistines and to feed a hungry enemy.

▶ Elisha was called to lead the Syrians blind to Samaria and to protect them from massacre (2 Kings 6:19–23).

It is only in the Old Testament—where kingdom and state were combined—that God used war as his means of establishing his people in the land and expelling their enemies.

The prophets declared that a day would come when swords would be beaten into ploughshares, and spears into pruning hooks (Micah 4:3; Isaiah 2:4).

The principle of non-resistance (Matthew 5:39–41; Romans 13:7; 1 Peter 3:9) was an essential part of the gospel of salvation (1 Peter 2:21–23; Philippians 2:5–15).

The Lord declares that vengeance is his province, not ours (Romans 12:19).

Jesus demanded that:

▶ We should love our enemies (Matthew 5:44), and that we should love our neighbours as ourselves (Matthew 22:39).

▶ It is extremely difficult to love someone while committing violent acts against them.

▶ Paul and James agreed with this emphasis (Romans 12:9–21; James 2:8).

The military option was never the one Jesus chose.

▶ Although Jesus had Zealots (violent revolutionaries) among his disciples—and was crucified by the Romans as if he were one—he always chose peace. When he approached Jerusalem the shout 'Save us now' *(Hosanna)* died out when instead of turning towards the fortress of Antonia to repel the Romans he turned right and cleansed the temple.

Jesus spoke against:

▶ The use of the sword (Matthew 26:52)

▶ His servants fighting (John 18:36)

▶ When Peter used a sword, Jesus healed his victim.

▶ Jesus rejected the use of legions of angels to defend himself on the cross (Matthew 26:53).

Among the apostles:

▶ Paul proclaimed that Christians used different weapons (2 Corinthians 10:4).

Jesus never identified himself as Messiah in terms of a military ruler. Rather he chose to see himself as the suffering servant of Isaiah 40–55.

As such he:

'*P*eace is liberty in tranquillity.'
MARCUS TULLIUS CICERO

KEY POINT

'*M*y religion is based on truth and non-violence. Truth is my God and non-violence is the means to reach him.'
MOHANDAS GANDHI

KEY POINT

'*W*e [Christians in war] are called to the hardest of all tasks; to fight without hatred, to resist without bitterness, and in the end, if God grant it so, to triumph without vindictiveness.'
WILLIAM TEMPLE

'*T*o be prepared for war is one of the most effectual means of preserving peace.'
GEORGE WASHINGTON

'*W*hen Christ came in to the world, peace was sung; and when he went out of the world, peace was bequeathed.'
FRANCIS BACON

KEY POINT

▶ Called for peace not war.

▶ Became vulnerable rather than dominant.

▶ Called for social justice.

▶ Extended salvation to the Roman enemy.

Both Jesus, and the writers of the epistles, called for a policy of non-resistance.

▶ They desired to overthrow evil, but by good actions, not violent ones (Matthew 5:39–41; Romans 12:17–21; 1 Peter 3:9).

The picture of Jesus as a suffering servant is that of a non-resistant lamb being meekly led out to be slaughtered (Isaiah 53:7).

▶ Jesus loved those who despised and rejected him.

▶ Jesus prayed for forgiveness for those who crucified him.

Until the Roman Emperor Constantine declared himself to be a Christian, the majority of Christians refused to serve as soldiers.

This may have been due to a desire to avoid the idolatrous practices associated with life in the Roman army. However, there are still significant numbers of Christians who take the same view today.

Can Both Answers Be Right?

These two attitudes—'a just war' or 'peace at any price'—are clearly incompatible with one another. Yet both claim the Bible as the basis for their view.

How can we draw ethical truth from both views? Here are some observations.

▶ We live at a different time in God's plan to that in which Jesus walked and spoke by Galilee. Perhaps the commands issued in the Sermon on the Mount await fulfilment when the kingdom is finally established. Some Christians have even claimed that until the kingdom fully comes we can ignore the instructions which Jesus gave when on earth.

▶ Perhaps the command not to 'kill' refers to an action conducted with malice or hatred. It is argued that the Hebrew word for 'kill' in the sixth commandment refers to 'murder' rather than the taking of human life in a just cause.

▶ While in warfare our killing is more objective. We can kill while still loving, not hating, our victim.

▶ Perhaps the New Testament has now replaced the Old Covenant. Warfare was legitimate then—as a divine concession to Israel's sin, when kingdom and state were united—but that no longer applies.

▶ Perhaps the end justifies the means. In Israel's day force was used for good purposes. That example still holds good for today.

▶ Perhaps it is inconsistent to take the life of someone who has yet to commit themselves to Jesus Christ. As Myron Augsburger has suggested: 'We cannot kill a man for whom Christ died ... we cannot take the life of a person God purposes to redeem.'

▶ Perhaps just as Jesus achieved much significance through his suffering, we must follow his

example—seeking to be servants not power-brokers (Philippians 3:10; 2 Corinthians 4:10; 1 Corinthians 10:33).

When the War Is Nuclear

When the concept of war becomes nuclear war the debate moves a major step forward.

Nine simple statements convey an impression of the magnitude of the problem.

▶ Human history was designed to end in a coming king, not in nuclear conflagrations.

▶ MAD is what the word suggests—Mutually Assured Destruction can never be within the will of God.

▶ The build-up of radiation through testing together with the proliferation of nuclear waste pollutes God's creation.

▶ The danger of human error—either in terrorism, accident or in a processing plant—is increased daily.

▶ Human creativity—a mark of being made in the image of God—is used to plot human destruction.

▶ It represents a vast waste of human energies and resources. Twelve million children die of hunger in the Two-Thirds World each year, while what the West spends on nuclear armaments in one year could solve the problems of hunger at a stroke.

▶ At the same time some poor countries spend more on weaponry than on health and education combined.

▶ It represents the potential indiscriminate destruction of innocent men, women and children.

▶ It could affect the climate, producing a nuclear winter.

Unilateral or Multilateral?

The recent reduction in tension as a result of the break-up of the old Soviet Union does not remove the possibility of either conventional or nuclear war. Individual ex-Soviet States and some Arab nations pose a potential danger. India and Pakistan both possess nuclear weapons that could be used in the next war between them.

Traditionally, Christians have been divided into 'pacifist' and 'just war' lobbies. More recently these lobbies have often come together to agree on a

---

The facts of the matter

Between 1484 and 1945 there were 278 wars.

Since 1945 there have been 133 wars worldwide. If the duration of individual wars is added together it totals 369 years. Each of these wars lasted, on average, for more than three years.

Between 1945 and 1976, on any average single day, 11.5 wars were taking place simultaneously.

Adapted from A. Gregory et al., editors, *Den Frieden entwickeln*, Gütersloh Verlaghaus, 1981

KEY POINT

'**F**rancis Bacon is a case in point. His moral confusion—the confusion at the heart of much of modern science—came from the assumption, echoing Plato, that human intellect could safely analyze and understand the natural world without reference to any moral principles defining our relationship and duties to both God and God's creation ... Since the onset of the scientific and technological revolution, it has seemingly become all too easy for ultra-rational minds to create an elaborate edifice of clockwork efficiency capable of nightmarish cruelty on an industrial scale. The atrocities of Hitler and Stalin, and the mechanical sins of all who helped them, might have been inconceivable except for the separation of facts from values and knowledge from morality.'
SENATOR AL GORE, *EARTH IN BALANCE*, EARTHSCAN, 1992

KEY POINT

'**P**eace is not made at the council tables, or by treaties, but in the hearts of men.'
HERBERT HOOVER

Is nuclear war morally different from conventional war?

'**T**he springs of human conflict cannot be eradicated through institutions, but only through the reform of the individual human being.'
DOUGLAS MACARTHUR

policy of nuclear pacifism.

But should the Christian ethical position call for unilateral or multilateral disarmament?

The Conclusion

Christians who seriously examine the ethics of war are likely to find that their conclusion will fall into one of three categories:

Militaristic. Maintaining that:

▶ Force is the only way to uphold peace.

▶ Patriotism and preservation of national identity must be preserved.

▶ Old Testament Israel provides a vivid illustration of these two attitudes.

This view is hard to support from a careful study of scripture.

Pacifist. Maintaining a firm commitment to never resist and never to fight—in any conflict.

However, can it be practical or even just to maintain a totally pacifist position?

Limited involvement. Maintaining that a restricted military response is acceptable if it protects the innocent victims of aggression. This would:

▶ Sanction involvement in a 'just war'.

▶ Agree to the support of armed services employed for national defence and the restoration of justice in other countries.

But is it reasonable to believe that wars can ever remain 'just'? Conflicts escalate.

It is clear that the latter two attitudes can both be sincerely held by Christians—yet they are in disagreement with each other. Whatever camp we are in, it will be an important example of our personal ethics.

The discipline is to work out our own convictions from a basis of scripture rather than from public opinion, the media, our family history, friends or any of the other key influences on our thinking. If there should be another war in our lifetime it could be of more than academic importance.

What About Homosexuality?

On the subject of homosexuality the Christian seems to be totally out of step with the rest of society. The rejection of the 'normality' of homosexual behaviour makes Christians appear narrow-minded and bigoted.

This is particularly true in the face of a culture where:

▶ Codes support positive discrimination in favour of homosexuals.

▶ Constant affirmation from the media.

▶ Even those who lived promiscuously—like certain entertainers who died of AIDS-related illnesses—are treated as heroes.

▶ It has been accepted that homosexuality is neither a disease nor a disability—but the

recognized sexual orientation of a large minority. At the same time:

▶ The Gay Christian Movement has a high public profile.

▶ There are churches, some describing themselves as 'evangelical', that are primarily for those involved in homosexual and lesbian relationships.

▶ It is widely accepted that the Church of England has active homosexuals among its clergy.

So how can we begin to work out a biblical ethic on the subject of homosexuality that is based on what the Bible says rather than in our own assumptions or prejudice?

The Case for Homosexuality

Those who see homosexual practice as being compatible with the teaching of the Bible do so because they believe the following:

That the sin of Sodom was not that of homosexuality but inhospitality (Genesis 19:8).

▶ The word 'know' is taken to mean 'get acquainted with' rather than referring to sexual intercourse.

▶ The violence that erupted came from the fear that Lot, an outsider, might have been entertaining enemy agents in his home. Sodom's sin is therefore seen as not simply that of 'sodomy'.

▶ Jesus mentioned the fate of Sodom and Gomorrah on three separate occasions without reference to homosexual malpractice (Matthew 10:15; 11:24; Luke 10:12).

▶ Sodom is regarded as being guilty of pride and selfishness, of social injustice and deceit, of greed and adultery (Isaiah 1:10–17; Jeremiah 23:14; Ezekiel 16:49–52).

▶ The Apocryphal books also mention Sodom's pride (Ecclesiasticus 16:8) and inhospitable attitude (Wisdom 10:8).

That the Levitical law which condemns homosexual practices (Leviticus 18:22) is now irrelevant and redundant. That same law:

▶ Condemned the eating of pork and shrimp.

▶ Banned wearing clothes made of mixed fabric.

These ceremonial laws—and many others—have been disposed of (Acts 10:15) in the new covenant made by Jesus.

That in order to understand the biblical condemnation of homosexuality, we must recognize its purpose. This was:

▶ To reject the idolatry associated with homosexual practices at the cultic shrines (Deuteronomy 23:17).

Therefore, it was the idolatry, not the homosexuality, that was wrong.

That the Old Testament prohibition of homosexuality must be seen against the cultural background of the time.

▶ Being barren was regarded as the equivalent of being cursed (Genesis 16:1; 1 Samuel 1:3–8).

▶ Children were regarded as a blessing from God (Psalm 127:3).

Is your instinctive reaction to the subject of homosexuality primarily based on your understanding of scripture or your own sexual feelings?

KEY POINT

'O*vert homosexuality* is physical sexual contact between members of the same sex. *Latent homosexuality* is having impulses and desires towards a member of the same sex which are unconscious, or if conscious are not sexually expressed . . . *Lesbian* or *sappho* are terms often referred to female homosexuality after Sappho, a female homosexual who lived on the Isle of Lesbos in ancient Greece. *Homophobia* is defined as the fear of being in contact with homosexuals and, in the case of homosexuals themselves, self-loathing.'

ALASTAIR V. CAMPBELL, EDITOR, *A DICTIONARY OF PASTORAL CARE*, SPCK, 1987

If homosexual practice was unacceptable amongst the Jews in the Old Testament does that necessarily mean it is wrong in Britain today?

Therefore, any sexual activity which could not produce offspring was rejected as unacceptable.

That Isaiah predicted a day of acceptance for homosexuals into God's kingdom (Isaiah 56:3).

That the case of the men of Gibeah is one of inhospitality rather than sexual perversion (Judges 19:23).

That Paul's rejection of homosexuality could be regarded as merely his own opinion.

▶ Twice in 1 Corinthians Paul expresses that he is voicing a private opinion (1 Corinthians 7:12, 25). So his condemnation of homosexuals (1 Corinthians 6:9) could just be the reflection of his own opinion—after all he also condemned men who grew their hair long! (1 Corinthians 11:4)

That Paul may only be referring to offensive homosexual acts rather than the private and faithful relationship of consenting adults.

That when Paul called homosexual conduct 'unnatural' (Romans 1:26) he could be declaring that such behaviour was 'unnatural' for heterosexuals. That does not mean he was issuing a condemnation of all homosexuality.

That Jesus never condemned homosexual conduct. If this issue was so important why was he so silent?

That the translators have blurred the true picture:

▶ The same word, *arsenokoitai*, is translated 'homosexual offenders' (NIV) in 1 Corinthians 6:9–10, and 'perverts' (NIV) in 1 Timothy 1:9–10. May a true understanding be that Paul rejects male prostitution, orgies, and the corruption of the young?

▶ This word could never be used of a loving, constant relationship between two people just because they happened to share the same gender.

That David and Jonathan enjoyed a homosexual relationship together.

▶ Jonathan 'loved' David (1 Samuel 18:3).

▶ Jonathan stripped in David's presence (1 Samuel 18:4).

▶ The two kissed each other (1 Samuel 20:41). Some have read a term meaning 'ejaculation' into this verse as well.

▶ David's mixed fortunes in his relationships with women have also caused some to assume that he was bisexual.

That moral standards have changed.

▶ That the right to privacy and freedom for consenting adults should guarantee homosexuals the right to an equal participation in the life of the church.

▶ That the sexual tendency of homosexuals is inherited, and they could not change their sexuality any more than the colour of their eyes.

The extent of the use of scripture to justify homosexuality may surprise many people. The key issue is how scripture is interpreted. The case against homosexuality appeals to many of the same verses but with different conclusions.

The Case Against Homosexuality

Those who see homosexual practice as not being compatible with the teaching of the Bible do so because they believe the following:

That Sodom's sin was that of homosexuality.

▶ The adjectives 'vile', 'wicked' and 'disgraceful' (Genesis 18:7; Judges 19:23) are not appropriate if Sodom's error was simply that of inhospitality.

▶ The fact that Lot offered his virgin daughters to satisfy the crowd does imply a clear sexual motivation to the actions of the men of Sodom.

▶ Of the twelve times that the verb 'know' (Hebrew, *yedha*) is used in Genesis, on ten of these occasions it refers to sexual intercourse. One of these is in the Sodom story itself, referring to Lot's daughters.

▶ Jude 7 clearly refers to the Sodom incident as one of homosexual lust run rampant. The same arguments apply to the situation at Gibeah (Judges 19:23).

That while sodomy was not Sodom's only sin, according to scripture it was certainly one of them.

▶ It is only possible to escape this conclusion by casting doubt on the authority of the biblical records.

▶ The testimony of second-century BC Palestinian writings made the same assertion as did Jude.

That to put the Levitical law against eating pork and shrimp in the same category as the law against homosexual acts is debatable. There was a major difference in the standard of punishment for these two prohibitions.

▶ Eating offences were punished by a few days of isolation.

▶ Homosexuality incurred the death penalty.

That if the law against homosexuality is to be seen as just part of the ceremonial law which is now redundant, then rape, incest and bestiality also can no longer be regarded as moral offences against God's law.

▶ These acts are all condemned in the same chapter as homosexual sins (Leviticus 18:6–14, 22–23).

▶ While the Gentiles did not possess the ceremonial laws, homosexual acts among them were also condemned by God (Leviticus 18:1–3, 25).

That this argument is settled by the fact that Jesus changed the dietary laws of the Old Testament (Mark 7:18; Acts 10:12). Yet homosexuality continued to be prohibited in the New Testament (Romans 1:26–27; 1 Corinthians 6:9; 1 Timothy 1:10; Jude 7).

That both homosexuality and adultery are condemned without any clear connection to idolatry (Leviticus 18:22; Romans 1:26–27). Homosexuality was not therefore only prohibited when linked to idolatrous practices.

That scripture never states that homosexual practices were sinful because no children could result from them.

▶ If to be childless was always a divine curse then

When is tolerance a virtue and when a vice?

'*T*he Bible clearly condemns certain kinds of homosexual practice (. . .gang rape, idolatry and lustful promiscuity). However, it appears to be silent in certain other aspects of homosexuality—both the "homosexual orientation" and "a committed love-relationship analagous to heterosexual monogamy".'

LETHA SCANZONI AND VIRGINIA MOLLENKOTT, *IS THE HOMOSEXUAL MY NEIGHBOUR?*, SCM PRESS, 1978

singleness would also be sinful. Both Jesus and Paul hallowed singleness by precept and practice.

▶ The significance of child-bearing was linked to populating the land with the people of God. Gentiles could not be involved, yet their homosexual practices were also condemned (Leviticus 18:24).

That to dismiss Paul's teaching against homosexual practice as just personal prejudice is to deny the revelation he consistently claimed from God (Romans 1:5; 1 Corinthians 2:13).

▶ Paul even concludes his first epistle to the Corinthians with the affirmation, 'What I am writing to you is the Lord's command' (1 Corinthians 14:37).

That to claim Paul is speaking only of homosexual 'offences' is not consistent with scripture.

▶ Elsewhere in scripture no distinction is made between different types of homosexual activity (Leviticus 18:22; Romans 1:26–27; 1 Timothy 1:10; Jude 7).

That Paul also speaks of idolaters and adulterers. But is it reasonable to assume that only offensive kinds of adultery and idolatry can be assumed to be evil?

That Isaiah's prophecy concerned 'eunuchs' not homosexuals. And eunuchs are asexual not homosexual.

That in Genesis, God ordained heterosexual relationships when he created male and female and instructed them to have children (Genesis 1:27–28). Thus:

▶ Sex was given a family context from the very beginning. It was introduced as the seal and content of marriage (Genesis 2:24; 1 Corinthians 6:15–17; Exodus 20:14–17; Hebrews 13:4).

That Paul's denunciation of homosexuality as 'against nature' is clearly referring to God's intention that sex is for men and women, not for men to engage together in anal intercourse (Romans 1:27).

That Jesus' silence on the issue is not significant as an argument from silence is always a weak one.

▶ To suggest that because Jesus never specifically denounced homosexuality does not mean he therefore approved of it.

▶ Jesus lived and worked in the Jewish world. While Paul wrote his letters to those whose cultural world was Roman and Greek. Homosexual practices were far more commonplace in the situations which Paul addressed than in those which Jesus encountered.

That the translators of the Revised Standard Version heeded the protests and adopted the form 'sexual perverts' in their second edition. This does not minimize the clear judgment of the New Testament.

That scripture takes no account of the length and consistency of a relationship as a justification or otherwise of its morality.

That the plain fact is that homosexual practice was a denial of God's natural order and unacceptable to him.

That there is no evidence that David was bisexual. Judging by the number of wives he had, David possessed a surplus of heterosexuality.

▶ The kiss with Jonathan was a common cultural greeting for men at that time. It did not occur when Jonathan stripped, but two chapters later (1 Samuel 20:41).

▶ Jonathan only divested himself of his armour and royal robe (1 Samuel 18:4).

▶ The emotion at their parting was weeping, not orgasm (1 Samuel 20:41).

That Christians want to affirm that basic moral principles do not change with the times.

▶ What scripture has ordained must remain the same.

▶ Human privacy and mutual consent cannot justify that which God has forbidden.

Putting it in Perspective

There is mistrust on both sides of the divide.

▶ The active homosexual accuses those who condemn his lifestyle as having started from the point of prejudice and homophobia.

▶ Those who condemn homosexual activity fear that those who advocate its practice are prejudiced by their own sexual preferences.

More than that, it is essential to understand that this debate may be about ethics but it is also about people—with emotions. Many have deep and painful inner struggles with their sexuality and need compassion rather than condemnation.

This debate is not without its tensions and regrets.

It is therefore important to affirm that which scripture powerfully declares, but to do so with an attitude of humility and not one of condemnation.

▶ Paul wrote: 'All have sinned and fall short of the glory of God' (Romans 3:23).

▶ Jesus warned of the dangers of arrogance when he said: 'If any one of you is without sin, let him be the first to throw a stone at her' (John 8:7).

Evangelicals have sometimes been tempted to place a greater emphasis on sexual sin than on other forms of moral failure. That is wrong.

▶ Paul places envy, selfish ambition, discord and fits of rage alongside drunken orgies, impurity and sexual immorality (Galatians 5:19–21). It is hard to claim that we are not guilty of the first part of the list, even if some may manage to avoid the second.

▶ Scripture does not give a hierarchy of sin, and we should not seek to invent one today.

If we are horrified at the mote of homosexual practice in the eye of our brother we should similarly be appalled at the beam of selfish ambition in our own.

There is also the danger of a homophobic reaction to those of a homosexual orientation. That is totally wrong. Homophobia is not a biblical response.

▶ We may disapprove of homosexual practice but can develop friendships with people of all orientations.

Was Paul's teaching on homosexuality the result of his own reaction to the overt sexual practice of many men of the time?

'Taken together, St Paul's writings repudiate homosexual behaviour as a vice of the Gentiles in Romans, as a bar to the Kingdom in Corinthians, and as an offence to be repudiated by the moral law in 1 Timothy.'
PETER COLEMAN

► Our disagreement is not a licence to ignore, reject or be paternalistic towards someone for whom Christ died.

There is also a temptation to compromise on an issue that can be so pastorally sensitive. It may seem more loving to hold back on what we believe the truth of the Bible to be—framing our ethic from a natural sense of compassion. That is a dangerous solution.

KEY POINT

<u>We need to take the scriptural teaching on an issue like homosexuality and use biblical models to apply it.</u>

In doing so we must remember:

► God's standards are not to be reduced by well-meaning Christians.

► God's love extends to the sinner, not the sin.

► God's servants should not be self-righteous but kind and compassionate.

It is important to affirm that it is not the orientation but the practice that God condemns. To wrestle with a constant urge to steal is not to sin. Only when we succumb to temptation do we merit condemnation.

Christians should love, help and support one another. Whatever the struggles they may personally endure we should always be open to help. And not just ourselves, but non-Christians too. Then our ethic is not sterile words, but God's love in action.

Living it All Out

Many accusations have been levelled against evangelical Christians. We have been charged with:

► Hiding away from involvement with the real world.

► Being so 'heavenly-minded' that we cannot be considered as being of any earthly use.

► Being simplistic and failing to explore and respond to those issues which confront society today.

► Confining our interest to moral rather than social issues.

► Self-interest, with an over-preoccupation with those issues which directly impinge upon ourselves.

► Burying our heads in the sand and ignoring our culture.

KEY POINT

<u>If we are to recover respect in society we must regain an understanding of the ethical implications of our faith.</u>

In order to do this, five requirements can be made of each one of us.

1. We must return to first principles. The Bible is where we begin. To fail to explore what scripture has to say about real issues is to deny our belief in the timeless authority of the Bible.

If we are to engage in a meaningful dialogue with the world around us then we must be convinced of the ground on which we stand.

<u>We must adapt church programmes and agenda to engage in a discussion of the real problems faced outside the church community.</u>

We must not simply keep to our own pet issues. Instead we should employ scripture to make it possible to respond to a whole range of issues constantly hurled at us by our culture, often by way of the mass media.

We are called to be able to give guidance and leadership from a biblical perspective, to counter the arguments and actions of our secular society.

2. We must adopt lifestyles that match our convictions. It is not enough to have views on a subject. We need to demonstrate the sympathy and compassion of Jesus in the way that we live.

If we wish to say something about AIDS, abortion, homelessness or homosexuality then our actions must match our words and, ideally, precede them.

Arid ethic statements have nothing to say to the single parent, the dying victim of AIDS, the African refugee, the lonely and rejected homosexual and the derelict vagrant on the streets. But compassion in action is very eloquent.

3. We must fearlessly address society. Rather than meekly conforming to the cultural ethics popular among our contemporaries we need to be prepared to offer an alternative which is both reasonable and reasoned.

If scripture is the revealed word of God, then it is relevant to the whole of humankind. If the lion of biblical teaching is to be uncaged then we must remove the bolt and let truth out!

This will mean a thorough examination of all the Bible has to say about ethical issues so we may adequately 'be prepared to give an answer to everyone who asks you to give the reason for the hope that you have. But do this with gentleness and respect' (1 Peter 3:15).

4. We need to learn how to disagree with one another. There is a clear distinction between those issues where the meaning of scripture is plain, and where it is uncertain.

There is a subtle difference between the two ethical illustrations we have used—war and homosexuality. While scripture clearly rejects homosexual practice it is far from clear on the issue of military service.

In one case we need to proclaim what scripture says—but with love and compassion. In the other we must carefully listen to one another, and respect opinions different to our own.

<u>Distinguishing between 'primary' issues and 'secondary' ones is important.</u>

► Where scripture declares its position we cannot dispute it.

► Where the meaning is not stated with absolute clarity we have the right to exercise private judgment.

5. Our ethics must determine our lifestyle. Even our brothers and sisters in Christ will not always be in agreement. So it is always wise to gain mature advice from those in Christian leadership.

It was to address just such a situation that Paul wrote in Romans 14–15. Christians were disagreeing over the secondary issue of whether or not they could eat meat which had been offered to idols.

<u>Paul responded with four principles which can govern our attitude to ethical issues today.</u>

In an After Hours event at Spring Harvest the 14-year-old daughter of two of the speaker team was invited to serve on a panel with her mother and grandmother. She was asked, what was the greatest pressure she faced at school? Her reply has gone down in Spring Harvest folklore: 'Explaining to my friends why I am still a virgin.'

KEY POINT

KEY POINT

In matters essential—unity,
In matters non-essential—liberty,
In all things—charity.'
THE APHORISM OF WITSIUS

▶ *Examine all available biblical evidence* and be fully persuaded in our own minds as to the proof of our ethical position.

▶ *Recognize that we must one day give an answer to God for our position.* We will all have to give an account to our Lord, Judge and King.

▶ *Recognize that we must not be guilty of actions or attitudes which would cause other Christians to stumble or fall.*

▶ *Pursue those things that create harmony and growth* in the character of one another.

Living in the light of our ethics will affect how we live in our homes, our church fellowships and our local communities.

To live in the light of a 'moral' or 'immoral' world is not to lock ourselves behind closed doors and hope the real world will go away. It is to venture out:

▶ Prepared to cling tenaciously to that which we know to be true.

▶ To challenge the assumptions and the lifestyles of those around us.

FOUNDATIONAL READING

David Cook, *The Moral Maze*, SPCK, 1983

Norman Geisler, *Christian Ethics*, Inter-Varsity Press/ Apollo, 1990

FURTHER READING

Michael Alison MP and David L. Edwards, editors, *Christianity and Conservatism*, Hodder & Stoughton, 1990

David Atkinson, *Peace in Our Time*, Inter-Varsity Press

Richard Bauckham, *The Bible in Politics*, SPCK, 1989

Anne Borrowdale, *Distorted Images*, SPCK, 1991

Florence Bulle, *God Wants You Rich*, BHP, 1983

Nigel M. de S. Cameron, *The New Medicine*, Hodder & Stoughton, 1991

Alastair V. Campbell, editor, *Dictionary of Pastoral Care*, SPCK, 1987

Tony Campolo, *The Success Fantasy*, Victor, 1980

Tony Campolo, *20 Hot Potatoes Christians Are Afraid To Touch*, Word, 1988

Tony Campolo, *Who Switched the Price Tags?*, Word, 1986

Michael Cassidy, *The Politics of Love*, Hodder & Stoughton, 1973

David Cook, *Dilemmas of Life*, Inter-Varsity Press, 1990

David Cook, *Living in the Kingdom*, Hodder & Stoughton, 1992

Edward Craig, *The Mind of God and the Works of Man*, Clarendon Press, 1987

Donal Dorr, *The Social Justice Agenda*, Gill & Macmillan Ltd., 1991

Martyn Eden and Ernest Lucas, *Being Transformed*, Marshall Pickering, 1988

Jacques Ellul, *The Humiliation of the Word*, Eerdmans, 1985

Jacques Ellul, *Violence*, Mowbrays, 1969

Charles Farah, *From the Pinnacle of the Temple*, Logos

David Field, *God's Good Life*, Inter-Varsity Press, 1992

Brian Frost, *The Politics of Peace*, DLT, 1991

Bob Gordon, *The Foundations of Christian Living*, Sovereign World, 1988

Os Guinness, *The Gravedigger File*, Inter-Varsity Press, 1983

A.E. Harvey, *Strenuous Commands*, SCM Press, 1990

Kathleen Heasman, *Evangelicals in Action*, G. Bles Ltd., 1962

William A. Heth and G.J. Wenham, *Jesus and Divorce*, Hodder & Stoughton, 1984

Richard Holloway, editor, *Who Needs Feminism?*, SPCK, 1991

Michael Keeling, *The Foundations of Christian Ethics*, T & T Clark, 1990

Andrew Kirk, *God's Word for a Complex World*, Marshall Morgan, 1981

Donal B. Kraybill, *The Upside-Down Kingdom*, Herald Press, 1978

Hans Küng, *Global Responsibility*, SCM Press, 1991

David Lyon, *Future Society*, Lion, 1984

John Macquarrie, *The Concept of Peace*, SCM Press, 1973

John Macquarrie and James F. Childress, *A Dictionary of Christian Ethics*, SCM Press, 1986

Roy McCloughry, *Taking Action*, Frameworks, 1990

Roy McCloughry, *The Eye of the Needle*, Inter-Varsity Press, 1990

Dan McConnell, *The Promise of Health and Wealth*, Hodder & Stoughton, 1990

Peter C. Moore, *Disarming the Secular Gods*, Inter-Varsity Press, 1989

René Padilla and Chris Sugden, editors, *Texts on Evangelical Social Ethics 1974–1983*, Grove Books Ltd., 1985

Wolfhart Pannenberg, *Christianity in a Secularized World*, SCM Press, 1988

Ronald H. Preston, *Religion and the Ambiguities of Capitalism*, SCM Press, 1991

Myron Rust, *Lord of the Marketplace*, Victor, 1986

Jack T. Sanders, *Ethics in the New Testament*, SCM Press, 1975

Jean-Paul Sartre, *Existentialism and Humanism*, Methuen, 1948

Francis Schaeffer, *A Christian Manifesto*, Pickering, 1982

Schluter et al., editors, *The Application of Christian Principles to Public Policy*, Jubilee Centre, 1992

Ronald Sider, *Christ and Violence*, Lion, 1979

Moises Silva, *Has the Church Misread the Bible?*, Apollos, 1987

Howard A. Snyder, *The Community of the King*, Inter-Varsity Press, 1977

R.C. Sproul, *Right and Wrong*, Scripture Union, 1983

John Stott, *Issues Facing Christians Today*, Marshall, 1984

Willard M. Swartley, *Slavery, Sabbath, War & Women*, Herald Press, 1983

A.N. Triton, *Whose World?*, Inter-Varsity Press, 1970

Kenneth Vickery, *Choose Health, Choose Life*, Kingsway, 1986

Andrew Walker, *Enemy Territory*, Hodder & Stoughton, 1987

Tony Walter, *All You Love is Need*, SPCK, 1985

Pete Ward, *Youth Culture and the Gospel*, Marshall Pickering, 1992

R.E.O. White, *Biblical Ethics—The Changing Continuity of Christian Ethics*, Volumes 1 and 2, Paternoster Press, 1979 and 1981

James Woodward, editor, *Embracing the Chaos*, SPCK, 1990

Christopher J.H. Wright, *Living as the People of God*, Inter-Varsity Press, 1983

David Wright, editor, *Essays in Evangelical Social Ethics*, Paternoster Press, 1979

Ravi Zacharias, *A Shattered Visage*, Wolgemuth & Hyatt, 1990

Not all of these books may be available at the event.

Evangelism
Living in a Lost World

CONTENTS

Book of the seminar day:
David Cook, *Dilemmas of Life*, Inter-Varsity Press

Introduction

The single word 'evangelism' creates a wide mixture of emotions.

▶ Hostility

▶ Excitement

▶ Embarrassment

▶ Inferiority

▶ Natural reservation

But—above all—it evokes

▶ Fear

American author Rebecca Manley Pippert points out that

KEY POINT

'Christians and non-Christians have one thing in common, they are both uptight about evangelism.'

Considering the level of dislike for this subject, it is surprising that evangelism is now being discussed with such unparalleled intensity around the world. There are:

▶ Conferences

▶ Consultations

▶ Projects

▶ Missions

▶ Calls to evangelize

▶ Research projects

Yet there is a wide gulf between discussing and planning and actually getting the job done.

In the United Kingdom more than 40,000,000 people are outside of the Christian church. That represents too many zeroes for most of us to cope with. That leads to twin dangers:

▶ We see evangelism as a special science, for a group of dedicated professionals

▶ We do nothing and feel guilty

Most of us are apprehensive about sharing our faith. Yet we have been called to risky living—to living on the edge. So how can we move beyond a recognition of the problem and begin to respond personally to the task before us?

Projects and Megaplans?

The 1980s were declared by the Evangelical Alliance as a decade of evangelism. The challenge led to a series of initiatives including the visits of Billy Graham and Luis Palau. As a result:

▶ Thousands of Christians were involved in prayer triplets, nurture groups and the mission meetings.

▶ Thousands made their commitment to Christ and have become part of local churches.

▶ A natural sense of exhaustion has accompanied the conclusion of a decade of intense activity.

▶ Despite considerable gains in fresh vision and new converts, a huge task still faces us.

Now, the 1990s are a decade of evangelism. This stems from the 1988 Lambeth Conference which issued a call to the Anglican Church to join with other Christians in a Decade of Evangelism during the 1990s.

In addition, the AD2000 movement has issued a challenge that the whole world should be evangelized before the year 2000. The call focuses our attention on a particular date, and on the global proportions of our task.

▶ New strategies and concepts have emerged to concentrate our energies on fulfilling the task.

▶ Fresh and innovative thinking has been combined with the resources of contemporary technology.

▶ The vision and skills of parachurch agencies have combined with denominational mission bodies to release new plans and resources.

All of this is designed to equip us to fulfil the commission of Jesus to reach the whole world with the gospel within our own lifetime.

Computers, statisticians and strategists have been devoted to solving the problem: 'How do we go and make disciples of all nations (Matthew 28:19), within our generation?'

It has been suggested that, to complete the task, we need:

▶ better plans

▶ better technology

▶ better equipment

▶ better structures

▶ better funding

To help make it happen:

▶ A whole new vocabulary has been introduced to communicate the objective

▶ Attempts are being made to link together all initiatives aimed at reaching people with the gospel on a global scale

Such action can harness vision within certain cultures. But others will merely feel intimidated by their failure to launch a 'gigaplan' or engage in a 'megaministry'.

Did you know?

We may, or may not, be encouraged to realize 'the extraordinary fact that, like it or not, all the essential elements of such a Great Commission global giganetwork are already in place: 42 million computers owned and operated by Christians, 100 million other screens or terminals, 4,000 Great Commission computer networks, 56 global networks, nine maganetworks, and vast armies of 50 million Christians who are expert operators, programmers or systems analysts... Giganetworking can thus be seen as an acid test for Great Commission effectiveness... There are 36 possible giganetworking relationships involving 72 one-way attitudes between the nine mainline Great Commission global meganetworks.'

■ Megaministry = a specific global or other large-scale ministry reaching or evangelizing over one million persons a day.

■ Megamissionary = a term coined for a missionary who is engaged in or working with a megaministry.

■ Gigaplan = a Great Commission gigaplan is a massive currently-expanding organized global megaplan for world evangelization which is expending over US $1 billion in a decade.

■ Megaplan = as a gigaplan but expending over US $100 million.

■ Master global plan = a possible global plan to evangelize the world which would encompass and incorporate the ministries of all other existing global plans, fitting them into some kind of master global framework.

Taken from David B. Barrett and James W. Reapsome, *Seven Hundred Plans to Evangelize the World*, New Hope, 1988

'In many quarters of the church evangelism is still considered a dirty word. It has the sniff of proselytising about it, of big meetings—and famous but perhaps simplistic and slick preachers. It is suggestive of illicit psychological pressure, and if it has a particularly notable impact, of mass hysteria. And yet... does not evangelism mean the spreading of good news? And if you have found good news, it is churlish indeed to keep it to yourself. If you are thrilled about it, why should you not show it?'
MICHAEL GREEN

'Witnessing is removing the various barriers of our self-love to allow Christ, living within us, to show himself to our neighbours.'
PAUL FROST

'If Christ lives in us, controlling our personalities, we will leave glorious marks on the lives we touch. Not because of our lovely characters, but because of his.'
EUGENIA PRICE

What were the three most significant factors in you coming to faith in Christ?

Witnesses Wanted

Without sacrificing vision or the ability to set goals and objectives it is important to restate a clear biblical principle.

KEY POINT

Our society may dictate that 'big is beautiful' but scripture appears to offer an alternative model. We are the answer.

Today, evangelism is almost exclusively thought of in terms of special events or special people. But that is not God's intention. God has always used people to spread his message.

The Way God Planned it

KEY POINT

Ever since the fall of humankind (Genesis 3) God's plan has been to restore people to a right relationship to himself.

God established covenants with Noah (Genesis 9:1–17), Abraham (Genesis 12:1–3; 17:1–22) and Moses (Exodus 20:1–26) that provided a way for this to happen.

▶ Israel was to be a light among the nations (Isaiah 42:6; 60:3) although her record was frequently one of failure.

▶ The coming Messiah was to not only bring Israel back to God but also to extend salvation to the Gentiles (Isaiah 49:6).

▶ Jesus was recognized as the 'true light' (John 1:9) and called himself 'the light of the world' (John 8:12). He told his followers that they also should be lights (Matthew 5:16).

▶ Paul, quoting Isaiah 49:6, applies the Messianic prophecy as a command to take the gospel to the whole world. And he tells the Philippians they are like 'stars in the universe' or 'lights in the world' (Philippians 2:15) bringing together the ideas of purity of life and witness to the surrounding darkness.

▶ In 2 Corinthians 4:3–6 Paul equates preaching Jesus Christ as Lord to light shining in the darkness.

God has always relied on people to example his message—to be models of the truth they preach as ambassadors from another realm (2 Corinthians 5:20).

KEY POINT

Jesus:

▶ Preached the message of the coming of the kingdom of God (Mark 1:14–15) and of salvation through his own work (John 3:17; 10:9).

▶ Used Isaiah 61:1–3 as his manifesto (Luke 4:18–19) linking the anointing of the Holy Spirit with the task of preaching good news.

▶ Trained his disciples to continue the task, sending out not just the twelve (Luke 9:1–6) but seventy-two followers (Luke 10:1–20) as well as individuals such as the Gerasene man he healed (Mark 5:18–20).

▶ In his great prayer (John 17) is concerned not just for his followers but for the subsequent generations who will believe because of their witness (John 17:20). The whole prayer is that they will, by the Father's aid, continue the work he has begun.

God has called each one of us to be his witnesses—light-bearers—at home, in our communities, throughout our nation and, ultimately, to the far corners of the globe.

KEY POINT

Through our prayer, conversation or actions, we are all called to bear witness to what we have seen and heard.

The apostles had a unique authority when they spoke. They were 'eye-witnesses' of what they had seen and heard of Jesus personally (Acts 5:32; 10:39; 13:31; 1 Peter 5:1; 1 John 1:1–4). Our witness is to be to:

▶ The truth we have learned

▶ Our own experience of Christ

The Chambers English Dictionary says:

> **'witness**—*knowledge brought in proof; testimony of a fact; that which furnishes proof; one who sees or has personal knowledge of a thing; one who gives evidence … bear witness—to give, or be, evidence.'*

Can God Really Use You?

Each one of us is the creation of the living God. When we have committed our lives to God he longs to equip and to use us to build his kingdom.

Strangely, we can believe that God can use us to speak, teach or worship. But we are dubious about our ability to introduce other people to his forgiveness and love.

This is not the result of sincere humility. Rather, it is doubt as to his ability to make us usable and effective.

Of course, there is value and sense in using gifted people, together with well-organized plans. Yet this should never lead to us ignoring the vast potential of each one of us. Nor should we be guilty of using them to do our job for us.

However, in truth:

'Our task as laymen is to live our personal communion with Christ with such intensity as to make it contagious.'
PAUL TOURNIER

'God's means of drawing people to himself has always been, and always will be, people. No amount of literature, recourse to sophisticated forms of communication, activity, or the hiring of gifted preachers, can ever substitute for personal relationships.'
STEPHEN GAUKROGER

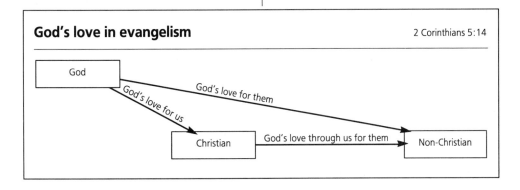

God's love in evangelism   2 Corinthians 5:14

God → *God's love for us* → Christian
God → *God's love for them* → Non-Christian
Christian → *God's love through us for them* → Non-Christian

Some definitions

Evangelical: (noun) A person who believes the historic truths of the Christian faith, and is committed to living out their implications.

Evangelism: (noun) The activity of sharing the Christian faith, with an aim that others will become followers of Jesus Christ.

Evangelist: (noun) A person involved in sharing the Christian faith. A role officially recognized by most Christian denominations and often a person's full-time vocation.

Evangelize: (verb) The act of sharing the good news about Jesus, with an aim that others will become followers of Jesus Christ.

Evangelistic: (adjective) A description given to an activity which has the aim of communicating the Christian message.

Evangelicalism: (noun) The overall evangelical movement, their beliefs and activities.

Issued by the Evangelical Alliance Press Office

▶ Few people are given the specific ministry of the evangelist (Ephesians 4:11), with the accompanying spiritual anointing to lead many people to faith in Jesus Christ.

▶ Few people have preaching and teaching skills.

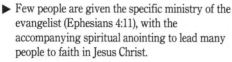

KEY POINT

But we have all been called to give testimony about our Lord Jesus and to his truth.

God Used People in Church History

Surveying the history of the church tends to do little more than throw up a lot of spiritual heroes. Men and women of God like Polycarp, Felicitas and Perpetua, Tertullian, Boniface, Wycliffe, Luther, Bunyan, Wesley, Moody, Billy Graham.

Just as important are the multitudes of ordinary people who simply told those around them about Jesus.

All Christians are witnesses. On a scale of 1 to 10 what kind of witness are you?

If you were called to testify in court as a character witness of Jesus, what would be the outstanding evidence from your life?

The early years of the church: AD30–500

Christianity spread with breathtaking speed throughout the Roman world.

Christianity was largely based on the key Roman cities—for example, Rome (Romans 1:7), Ephesus (Acts 19:1—20:1), Corinth (Acts 18:1–18), Athens (Acts 17:16–34)—initially in Asia Minor, Greece and Italy.

The message spread along the trade routes mainly through the planting of churches to North Africa (Alexandria and Carthage), Syria, Spain, France (notably Lyon), Central Europe and even to Britain.

These churches then became missionary communities seeking to evangelize their localities.

Most converts were attracted through casual contact with Christianity and its followers. Often interest was aroused by:

▶ witnessing a martyrdom

▶ observing the way Christians cared for strangers

▶ receiving hospitality from the church

Church growth was often immediate, wide-spread and sustained. By the year AD150:

▶ Flourishing churches existed in nearly all the Roman provinces from Syria to Rome.

'*E*loquent speeches, visual aids, films, seminars and discussion groups are, after all, no substitute for the daily, un-spectacular witness of the rank and file Christian. If that witness is consistent and open, then no improvement in tactics or strategy will better it as a means of winning people for Christ. If it is not, then no evangelistic programme, no matter how ambitious or sophisticated, will make the slightest impact. That is a lesson we have been slow to learn.'
DAVID WINTER

▶ To the west there were churches in such far-flung outposts as Gaul (modern France). Christianity had already arrived in Britain.

▶ To the east, there were churches beyond the fringes of the Roman empire. Strong churches could be found in the major cities.

▶ The churches of Alexandria and Carthage were probably already in existence by this time.

Referring to the Roman world, Justin Martyr—the Christian apologist—maintained that the gospel had spread among all classes of people. He said,

'*There is not one single race of men, whether barbarians or Greeks, or whatever they may be called, nomads or vagrants, or herdsmen dwelling in tents, among whom prayers and giving of thanks are not offered through the name of the Crucified Jesus.*'
DIALOGUE WITH TRYPHO

Paul's extensive missionary journeys, together with the initiatives of other apostles do not begin to explain the fantastic growth of the early Christian church.

The plain fact is that the gospel was not spread throughout the Roman world by either preachers or professionals. The growth and spread of the church was due to thousands of anonymous believers who simply gossiped the gospel, and discussed their new-found faith with their friends and contemporaries.

These unrecorded witnesses:

▶ Were scattered throughout the Roman world—as traders, business people, refugees, soldiers and the like.

▶ Mainly gathered in private houses, using them as evangelistic outposts.

The spread of the gospel was greatly helped by:

▶ The ease of travel and the common language and culture of the Roman world.

▶ The long period of peace and stability—the Pax Romana—which provided safety and trust.

▶ The spiritual failure of the existing 'mystery religions', creating a hunger for truth.

▶ The persecution of the secular authorities: pagans were deeply impressed by Christian patience in the face of extreme suffering.

▶ The quality of their lives—and the conviction of the message they carried.

Case history

In the second century AD one of the earliest Christian apologists, Justin Martyr, gave his life in the cause of the gospel.

He was interrogated in a hostile pagan court:

Judge: Where do you have your meetings?

Justin: Wherever we can. Our God fills heaven and earth.

Judge: Tell me where!

Justin: I live upstairs in the house of Martin . . . If anyone wishes to come in to me there, I pass on to him the true doctrine.

Quoted in John Foster, *The First Advance*, SPCK, 1972

Are you prepared to suffer in order to advance the kingdom of God?

KEY POINT

*E*vangelism was, 'a very daunting prospect... involving social odium, political danger, the charge of treachery to the gods and the state, the insinuation of horrible crimes and calculated opposition from a combination of sources more powerful perhaps than at any time since.'
MICHAEL GREEN

Case history

Stories of personal heroism and devotion are found among evangelistic pioneers in the early church. Two young men, Aidesius and Frumentius, were ship-wrecked on the Red Sea and taken into slavery at the Ethiopian court.

Despite encountering considerable opposition from the king they gained his eventual favour, were awarded high office at court, and won a number of converts.

From their efforts came the birth of the Ethiopian Church around AD330. A few years later Frumentius was consecrated as its first bishop.

KEY POINT

It was the way that the individual believers lived within pagan society that carried the greatest impact.

The Emperor Julian, who persecuted the church was forced to admit, 'Through the loving service rendered to strangers ... the godless Galileans care not only for their own poor but for ours as well.'

KEY POINT

The combination of Christian compassion and spoken evangelism has always been an essential component of effective witness.

Too often evangelism is solely perceived as that moment of climax when someone finally commits their life to Jesus Christ. But there may have been many steps along the road before an individual arrives at that ultimate destination.

Each point in a person's spiritual pilgrimage is the product of evangelism, either through the reading of scripture, the direct intervention of the Holy Spirit without use of a human intermediary, or through the involvement of another individual.

So Why Don't We Witness?

KEY POINT

When it comes to talking about our faith, few of us rise to the occasion.

▶ We feel that we will look foolish and lose our credibility.

▶ We don't want to spoil our relationship with friends or neighbours by suggesting that we are superior to them.

▶ We don't want to force our opinions on them.

▶ We don't want to raise a subject, like religion, which can be a 'turn-off' to our friends.

▶ We don't know enough doctrine; we are uncertain about the content of our faith.

▶ We are not certain whether we would be able to answer the questions we might be asked.

▶ We fear that they might reject our message—and, therefore, us.

▶ We doubt that we can explain why Christianity is the only way to a personal relationship with God.

▶ Our insecurities create problems for us. We wonder if our lives would stand up to the assessment of our friends if we began to share Jesus with them.

▶ We might tremble at what their initial reaction would be.

The cage of evangelism

Some of the bars which lock us into our private spiritual world include:

Methodology	locked into techniques
Guilt	not doing it
Weakness	personal inadequacy
Example	leaders don't, why should we?
Contraception	don't want the problems that 'new babies' create
Failure	my friends don't get converted
Cowardice	fear of people
Complacency	like the local church the way it is
Minority	most Christians don't do it anyway
Rejection	rebuffed by individuals
Irrelevance	not connected with the real world
Sterility	same old theme
Loneliness	inadequate support
Insularity	no non-Christian friends
Unbelief	God couldn't use me
Enemy action	spiritual warfare
Shame	the local church is not what it should be like

Checkout:

Tick which three of the following most apply to you.

I seldom talk about Christianity with others because:

☐ I am afraid I will cause offence

☐ I really don't know what to say

☐ I feel this isn't my job

☐ I don't think I have the answers to people's questions

☐ I don't think my relationship with God is good enough

☐ Though I do have faith in God, I seldom experience his power in my life

☐ I am afraid of being rejected

☐ I worry that people will think I'm a hypocrite

☐ I am just not motivated to share my faith

☐ I would be embarrassed

☐ I don't like setting myself up as an expert

☐ I believe Christianity is a private matter between me and God

☐ I have seen other Christians 'witnessing'; I would be embarrassed to do that

☐ I don't have enough opportunities

☐ I don't think my friends would want to know anyway

☐ I might lose a friend

Adapted from John Grayston, editor, *Care to Say Something?*, Scripture Union, 1982

What is the real reason why you are reluctant—if you are—to share your faith?

How has God used you recently to help someone move on further in understanding God's love and forgiveness?

These fears are perfectly natural—and almost universal. Not just at first but every time.

It does not have to be this way.

▶ The Holy Spirit is never more with us than when we are seeking to share our faith (Acts 1:8).

▶ Jesus promised us that his 'yoke is easy' and his 'burden is light' (Matthew 11:30). This includes the yoke of 'witness'.

▶ God calls us to be faithful. Our success lies in being obedient to his call on our lives, not in seeing instant results.

Evangelism is not about success or failure. It is about being faithful to the abilities God has given to us.

If we can get this right, it could be the beginning of a significant evangelistic momentum which the Holy Spirit could use to create a major impact throughout the United Kingdom.

KEY POINT

What Is Our Message?

Our message is the full counsel of God as revealed in scripture. In evangelism this usually means focusing on the life, death and resurrection of Jesus Christ; who he is and what he has said.

There are many aspects to the Christian message but becoming a Christian demands some basic steps.

▶ Recognizing we need help (Romans 3:23).

▶ Being ready to turn our back on everything we know to be wrong (Acts 2:38).

▶ Putting our trust in Jesus to make things right with God (1 Peter 2:24).

▶ Inviting Jesus to be in charge of our life (John 1:12).

Evangelism Starts With People

KEY POINT

Unlike the religious leaders of his day—who preferred to stay in the safety of their private and professional networks—Jesus invested time with non-religious people.

Often these friends of Jesus represented an unlikely choice. Like:

▶ Zacchaeus (Luke 19:2)

▶ Publicans and prostitutes (Luke 15:1)

However:

KEY POINT

Most people who become Christians as adults lose normal social contact with non-Christians within two years.

The main reasons are:

▶ The church keeps them too busy to maintain friendships

▶ It avoids the need to cope with confronting non-Christian standards

▶ It is more comfortable to be among those who

share your values and views

This means that there is a need to give priority to sharing the gospel, as soon as possible, with the friends and family of new converts.

One Korean pastor asks each new convert, 'Who do you know that we could invite to a meal so that I can explain to them what has happened to you.'

It is vital to widen our circle of influence—particularly for those who have been brought up almost exclusively in the environment of the church.

Opportunities for developing an active Christian presence in society

▶ **Neighbours**—developing friendship and support for neighbours, baby-sitting, Avon, casual conversation, meals and so on.

▶ **Leisure**—sports centres, golf clubs, aerobic societies, adult education—join!

▶ **Community**—resident associations, Neighbourhood Watch schemes, local radio, community associations, Samaritans, community newspaper and so on.

▶ **Schools**—The PTA, governors or general school social activities.

▶ **Volunteers**—voluntary activities in the community including Citizens Advice Bureau, Relate and other groups.

▶ **Groups**—Women's Institute, Mothers' Union, Young Farmers, Scouts and Guides, Territorial Army and so on.

▶ **Medical**—hospital and hospice visitation, counselling support groups and so on.

▶ **Elderly**—visitation, shopping, transport, support to old people's homes.

▶ **Trades Unions**—works councils, staff and professional associations.

▶ **Politics**—local and national political societies and discussion groups.

▶ **Disadvantaged**—soup kitchens, work with homeless, single parents, physically disabled and so on.

▶ **Environment**—action groups, garbage disposal, decorating and gardening schemes within the community.

These initial suggestions are only a beginning. There are many more opportunities. Some would relate to a distinctive situation in our own community. Others would be a response from our community to a local, national or even an international need. For example:

▶ When some friends heard of the desperate plight of Romanian children they organized a town-wide support scheme. They organized the venture as Christians, but involved the whole community.

It would lack integrity to become involved in an activity for which we sustained no interest other than viewing it as a potential platform to 'get' people. Also:

▶ None can become involved in every opportunity that is presented

KEY POINT

KEY POINT

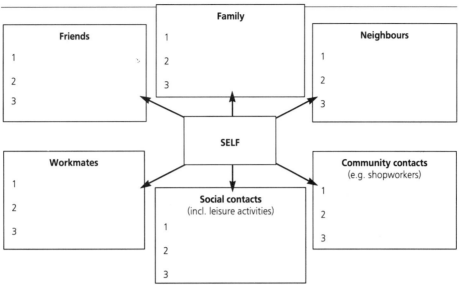

Networks for personal friendship

Family
1
2
3

Friends
1
2
3

Neighbours
1
2
3

SELF

Workmates
1
2
3

Social contacts
(incl. leisure activities)
1
2
3

Community contacts
(e.g. shopworkers)
1
2
3

Complete the diagram by filling in the names of the relationships you already have with non-Christians which could be used as a platform from which you can share the gospel. Use the diagram to pray for them by name.

▶ We need the support of our local church or fellowship

▶ We must make sure that it is God's opportunities we take, not those of our own creation

KEY POINT

People Are Not Objects

To think of people merely as potential converts is to deny their human dignity.

God created humankind to live socially together—as friends and neighbours—sharing the joys and pains of life. It is out of this experience that we are to share God's love.

Each of us should be able to identify their own social network. This will include neighbours, friends, workmates, those who share the same social interests.

In addition each of us will have specific networks:

▶ For a non-working parent with young children it will be others in a similar position—met at the school gates or the playgroup

▶ For a factory-worker it will be those with whom they work

▶ For those at school or college it will be their personal friends

Our responsibility is to be:

▶ personally involved with other people

▶ expressing the character of God in the way we live

▶ being ready to answer the questions that are provoked by our lives

It is in this context that the Holy Spirit will create the opportunities for us to witness.

Only the Holy Spirit can translate friendship and personal acquaintance into a hunger on the part of the non-Christian to discover more about Jesus Christ.

It is a big step between someone having contact with Christians and them actually being interested in Jesus. (See diagram on page 62.) But there are some principles to follow.

Live an attractive lifestyle: A loveless, joyless, narrow and legalistic Christian lifestyle is unlikely to be attractive to anyone.

A generous, warm, compassionate and caring lifestyle is a key factor and one which the early Christians clearly possessed.

Their characters displayed the fact that they had found someone who had changed their lives.

If we display personalities that radiate humour, kindness and concern then we are not likely to be friendless.

Share interests with others. If all we can talk about are 'Christian things' then we will be left with only Christian friends. Developing an active genuine interest in other issues creates a more rounded personality and provides genuine contact-points with non-Christians.

Be interested in others. Good contact points are birthdays, anniversaries. Also an interest in problems or celebrations, high-points or low-points, where we can show a sincere interest and concern.

This should not be one-way traffic. The non-Christian can show interest, sympathy and concern for us as well—indeed often we have more to learn than to teach in this area.

Look out for the lonely. There will often be a 'lame dog', someone ignored within our circle of acquaintances. Give them time and concern.

Listen more than you speak. There's no point shouting 'Jesus is the answer' when nobody is asking the question.

Be ready with answers. Actions may speak louder than words but actions without words are not enough.

Don't point the finger. Don't come across as superior. It is not helpful to accuse people of having shallow, frustrated, alienated, purposeless, lonely and meaningless lives.

KEY POINT

How many of your best friends are non-Christians?

What has been the most effective evangelistic activity you have taken part in recently?

'*E*very Christian in Britain today has a network of relationships: family, neighbours, colleagues at work, friends, people met at the squash courts or while waiting outside school to meet the kids.'

LAURENCE SINGLEHURST,
EDITOR, *THE EVANGELISM
TOOLKIT,* CWR

Twelve hints on developing conversation with non-Christian friends

▶ Don't artificially try to direct every casual conversation towards 'spiritual issues'.

▶ Show genuine interest in the subjects your friend wants to discuss.

▶ Be prepared to put forward a Christian perspective on issues, without being too threatening or personal.

▶ When given an opportunity share your faith, don't duck it. This may be the moment.

▶ Pray and look for the Holy Spirit to give wisdom and direction.

▶ Be prepared for the long haul. It is rare for friends to be instantly ready to discover faith.

▶ Use the opportunities for discussion raised by TV programmes, current events and so on.

▶ There is a great deal of potential in a simple testimony as to what God has done in your own life—but avoid 'hype' and religious language.

▶ Don't take yourself too seriously. Humour, even at your expense, never did anyone any harm.

▶ Ask probing questions, where appropriate, in order to discover your friend's personal position and perspectives.

▶ Don't be afraid to say 'I don't know—but I will find you an answer.' Then find one.

▶ Don't push too hard.

Ideas file

Be ready to share at a practical level.
A man became a Christian through the 'ministry' of a lawn-mower! His Christian neighbour offered the use of his powered machine to help him out. After about six weeks the man was so impressed that he started asking questions about the Christian life, and eventually made a commitment to follow Christ. By sharing your resources you can actually show, and not just tell.

Find relaxed ways to introduce your networks to your Christian friends.
Invite people round for dinner—a few Christians together with some non-Christian friends. The idea is to relax, be normal. Don't push your faith, don't hide your faith. Be welcoming, and don't invite the kind of believers who can't cope with the real world and real people. Always make sure that the Christians are outnumbered.

Be thoughtful and supportive in times of stress.
'Get well soon' cards can be a non-threatening statement of care. Drop into the hospital, take some fruit, offer to watch neighbours' plants, keep an eye on the house when they have to be away, offer to be a telephone contact for relatives.

Hold a party for your neighbours.
Hold a barbecue—and invite your neighbours. Take the initiative, invite that lady next door in for a coffee and a chat. Don't play Spring Harvest worship tapes as background music.

Join in with positive local events.
Christians can be really good at asking everybody to be involved in their events, but show little interest in everything else that's going on locally. Good contacts can come from putting a float in the annual carnival though not necessarily with a Bible theme. As a result of this you will find conversations beginning—'Oh yes, I saw your lot in the parade . . .' Join a political group, find a club that caters for a hobby that you have, get fit at the local health club, get involved in the community associations.

Be a good listener.
As a Christian you have Godly wisdom—gently make it available! If people start asking you for advice, don't be an irritating know all quoting endless scriptures. Pray that God will help you to present his wisdom in a down-to-earth, non-religious way. Expose your faith, don't impose it.

Taken from Laurence Singlehurst, editor, *The Evangelism Toolkit,* CWR

Conversation is a two-way process. Be a good listener. This is often far more important than being a good speaker.

Pray: As someone has said, if you want to talk to John about God, first talk to God about John.

Understanding the Process

Evangelism is not just that moment of personal surrender. It equally involves each point in the process of bringing an individual from a total lack of awareness of God through to a recognition of their need of him.

KEY POINT

'*P*eople were drawn to Jesus both by His supernatural ministry, and His warm personality.'
LAURENCE SINGLEHURST

KEY POINT

Steps to Christ

Changing attitudes — *Changing knowledge*

10 Decision to surrender to Christ
9 Acceptance of the implications
8 Acceptance of Christian truth
7 Understand the implications of this
6 Grasp the truth about Jesus
5 Decide to investigate Jesus
4 Interest in Jesus Christ
3 Contact with Christians
2 Some awareness of God
1 No awareness of God

Adapted from Laurence Singlehurst, editor, *The Evangelism Toolkit,* CWR

For most people becoming a true follower of Jesus involves a journey of discovery and understanding.

Some start with a little knowledge, others with a lot. But few, if any, start from a point of knowing enough to make an informed and rational decision.

They may also need to change their attitude towards Jesus and the church. Growing knowledge must be combined with a positive approach if they are to be converted.

Mahatma Gandhi knew all about Christianity and had a positive approach towards Jesus, but never became a Christian because he had a very negative attitude towards the church.

Our task, as a witness, is to help people move on in their journey towards understanding the truth about God and how it should impact their life.

KEY POINT

From Friendship to Facts

This is the process needed to move from step 5, 'decide to investigate Jesus' to Step 7, 'understanding the implications of the gospel' (see chart above).

Once someone's interest has been aroused, the task is then to respond to the ignorance and wrong understanding that they are likely to have.

KEY POINT

Steps to Christ

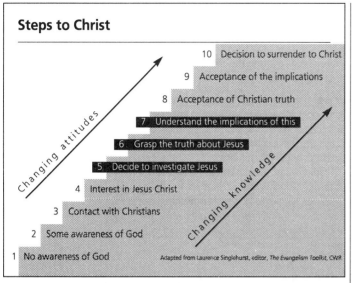

10 Decision to surrender to Christ
9 Acceptance of the implications
8 Acceptance of Christian truth
7 Understand the implications of this
6 Grasp the truth about Jesus
5 Decide to investigate Jesus
4 Interest in Jesus Christ
3 Contact with Christians
2 Some awareness of God
1 No awareness of God

Changing attitudes
Changing knowledge

Adapted from Laurence Singlehurst, editor, *The Evangelism Toolkit*, CWR

The idea is to meet briefly each week with two others, when you all identify three people who you feel you should pray for concerning their need to know God. You also pray for one another in your steps to speaking to them about Jesus.

As well as praying, the group can also encourage and help one another—as well as give combined input on particular questions and needs.

From Facts to Faith

This is the process needed to take someone from step 8, 'Accepting that Christianity is true' to step 10 'Deciding to surrender to Christ'.

Steps to Christ

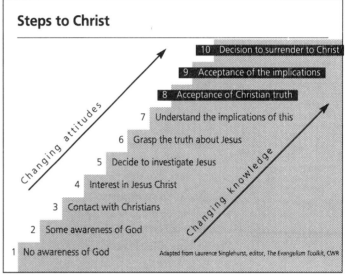

10 Decision to surrender to Christ
9 Acceptance of the implications
8 Acceptance of Christian truth
7 Understand the implications of this
6 Grasp the truth about Jesus
5 Decide to investigate Jesus
4 Interest in Jesus Christ
3 Contact with Christians
2 Some awareness of God
1 No awareness of God

Changing attitudes
Changing knowledge

Adapted from Laurence Singlehurst, editor, *The Evangelism Toolkit*, CWR

> '*I*n an age when facilities for rapid communication of the Gospel are available to the church as never before, we are actually accomplishing less in winning the world for God than before the invention of the horseless carriage.'
> ROBERT E. COLEMAN

This needs to be transformed into an understanding of the truth about Jesus.

The ability to do this does not require a mass of education. But, we do need to be clear as to what we believe and why. In truth, few of us have all the answers, but we should be able to explain the basis of our belief.

You Don't Need to be a Genius

If it all sounds too difficult, remember:

▶ Peter and John were called αγραμματοι and ιδιωται (uneducated laymen) by the Jewish Sanhedrin (Acts 4:13).

▶ Jesus had promised that the Holy Spirit would teach his people all they needed to say (John 14:26; 15:26–27).

It is never easy to translate our understanding about Jesus into language that will avoid confusing the non-Christian. This is one way of doing it:

> '*But God liked us!*
> *He liked us too much to let us continue crawling through life.*
> *He wanted us to be able to walk with him.*
> *So he sent his son Jesus.*
> *God became man when Jesus was born in a smelly cowshed.*
> *Homeless at his birth, he knew no real security in his life except that of doing what God wanted.*
> *Called 'devil' by his neighbours, he gave all the opportunity to know God as father.*
> *Having nothing to call his own he gave healing and sight to those who needed it.*
> *Misunderstood by his family and friends, he brought a message from the heart of God.*
> *Established religion put Jesus down when he came in order to pick me up.*
> *And by a city rubbish-dump, he did just that.*
> *He died.*'
>
> C. CALVER AND J. OLIVER, *GETTING IT TOGETHER*, CPO, WORTHING

We will learn from our mistakes. But each of us has a responsibility to learn to: 'Always be prepared to give an answer to everyone who asks you to give the reason for the hope that you have. But do this with gentleness and respect' (1 Peter 3:15).

Support from other Christians is important.

Many have found help in the idea of a 'triplet approach'.

> '*T*here is only one way not to be won over by love, and that is to flee from it.'
> NAPOLEON

> '*T*his seems a cheerful world, Donatus, when I view it from this fair garden under the shadow of these vines. But if I climbed some great mountain and looked over the wide lands, you know very well what I would see. Brigands on the high road, pirates on the seas, in the amphitheatres men murdered to please the applauding crowds, under all roofs misery and selfishness. It is a really bad world, Donatus, an incredibly bad world. Yet in the midst of it I have found a quiet and holy people. They have discovered a joy which is a thousand times better than any pleasures of this sinful life. They are despised and persecuted, but they care not. They have overcome the world. These people, Donatus, are the Christians . . . and I am one of them.'
> A CYPRIAN TO DONATUS, THIRD CENTURY AD

One of the greatest experiences for a Christian is to bring someone to a personal faith in Jesus Christ.

When someone has reached the point of an acceptance of Christian truth, we need to allow the Holy Spirit to lead them to an actual commitment to Jesus Christ. We become the midwife at a spiritual birth.

There can often be excuses offered that will delay birth. Faced with the challenge of surrender to Jesus, people will often begin to make excuses. Here are some examples and some relevant Bible verses to use to aid the birth.

▶ I haven't time (Isaiah 55:6; Galatians 6:7)

▶ I can be a Christian without going to church. (But Jesus didn't demonstrate this: Luke 4:16)

▶ I have always been a Christian (John 1:13; 2 Timothy 3:5)

▶ I have been baptized and that's enough (Romans 2:28; Acts 8:13–21)

▶ I've always done my best (James 2:10; Matthew 22:37–39; Galatians 3:10)

▶ I will do it later (John 4:25–26)

▶ I don't know what I am getting into (1 John 4:18)

▶ I'm afraid of the future (John 14:1)

Introducing Them to Jesus

One other factor may also keep someone from making their commitment to Jesus Christ.

KEY POINT

> '*E*vangelism is basically a matter of truth. Is it true that there is but one God, and he a God of perfect holiness and perfect love? Is it true that he has come to our world in the person of Jesus of Nazareth to show us what he is like, and to reconcile us from our alienation into his family? Is it true that the living God can come and indwell a man's life, and transform him utterly? If it is, then it is not only permissible for a Christian to spread such good news; it is incumbent upon him.'
> MICHAEL GREEN, PREFACE TO DAVID WATSON, *I BELIEVE IN EVANGELISM*, REPRODUCED BY PERMISSION OF HODDER & STOUGHTON LTD, 1976

KEY POINT

How often do you pray for the conversion of your non-Christian family and friends?

KEY POINT

'*I*t's been two years since I was saved and delivered. Now I'm plugged in, planted, and committed to a good body. God has been moving, and I've been stepping out in the gifts. I can hardly believe how God has been using me! I have developed one new problem, though. It seems that all my old friends just don't understand me any more. When I share about my redemption, that I've been washed as white as snow, and that I desire to follow the Lamb, they seem to tune me right out. I guess they're just convicted when they see that I'm on fire.'

BOB COHEN, 'THEY SPEAK WITH OTHER TONGUES' IN *TODAY'S CHRISTIAN*, SUMMER 1988

'*P*hilosophers have only *interpreted* the world differently; the point is, however, to *change* it.'

KARL MARX

They may think that becoming a Christian also involves saying 'yes' to a whole set of rules, regulations and observances. They need to see the truth of Galatians 5:1—that Jesus came to set them free.

So we must take care not to wrap the message of the gospel in a package of extras that spring from our culture rather than from scripture.

A new lifestyle should be the natural choice of someone who becomes a Christian but it should not be seen as what makes a person a Christian.

Leading a person to Christ—bringing about their spiritual birth—involves three things.

▶ They must recognize their own personal sin and failure and what God thinks about it.

▶ They must see that the death of Jesus achieved forgiveness and freedom from the penalty and guilt of sin if they will turn from their old self-centred lifestyle and give their life to Jesus.

▶ They will need to ask the resurrected Jesus to come into their lives to rule and reign as their Lord and king.

It is their prayer of personal surrender that represents the crucial moment in spiritual rebirth. You may get them to:

▶ Pray out loud in your presence

▶ Follow you phrase by phrase as you pray

▶ Get them to pray alone, if they are a very private or nervous person

The challenge of Jesus was that:

▶ People should deny themselves, accept a personal cross, and follow him (Matthew 16:24; Mark 8:34; Luke 9:23).

▶ The Christian life will not be an easy one (Matthew 5:11–12; John 15:20).

Those who first followed Jesus knew that it would cost them their reputation, their friends, their possessions—even their life. We must make sure that someone considering following Jesus is equally clear what the cost might be.

Helping Them Follow Jesus

Having led someone to Jesus, we have a responsibility to help them understand what has happened and what they should do now.

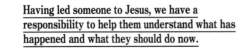

Following Jesus

15	Sharing their faith with others
14	Learning the Christian disciplines
13	Learning the basics of their faith
12	Experiencing change in their life
11	Gaining confidence in their decision

The five steps all begin at the moment of conversion and will continue for a long time afterwards.

Immediately they need some help to ground them in their new-found faith.

Some people immediately 'know' something has happened.

It is as if a great weight has fallen from their shoulders. It may be a sense of forgiveness for sins, a feeling of belonging, an intuitive conviction of the truth they have come to believe or a sense of inner strength or purposefulness.

Others may have no emotional experience at all. It is vital to stress that feelings are not the test of what has happened. When their feelings change the love of God for them will still be the same. Instead of counting on feelings, encourage them to look for positive changes in their life.

Some people come to faith slowly.

For them there is no moment of crisis. Either they have grown up in a Christian environment and can not remember a time when they did not trust Jesus. Or they now know they trust him but have reached this point gradually.

The key difference between a Christian and a non-Christian is simple—a Christian receives the Holy Spirit at conversion (Ephesians 1:13–14). It is important to help a new Christian see this—without necessarily going into detail—and to pray for them to be filled with the Holy Spirit and for his strength to help them in their new life (Acts 2:38).

We should not underestimate the importance of the support that a new Christian needs.

We have a part to play in helping new Christians to grow to maturity. When a baby is born into a human family it leads to major changes. Timetables are rewritten. Priorities are redefined. So it should be when we are involved with a spiritual birth.

▶ We need to give our time—including spending some of it on their territory and with their friends and lead by example.

▶ We need to demonstrate how the Christian life is lived by giving opportunities for them to observe our lives.

Beware of imposing a rigid structure on the fragile believer. They need love and support not a whole load of new rules, regulations and books.

Some converts immediately experience rapid change in their behaviour. Others need instruction to see that their actions are contrary to God's laws. Change may be most noticeable to them regarding their inner desires and attitudes. Selfishness—that most basic of sins—may not disappear overnight but may suddenly be more obvious to them. New Christians must be assured that although change is to be expected, perfection is not.

They should be encouraged to tell others about their conversion. Public confession of faith in Christ is part of the process of salvation (Romans 10:10). Trying to be a secret disciple does not work—although in some cultures and other countries great discretion may be needed. It may help if immediately after their prayer of commitment they are encouraged to tell someone nearby—preferably a sympathetic Christian of their decision to follow Christ. This can prepare them for the more sensitive

---

'*E*vangelism is neither to convert people, nor to win them, nor to bring them to Christ, though this is indeed the first goal of evangelism. Evangelism is to preach the gospel.'

JOHN R.W. STOTT

KEY POINT

Have you the confidence necessary to help another person make their initial commitment to Christ?

'*I*n the church's mission of sacrificial service evangelism is primary.'

LAUSANNE COVENANT

task of telling those they love.

Growing towards Christian maturity will involve them:

▶ Becoming part of a local church which maintains biblical truth and offers lively support and fellowship (Hebrews 5:11–14; 10:24–25).

▶ Being part of a nurture group, or Start-Right class, which will encourage them to move on in their relationship with God (Colossians 3:15–17).

▶ Reading and learning from the Bible for themselves (2 Timothy 3:14–17).

▶ Learning how to pray (Luke 11:1–5).

Evangelism and the Holy Spirit

Evangelism is not about convincing someone with arguments that they are wrong and we are right.

Although this is part of the story it is not the whole story by any means.

The Holy Spirit is God the Father's gift to our evangelistic enterprise. Without him we could do nothing.

The Holy Spirit:

▶ Gives us the love for others that motivates our evangelism (Romans 5:5; 10:1; 2 Corinthians 5:14–20).

▶ Guides us in proclaiming the truth about Jesus (John 14:17, 26; 15:26; 16:13).

▶ Without him all our own efforts would be worthless (John 16:8–11).

We pray:

▶ To be filled with the Holy Spirit as we go

▶ That he will work in bringing conviction of sin, illumination of the truth and fear of God into non-Christians' lives—these are all things we cannot do

▶ That he will lead us and guide us to the right people at the right time

Prayer and Spiritual Warfare

Evangelism is God's work. He takes initiatives in people's lives, through the work of his Holy Spirit.

And he calls us to cooperate through our prayers. See:

▶ Paul (Acts 9:1–9) needed Ananias (vv. 10–19)

▶ The Ethiopian (Acts 8:26–39) needed Philip

▶ Cornelius (Acts 10:1–8) needed Peter (vv. 9–48)

There is a clear link between prayer and irresistible evangelism.

People who seek God are transformed so that unbelievers can see the truth of Christ in them.

In Acts 1 and 2, the dejected disciples prayed and God filled them with his Spirit, enabling them to reach the diverse cultures in Jerusalem.

The impact of prayer can be seen today in significant worldwide church growth. The phenomenal church growth in Korea, Indonesia and North-East India is directly linked to prayer

KEY POINT

KEY POINT

KEY POINT

Evangelism and the Holy Spirit as demonstrated in the book of Acts

The whole book of Acts shows how the Holy Spirit can give us the ability to serve God and to be his witnesses to the ends of the earth (Acts 1:8).

The Holy Spirit empowered them to:

Speak for God

■ In their own language (Acts 2:14, 37)

■ In other languages (Acts 2:6–11)

■ In debate (Acts 6:10)

■ Boldly (Acts 4:29, 31)

Discern truth from error

■ Within the church (Acts 5:1–6)

■ In society (Acts 8:9–24; 13:9–12)

Gain specific guidance

■ To start a new work (Acts 13:1–3) in a new location (Acts 13:4–5) with new people (Acts 15:40)

■ To do the unexpected, for example to leave a successful public ministry for private encounter (Acts 8:4–8, 26–31)

Serve others

■ Through administration (Acts 6:1–6)

■ In famine relief (Acts 11:27–30)

■ By signs and wonders (Acts 3:1–8)

■ By meeting physical needs (Acts 16:33–34)

■ In justice (Acts 6:1–2)

■ In delivering from demonic forces (Acts 16:18)

Be faithful

■ Pray effectively (Acts 12:5–17)

■ Endure threats and physical abuse (Acts 4:21–25; 5:40–42)

■ Face martyrdom (Acts 7:54–58)

---

movements there.

This should encourage us to see prayer as a foundation for our evangelism. Remember:

▶ Include prayer as an integral part of the preparation of any evangelistic activity, and continue long after its completion.

▶ Constant prayer changes the spiritual climate of an area and makes people more responsive to Christ.

▶ God's response isn't automatic. Praying may not give the answers you expect. God looks for three things: a heart after God, humble dependence on him, and a life that is holy.

▶ It's the prayer of 'the righteous' that is effective (James 5:16, NRSV).

▶ Prayer increases our concern and love for those we pray for. It is motivational.

There are many creative ways to participate in prayer as it relates to evangelism. These include:

▶ A praise march

▶ A prayer walk—very different from the first and much quieter

- Prayer triplets
- Dawn prayer meeting
- 24-hour prayer chain
- Using the local newspaper to identify needs and issues—give everyone a page
- Street prayer—all Christians in the street regardless of their church meet to pray for neighbours

The Office of Evangelist

KEY POINT

The office of evangelist stands alongside those of apostles, prophets and pastors/teachers (Ephesians 4:11).

This is a leadership role given to those who are especially motivated and effective:

- In sharing their faith
- In drawing a positive response from their hearers
- In motivating others to join in the task

While a few may gain national recognition as evangelists, those with this calling from God are to be found in every congregation and age-group—both male and female.

It is vital that they should be:

- Recognized by the congregation
- Suitably resourced and trained
- On the receiving end of encouragement in their task which is all too often a lonely one

KEY POINT

No Christian can justifiably claim that evangelism is not their responsibility because they have not been given the gift.

The 'gift of evangelism' is conspicuous by its absence in the lists of spiritual gifts in Romans 12:6–8, and 1 Corinthians 12:4–11, 27–30. There is no specific gift of evangelism because any of the spiritual gifts can be used evangelistically.

The gifts were given to be part of extending the kingdom of God. The prime gift of God to each one of us to further this aim is the presence of the Holy Spirit himself—*the* witness to Jesus. He gives his Spirit to enable each of us to carry out his will.

KEY POINT

We are to use whatever gifts—spiritual and practical—that we do have to further the evangelistic task of the church.

Hospitality, catering, writing skills, financial support, typing, driving, can all work together with preaching, healings, words of knowledge and faith to make things happen.

Jesus the Evangelist

KEY POINT

There can be no finer example of effective evangelism than that of Jesus.

If we followed his model, it would be hard to go wrong. In John 4:1–42 Jesus encountered a woman at a well.

- He did not have to go through Samaria. No self-respecting Jew would have done so. But the Father had arranged an appointment for his Son (John 4:4).

- He was concerned with one single individual, rather than with a vast multitude. Even one person apart from God, was important to Jesus.
- He asked the woman to do him a favour—placing himself in her debt (John 4:7).
- He was not put off by the knowledge of her background and personal immorality (John 4:18).
- He defied personal exhaustion and social convention to speak alone with a woman (John 4:6).
- He began with her interest, which was water, not conversion (John 4:10).
- He made her curious and then thrilled her heart with his explanation of living water (John 4:10, 13–14).
- He challenged her dismissal of him (John 4:10).
- He pointed out her sin—graciously but firmly (John 4:18).
- He told her who he was, doing so at the point when she procrastinated (John 4:25–26).

As a result:

- The whole village came to Jesus (John 4:30).
- Many found Jesus because of the woman's testimony (John 4:39).
- Others believed once they heard Jesus for themselves (John 4:41).

This is a riveting story because it portrays profound principles:

- When we meet Jesus, we have something to share
- When our lives demonstrate the truth of our words—and we allow both to show—people are drawn to Jesus for themselves

Evangelizing Men

Of the adult church members in the United Kingdom, six out of ten are women while only four out of ten are male.

KEY POINT

The British church has suffered this imbalance for years.

The most likely reason for this problem is one of history. Two World Wars took men from the church for long periods—leaving the programmes to be developed for those who remained behind. Thus our churches have extensive activities for women and children—but not for men.

To reach men with the gospel we need to present the message in both style and content so that the ordinary unchurched man will listen. It must be clear and relevant.

KEY POINT

Long-term friendship is the most effective method to reach anyone—including men. This can be supplemented by special activities such as:

- Personal witness in pubs and clubs
- Businessmen's breakfast/lunch clubs
- Sports teams
- Church-based car maintenance courses
- 'Agnostics Anonymous' or 'Just Looking' groups
- Gardening/Allotment cooperatives

'The finest opportunity for evangelism in Britain today probably occurs at 3.15 most afternoons, at the school gate. There the nation's most gifted evangelists meet their contemporaries. They share the same problem (children!), have a brief opportunity to learn of each other's needs, and are not there for long enough to be boring. Day by day a foundation is built of friendship, with the eventual possibility of sharing faith in Jesus. What better ministry could there be?'
CLIVE CALVER

- ▶ Political/Trades Union activity
- ▶ Paternity courses
- ▶ Finance/debt/management seminars
- ▶ Home entertaining
- ▶ Outings to sports events

Evangelizing Children

KEY POINT

The importance of reaching children with the gospel during their formative years has long been recognized as vital.

- ▶ Bringing up children to know God is the prime responsibility of Christian parents (Psalm 78:1–7; Proverbs 1:8; 2 Timothy 3:15).
- ▶ Jesus dealt with unhelpful attitudes towards children in his disciples (Matthew 19:13) and in spiritual leaders (Matthew 21:15).

Non-Christians no longer send their children to Sunday School. In the mid-fifties around fifty per cent of the nation's children had a link with the church Sunday Schools (BBC survey in 1955). The corresponding figure in 1989 was only fourteen per cent (English Church census).

Junior Church and Sunday Schools still remain the most significant activity in bringing children to faith in Christ. However, this tends to be a means of educating the children from within the church family as the habit of unbelievers sending children to Sunday School has largely died out.

Nevertheless, some pioneering initiatives are making a significant impact through established programmes for children in the church.

Ideas to reach children

- ▶ **Housing estate programme**
- ▶ **Family fun nights**
- ▶ **Nursery playgroups**
- ▶ **School assemblies**
- ▶ **Children's open airs**
- ▶ **Family guest services**
- ▶ **Home-based events**
- ▶ **Seasonal events**
- ▶ **Outings**
- ▶ **Short-term clubs**
- ▶ **Summer holiday weeks**

Evangelism Through Small Groups

KEY POINT

The small group has many advantages in evangelism.

- ▶ Mothers and toddlers and other peer groups bringing together those who have a natural linking.
- ▶ Aerobics class. Activity-based groups with appeal to Christian and non-Christian alike.

*T*wo nine-year-olds asked if they could become part-time Christians because: 'We don't much like what happens in church on Sundays but we'd like to be Christians for the rest of the week.'

QUOTED IN LAURENCE SINGLEHURST, EDITOR, *THE EVANGELISM TOOLKIT*, CWR

- ▶ Neighbourhood groups. Meeting together on the basis of housing to foster friendship, discuss common concerns, security, children and so on.
- ▶ Social activities. OAP outing, youth group socials, family away-days, the possibilities are endless. Rather than one-off activities these can be part of a planned programme.
- ▶ Video film nights. Invite some people round for refreshments and a video. Secular as well as Christian films can be used to provoke discussion.
- ▶ 'Meet our friend'. Interesting guests, minor celebrities, overseas visitors and so on, can all be the stimulus for an open home gathering.
- ▶ Seasonal activities. Christmas, New Year, Harvest, Easter and so on.

Other small groups are ideal to help people discover the truth about Jesus and to grow as a new Christian:

- ▶ Enquirers groups—for those on the fringe of the church seeking to learn about the Christian faith.
- ▶ Evangelistic Bible-discovery groups—where they at least see the Bible as worth looking at and work their way through one of the gospels.

Evangelism and the Local Church

Each Christian is called to be a witness. But this should be in the context of the local church. After all, the church is not just a club to serve its members—keeping them happy and busy.

The church is intended to be a mission station:

KEY POINT

- ▶ Showing the character of Jesus through the activities of its members
- ▶ Equipping its members for works of service—including evangelism
- ▶ Building up its members—and new believers—in their faith

First Principles

Spontaneous evangelism—taking opportunities as they arise—is generally an individual activity. While organized evangelism is primarily the responsibility of the local church.

A healthy church will have:

- ▶ Evangelistic goals
- ▶ A long-term strategy to achieve its goals
- ▶ Immediate plans and actual activities as part of the strategy

The purpose of the global church is to make sure

The Great Commission

'Go and make disciples of all nations, baptising them in the name of the Father and of the Son and of the Holy Spirit and teaching them to obey everything I have commanded you. And surely I am with you always to the very end of the age.'

Matthew 28:19–20

that every person has the opportunity to hear the good news about Jesus in a way in which they can understand. The task of each local church is to be responsible for a part of this commitment.

Locally, it is foolish to attempt to separate evangelism and mission.

▶ Our local activities in evangelism contribute to the global task of mission.

▶ A missionary church should be committed to local evangelism.

▶ An evangelistic church should be actively supporting mission beyond its own locality.

The responsibility for drawing up the local church goal strategy is the task of its leadership. However, many church leaders are overwhelmed with immediate pressures. Keeping the church running and the congregation happy prevents them being able to lift up their eyes and look on the fields which are 'ripe for harvest' (John 4:35).

Ideally, every church should have a timetable to set and review its goals, strategy and plans.

How to Get Started

It is essential to know the facts. In particular:

▶ What resources are available—people, opportunities, experience, skills, finance and material resources.

▶ What are the real needs of the people in the community. Who are they, where are they and what do they feel and think?

An effective way to discover answers to these questions is to ask. Two surveys can help.

A Survey of the Church

Such a survey should enable the local church leaders to have answers to questions such as:

▶ What sort of people do you have in your church?

▶ What sort of roles and tasks are they fulfilling?

▶ Are there those already involved with particular sections of society?

▶ Are there those who are looking for a role but who are not sure what they should do within the church?

▶ Are there any new Christians who have enthusiasm, and a concern to reach out to friends and colleagues?

▶ Where do these different groups of people, with evangelistic potential, live?

▶ What previous experience do they have?

▶ What gifts and skills do they feel they have?

A Survey of the Community

A person or small team could undertake this survey and report back to the whole church.

Much of the information needed is available from public sources—the library, local council, electoral roll and so on. A simple survey like that on page 69 will help to:

▶ Understand the people themselves, their attitudes and beliefs.

▶ Form a more accurate picture of the locality.

▶ Discover strengths and weaknesses of the community.

▶ Raise the profile of the church. Introduce yourself as coming from the church.

▶ Demonstrate Christian concern. Ask them about any felt community needs.

▶ Help future targeting by discovering the different types of people resident—which households have children who might be interested in a Holiday Club and so on.

▶ Prepare the way for further contact. Offer to return again, especially if they are lonely and isolated. Have questions that you cannot answer, show an interest in Christianity, have a desire to be involved in a community-based activity.

The results of the survey should enable you to be alert to:

▶ Specific felt needs in the community

▶ Any neglected section of the community

▶ Lonely or needy individuals

▶ Any sub-groups with their own cultural distinctives, group activities and lifestyle

▶ Any potential bridge-building opportunities

As a result of such a survey a new church in South Wales discovered that the nearest doctor's surgery was several miles away and virtually inaccessible by public transport. As a result, the main felt need of the estate was for a health centre.

So a petition was organized and presented to the local council. Although the campaign failed, it firmly established the church's credentials with the neighbourhood.

Local Initiatives

We have the privilege and responsibility to share the good news about Jesus with those who are in contact with us.

But there are many in our neighbourhood and society who have no contact with Christians. We need to find effective ways to reach them.

Go where they are

There is a vast number of ways in which a local church can impact its community. The following ideas come from *The Evangelism Toolkit* published by CWR.

Contact—some ideas:

▶ **Church newspaper.** Print a church newspaper or magazine. Include testimonies, stories and photos that cover the different cultures and age-groups of the community.

Perhaps review a few of the restaurants in your area. Point out some local parks or places of interest. State clearly that this newspaper comes from your church. Go for quality. This could not only be a resource for door-to-door, but also for your open-air outreach.

▶ **Door-to-door.** Regular visits by the same team with good literature to leave behind.

continued on page 70

'*T*he church exists by mission as a fire exists by burning.'
EMIL BRUNNER

KEY POINT

Community Survey

1	**Age**	Under 21 ☐ 21–45 ☐ 46–65 ☐ Over 65 ☐
2	**Sex**	Male ☐ Female ☐
3	**Occupation**	_____ Unemployed ☐
4	**Do you/your partner work locally?**	Within 1 mile ☐ 2–5 miles ☐ Further ☐
5	**How long have you lived in this area?**	Under 1 year ☐ 1–5 years ☐ 6–10 years ☐ Longer ☐
6	**How many people do you talk to in a day from outside the home?**	*(Face-to-face)* _____
7	**Would you and your neighbours visit one another?**	Several times a week ☐ Occasionally ☐ Rarely ☐ Never ☐
8	**What sort of neighbourhood is this generally?**	Friendly ☐ Unfriendly ☐
9	**What do you see as the main problems in the area?**	_____ _____
10	**What facilities do you think are lacking in this area?** (a) Generally, e.g. leisure, help with difficulties, etc. (b) For different groups, e.g. elderly, young people, unemployed, women, etc.	 _____ _____ _____ _____
11	**Who would you look to for help in a time of crisis?** *(Can tick more than one)*	Cope on your own if at all possible ☐ Doctor ☐ Church ☐ A neighbour ☐ Family member ☐ Friend ☐ Other ☐ *(specify)* _____
12	**Where would you recommend someone to go locally if they want to** (a) Meet new people (b) Have a good time (c) Have advice about a personal problem	 _____ _____ _____
13	**If you have any questions about things like life after death, the meaning of life, etc. to whom would you talk?** *(Can tick more than one)*	Family ☐ Friend ☐ Someone that is 'religious' ☐ Other ☐ *(specify)* _____
14	**Do you attend church?**	Regularly ☐ Rarely ☐ Never ☐

Called to action

15	**What would you like to see the church do in this area?**	_____ _____ _____ _____
16	**What do you think of the church today generally?**	_____ _____

Thank you very much for your help in completing this questionnaire
This Community Survey has been reproduced with the kind permission of Fount Publishers.

▶ **Welcome newcomers.** When new people move into your area pay them a welcome visit. Ask if you can help them. Give them an information pack with details of the best schools, restaurants, doctors and so on—and your church.

▶ **Street parties.** Encourage people in your church to have a barbecue, or organize a street party, and invite their neighbours. This could include a light programme of drama and songs from church members.

▶ **Special services.** Christmas, Easter, Harvest. Have a Christmas Carol service each year and invite the people you have contacted in the past 12 months. During the service present the gospel message in an attractive but penetrating way. Use specially prepared invitations.

▶ **Produce a cassette for distribution in your area.** This could include testimonies and music together with an explanation of who you are and when and where you meet. A contact phone number for enquiries or requests for practical help or prayer is essential.

▶ **Street discussion group.** You could set up a discussion group for those people in a particular street or group of streets who have shown an interest in Christianity, or are in need of friendship.

In the Streets

Proclaiming the gospel in public places has a history all the way back to the day of Pentecost. We should not take for granted the freedom we have to engage in this method.

There are a variety of ways to use this opportunity:

▶ Conversation

▶ Preaching—short, carefully prepared and to the point

▶ Praise and worship—a group of no less than 20 people—happy and singing—will draw a crowd

▶ Creative ministry—dance, drama, mime

▶ Sketch boards—street artists usually draw a crowd

▶ Testimonies—brief and personal, about two minutes long.

▶ Literature

▶ Praise marches and pageants—decorated trucks, colourful banners, fancy dress

▶ Gifts—give away mince pies, coffee, cakes, cards, pizza—a good illustration of 'grace'

Nationally Coordinated Initiatives

Special initiatives like the *Decade of Evangelism* will unite the activities of many churches. Specific projects like *March for Jesus* and *On Fire* will provide fresh opportunities for evangelism in many areas.

Church Planting

KEY POINT

Planting churches from scratch—or by sub-dividing an existing church—is a real opportunity for growth.

> ### The 'On Fire' project
>
> ### What is 'On Fire'?
> Managed by the Oasis Trust, 'On Fire' is an interdenominational project to raise the consciousness of Pentecost to our nation and bring its message to our society.
>
> On Saturday 21 May 1994 a simultaneous series of carnivals, bonfires, and barbecues will act as a catalyst for evangelism and mission opportunities in local communities on a town-wide basis.
>
> Resource and training material for a wide range of evangelistic projects and events, for all ages, will be designed to follow naturally from an inter-church Lent course on evangelism.
>
> The strength of 'On Fire' depends on local churches working together and the national church bodies and associations planning and preparing together.
>
> 'On Fire' will be a contribution to the Decade of Evangelism, encouraging evangelism in the middle of the Decade and during the United Nations 'Year of the Family'.
>
> ### Why Pentecost?
> Flames reflect the fire of Pentecost and underline the theological significance of this festival. Pentecost is when the Easter message 'went public', and so is a natural time for evangelism.

It must be seriously considered as a method to reach the unreached communities without their own local church.

▶ It encourages church members to exercise new gifts and responsibilities

▶ It takes the church to where the people are

Only make a commitment to plant a new church if you are:

▶ Prepared to lose some of your best people (Acts 13:1–3).

▶ Prepared to commend some of your best people into the areas where they have a ministry in reaching the unreached.

▶ Willing to support financially and prayerfully those who are committed to the task.

Cross-Cultural Evangelism

It is one thing to seek to evangelize someone of our own culture—who shares our language, standards of normal behaviour and experience of life. It is quite another to seek to reach those of a different culture.

One missionary strategist has defined four different kinds of evangelism.

▶ **E1** Evangelism of those who are within the existing church structures.

▶ **E2** Evangelism of those on the fringe of the church—lapsed and nominal members, family members, church contacts and so on.

▶ **E3** Evangelism of those outside the church but within our own culture.

▶ **E4** Evangelism of those outside of our culture—whether across the fence or across the ocean.

The first three kinds of evangelism listed above we easily understand—while overlooking the priority of the fourth.

KEY POINT

483 million people in the world will only ever hear the good news about Jesus if someone *from another*

culture than their own brings them the message. 2,310 million still need to hear, but do have some Christians in their culture.

There are also 3,628 distinct 'people groups' with their own culture who do not have the New Testament in their own language. Of these 1,800 have a missionary but only 600 have a church.

In the United Kingdom, the majority of the population share a white European culture. However, there are:

▶ 1.2 million Muslims
▶ 0.3 million Hindus
▶ 0.5 million Sikhs
▶ 0.121 million Buddhists

While, at the same time within the white European culture, there are sub-cultures often overlooked by a predominately middle-class church:

▶ The 'working class'
▶ The 'upper class'
▶ Those who are blind
▶ Gypsies and 'travellers'

Some differences in culture are easy to understand:

▶ Language
▶ Religion
▶ Social customs
▶ Public institutions

Others can be more subtle:

▶ Age

Culture—a definition

The short version:

Culture—The totality of a person's normal behaviour and attitude in their own society.

The long version:

Culture—An integrated system of beliefs, values, customs and institutions which bind a society together and gives it a sense of identity, dignity, security and continuity. (Willowbank Report 1978)

▶ Social class
▶ Vocabulary
▶ Superstitions
▶ Education

Some people are more naturally gifted than others in sharing the news about Jesus with those of other cultures. But we can all play some part.

Differences in culture can be solved but they do make the clear communication of the gospel more difficult.

Dr Roy Pointer identifies four different approaches to cross-cultural communication.

▶ **Isolation**—where the communicator remains in his own culture and is totally isolated from those he is seeking to reach. The result is non-communication in spite of the fact that the communicator may well believe that he has faithfully proclaimed the message.

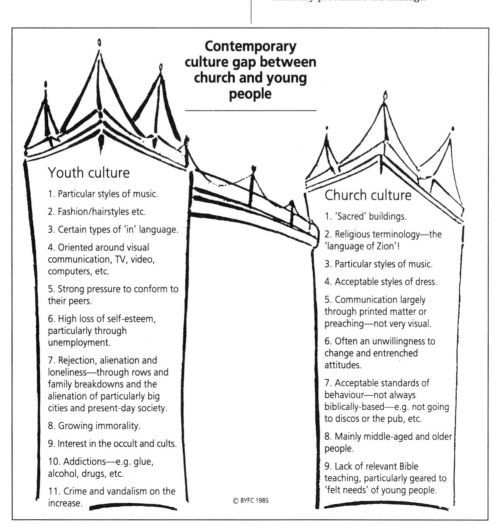

Contemporary culture gap between church and young people

Youth culture

1. Particular styles of music.
2. Fashion/hairstyles etc.
3. Certain types of 'in' language.
4. Oriented around visual communication, TV, video, computers, etc.
5. Strong pressure to conform to their peers.
6. High loss of self-esteem, particularly through unemployment.
7. Rejection, alienation and loneliness—through rows and family breakdowns and the alienation of particularly big cities and present-day society.
8. Growing immorality.
9. Interest in the occult and cults.
10. Addictions—e.g. glue, alcohol, drugs, etc.
11. Crime and vandalism on the increase.

Church culture

1. 'Sacred' buildings.
2. Religious terminology—the 'language of Zion'!
3. Particular styles of music.
4. Acceptable styles of dress.
5. Communication largely through printed matter or preaching—not very visual.
6. Often an unwillingness to change and entrenched attitudes.
7. Acceptable standards of behaviour—not always biblically-based—e.g. not going to discos or the pub, etc.
8. Mainly middle-aged and older people.
9. Lack of relevant Bible teaching, particularly geared to 'felt needs' of young people.

© BYFC 1985

▶ **Extraction**—where the communicator educates someone from another culture into his own culture. Result—the two now understand each other but are still unable to effectively communicate with those of the culture from which the one who was communicated with came.

▶ **Identification**—the communicator borrows from the language and thought forms of those with whom he is communicating. Result—people understand.

▶ **Reciprocation**—the communicator so fully identifies with and enters into the culture of the other that a genuine exchange of information can take place. Result—effective cross-cultural communication.

KEY POINT

Cross-cultural evangelism will only be effective when we are able to enter into 'their world' and identify with them.

Our example is the way Jesus abandoned the culture of heaven to absorb totally, and identify with, the culture of earth.

Steps to effective cross-cultural evangelism

In order to be effective in cross-cultural evangelism it is essential to have:

▶ **A willingness to learn.** Observation, listening and learning about the world is essential.

▶ **A willingness to be flexible.** To quote Paul, 'To the Jews I became a Jew ... To those under the law I became like one under the law ... To the weak I became weak ... I have become all things to all men so that by all possible means I might save some' (1 Corinthians 9:20–22).

▶ **A willingness to go.** Minority cultural groups in the United Kingdom are less likely to have a local church which is part of their own culture— particularly in the Asian communities. It requires people to enter their world—if only temporarily—if they are to receive the gospel. This may be by deliberately choosing to shop at a corner shop owned by someone from the Asian community. Or by moving home in order to make a day-to-day contact.

▶ **A willingness to identify.** Jesus left his own home and came to live with us. Paul went to both Jews and Gentiles and lived their lifestyles that he could bring the gospel to them. The most powerful way to identify is to live with the people as they live. In the nineteenth century, Hudson Taylor shocked Victorian Christians by his willingness to live as a Chinese in order to take the gospel to China. His example contradicted the Imperialist philosophy of the time, but it worked.

▶ **A willingness to love.** More than words, love expressed in action is the great communicator. When middle-class pentecostal pastor David Wilkerson left his country church to witness to the New York street gangs he broke almost every rule in the communication text book except one. He showed the teenage rebels that he loved them.

▶ **A willingness to build bridges.** The gap between the church and the cultural group

---

What are the 'nations'?

When Jesus spoke of us 'making disciples of all nations' (Matthew 28:19) he was not referring to the great nation states such as the United Kingdom, France, Germany or Japan.

Jesus used the word ἔθνη (*ethne*) which refers to an ethic group. This is a term wider than that of 'tribe' or 'clan' but one that differentiates between 'people groups' who each have their own language, culture, religion and social structures.

A modern country will contain a number of '*ethne*'. The great commission challenges us to take the gospel to each and every people group within every country.

---

targeted must be spanned. This could be by planting a new church which embraces the acceptable aspects of that culture. People are most at home when they can embrace new beliefs without abandoning the security of familiar music, language, styles of meeting, dress, food, leisure and customs.

To the Whole World

The message that we are to share is for the whole world.

KEY POINT

Jesus told his disciples (Acts 1:8) that they were to be his witnesses in:

▶ their home town
▶ the regions beyond it
▶ 'to the ends of the earth'

A challenge as large as this is the task of the whole church.

On a more global scale the DAWN (Disciple A Whole Nation) project is encouraging the planting of seven million new churches worldwide. The AD2000 Movement serves to focus attention on the challenge to reach our world with the gospel before the conclusion of this millennium.

France is an excellent illustration of the needs and benefits of church planting. It is a country even more secularized than Britain. Only 14–15 per cent of nominal Roman Catholics—the majority of the population—even go to Mass. Evangelicals are a mere 0.6 per cent of the population—less than one-tenth of the size of British evangelicals.

Twenty-five years ago there were few evangelical churches outside Paris, Alsace, the South-West, and the major cities. Since then the church planting has steadily taken place. As a result:

▶ Few medium-sized towns are now without an evangelical congregation.

▶ Churches are small—often 30–40 adults—but many have already had the experience of sub-dividing and starting a daughter church.

This still leaves the overwhelming majority of local communities without a witness. Outside of Paris, France is a nation of villages—but growth is continuing and with outside help can advance into these areas too.

Evangelism and Church History

The Apostles, particularly Paul and Barnabas, played a major role in the growth of the church.

▶ Peter preached in Rome.

▶ John maintained a long and successful ministry in the province of Asia.

Tradition also suggests that:

▶ Mark was involved in the foundation of the church in Alexandria.

▶ Thaddeus may have helped to establish the church in Edessa.

▶ Thomas carried the Christian message to India.

As early as the third century the theologian, Origen (AD185–254), foresaw the possibility that one day the whole world could be evangelized. He encouraged the church to pursue this task, and noted that, 'Many people, not only barbarians, but even in the Empire, have not yet heard the word of Christ.'

To address this kind of situation, Bishop Cornelius of Rome sent missionary bishops in AD249 to evangelize strategic situations. Included in this project were seven cities in Gaul—Tours, Arles, Paris, Limoges, Clermont, Toulouse and Narbonne.

▶ By AD250 a significant Christian minority could be found in several countries to the east of the Roman Empire.

▶ By AD300, the strong Christian groups which existed in almost every province of the Roman Empire had become a majority in parts of Africa and Asia Minor.

▶ Osrhoene—with its capital Edessa—and later the country of Armenia, adopted Christianity nationally.

In AD312:

▶ The Emperor Constantine himself gave his official support to the Christian faith.

During the fourth century the church saw a decline in its moral standards, while the introduction of certain pagan practices weakened its spiritual integrity. As a reaction, there came the rise of the monastic movement.

Egyptian monks travelled widely, evangelizing in Britain, Ireland and other parts of Europe. It is interesting to note the reports of healings, exorcisms and miracles, signs and wonders which accompanied their preaching of the gospel.

The thousand years of uncertainty: AD500–1500

During the years AD500 to 1500 the witness of the church waned. It is easy to see why.

▶ The rise of Islam and its military conquests

▶ The fusion of the church and state

▶ The division of the church into its Eastern Orthodox and Roman Catholic components

▶ The forcible baptism of tribal populations by the Emperor Charlemagne, which multiplied the number of nominal Christians

Celtic believers

The labours of Patrick in Ireland were followed by intensive Celtic evangelism. Columba also established the monastery of Iona.

The evangelization of Britain was furthered through the activity of Aidan and the Celts in the north, supplemented by the Roman-sponsored Augustine in the south.

Christian expansion in Britain was so successful that British evangelists were soon at work in the more pagan parts of Europe as well as at home.

▶ British missionaries were involved in Sweden.

▶ Willibrand took the gospel to the Friesian Islands.

▶ Boniface took the gospel to Germany.

▶ Wilfrid, the former Bishop of York, spent his retirement evangelizing heathen Sussex.

Case history

The way Armenia became Christian makes a compelling story. A pioneer missionary, Gregory, was ordered to lay garlands on the altar of the goddess Anahit. On refusing, he was imprisoned and tortured.

The quality of Gregory's endurance under persecution persuaded the king of Armenia to turn to Christ. The two then worked together to make the kingdom Christian.

Case history

Warlike Goths were scarcely prime potential for evangelization. Ulfilas was half-Goth and became the key instrument used by God to establish a church among these people.
From AD343–383 Ulfilas laboured in evangelism among the Goths, he nurtured converts and translated nearly the whole Bible into their language.
The result was the preservation of the Western church and the enabling of its northern advance. The cost to Ulfilas was hardship, pain and continual danger to his life.

Case history The Celtic Missionaries

The challenge that the Celtic missionaries faced is the same as that experienced today by Two-Thirds World Christians sharing their faith in the United Kingdom.

Celts were carrying the gospel back from churches on the outskirts of the Christian world into unevangelized areas closer to its centre!

Fragile hide-covered wooden coracles were their means of transport as they traversed dangerous seas. With a faith based on disciplined prayer—and exhibiting boundless energy—they moved out from monasteries to engage in missionary preaching.

The heroes of this movement include Patrick, who was forcibly taken to Ireland as a slave. As a young man Patrick developed a rigorous prayer life. He would be up before daybreak in snow, rain, hail or fine weather in order to meet with his God.

After his escape from slavery he returned home but God called him in a vision to return to Ireland as a missionary. He is reported to have visited his former master in order to seek to convert him, but the man committed suicide at Patrick's approach.

Patrick did succeed in confronting the Druids, whom he defeated by miraculous means, and initiated a movement by which many came to Christ.

Columba was a man of similar calibre. Blaming himself for causing a battle, he undertook the lifetime penance of establishing a group of monasteries as mission stations. From his island base of Iona he witnessed his missionary monks setting sail on their evangelistic initiatives to Scotland and the North of England. One almost feels sorry for the pagan King Brude who provoked Columba and his monks into singing psalms outside his gates—his conversion was inevitable!

In the sixth and seventh centuries Aidan and Cuthbert walked the hills of northern England carrying the gospel to the poor. Men like Columba and Gall drew whole tribes to Christ in France and Switzerland. Indeed, if tradition can be believed one of the Celtic evangelists, Brenden, took his coracle to America and was the first to carry the gospel to the continent. Holy lives, careful organization, pioneering spirits, spiritual practices and the message of Jesus were the tools of this evangelistic revolution.

Case history

It was inevitable that missionaries followed after the soldiers. Conquest of a people provided the church with a real opportunity to seek their conversion. But Christianity did not always follow the sword, on one occasion it followed an axe.

Boniface was born in Crediton, Devon, around AD680. He served as an evangelist to the Friesian Islands and then extended his missionary activities into Germany. He struggled unsuccessfully against the local folk-religion and pagan rites. Eventually he decided on a head-on clash. Seizing his axe he decided to chop down the sacred oak at Hesse which was dedicated to the god, Thor. As his axe bit into the trunk a mighty gust of wind joined Boniface in felling the tree which crashed down in four fragments forming a cross. Thor failed to retaliate, paganism ended in Hesse, and with an enhanced reputation Boniface continued his preaching. (An early illustration of signs and wonders in Germany!)

Again the major impact in evangelism came from the part played by ordinary Christians. For example, it was the witness of Celtic and Anglo-Saxon converts—working out from major biblical-missionary centres like Lindisfarne—who made the biggest contribution in leading the Northern European tribes to Jesus Christ.

Meanwhile, Ireland provided large numbers of 'ordinary' Christians committed to evangelistic witness. From around the year 510 groups of disorganized wandering hermits, the Irish 'Peregrin' travelled Europe as pilgrims for Christ.

▶ They migrated throughout Europe for 400 years in what has been described as one of the greatest missionary feats of all time.

▶ They used writing-tablets as their major piece of equipment.

▶ They carried the gospel to the Alps, Germany, the Danube, Italy, the Orkneys, the Faroe Islands and Iceland reaping thousands of converts.

One single Irish missionary, Columba, took the gospel through Europe almost as far as Rome.

The rampaging Vikings burned churches and monasteries, massacred Christians and sold monks into slavery. But, this unparalleled devastation of Britain and continental Europe did not result in a victory for paganism.

Not only did missionaries from Britain reach into Scandinavia, British Christians also saw the Viking invasions of the British Isles, and Britons experienced conversion to pagan Nordic religion.

The invading Vikings, in turn, felt the impact of the gospel. One highly significant factor was the translation of a Christian library into the common language sponsored by the Saxon king, Alfred of Wessex.

Constantinople had served as the sponsor for Cyril and Methodius, two missionaries who took the gospel to the Slav peoples. They also introduced the alphabet which is still used today, and reduced their language to written form so they could understand the biblical record.

Meanwhile, East Bulgaria became the battleground for the final 'missionary' outreaches of Rome and Constantinople. This period was notable for the conversion of the Poles, the Hungarians and the Russians.

During the medieval period efforts were made to convert the remaining heathen tribes in Europe. At this time missions among the Muslims were introduced by Francis of Assisi.

The militarism of the Crusades did not provide a good background for such activities. But Francis' order of travelling preachers took their evangelistic zeal to almost every part of the then known world.

By AD1400, Franciscan missionaries could be found from Lapland to the Congo, and from the Azores to China.

There were people like Ramon Lull, who was nicknamed 'the Fool of Love'. A missionary of unique foresight and understanding he established a missionary training school and language centre on his native island of Majorca. His study of Islam led to attempts to develop means of presenting the gospel to Muslims. Ultimately his 'foolish love' took him to North Africa where he preached and was martyred around AD1315.

An unwritten chapter in the expansion of the church is largely hidden activities of groups which existed outside the mainstream of church life.

While we know little first-hand detail of the activities of such groups (most surviving information comes from their persecutors), a strain of simple faith and practice served to unite a variety of minority groups:

▶ the Waldensians in France, Italy and Central Europe

▶ the Hussites in Bohemia

▶ the Lollards in England

The Waldensians were founded in Lyons by Peter Waldo, a wealthy merchant, who after his conversion in 1176 gave away his wealth adopting a simple lifestyle and preaching to the poor. He had great appeal to the illiterates and others repulsed by the wealth and moral laxity of the established church.

The group were quickly condemned for unauthorized preaching of the Bible and excommunicated by Pope Lucius III in 1184.

They fled from Lyons and preached wherever they went. They came to reject the authority of the church and the Pope, prayer for the dead, most 'Holy Days', taking oaths, praying to saints and eventually buildings and all the paraphernalia of the church.

They survived in Central Europe until the end of the fifteenth century and had a significant influence on the thinking of many of those who were to lead the Protestant Reformation.

Jan Hus (1374–1415) is today a great hero in the Czech Republic. A priest and a scholar he taught at Prague University.

Hus taught the authority of scripture over that of the church, and emphasized the importance of preaching, purity of life and personal piety. He condemned superstition in the churches and the sale

'**M**en are wont, O Lord, to die of old age, through the failure of natural warmth and excess of cold; but . . . thy servant . . . would rather die in the glow of love, even as Thyself'
RAMON LULL, *BOOK OF CONTEMPLATION*

KEY POINT

Case history

Francis of Assisi was a missionary at heart. His saintly life—though not all his reported theological pronouncements—should earn our admiration and esteem.

During the fifth crusade, in 1219, Francis appeared at the court of the Sultan of Egypt. Convinced that the beauty and simplicity of the gospel, not military force, would win a Muslim ruler he preached with courage and boldness.

A defenceless man in poor clothing, his holy lifestyle won him a respectful hearing.

of indulgences for the dead.

While travelling to Constance to defend his views before a church council he was seized, tried and burnt at the stake. In response the Czechs formed the Hussite church which lasted until 1620 when it was forcibly re-integrated into the Roman Catholic church.

The Lollards based their teaching on the sole authority of the Bible and the need for personal faith. Though frequently persecuted they condemned the corruption and injustices of the clergy and demanded a moral purity which matched the teaching of the gospels. They lived in poverty, challenging ordinary people to turn to simple faith in Jesus.

A group about which we know more is the **Nestorian** church.

▶ They possessed numerous monasteries and missions.

▶ They exhibited a special concern for both the spiritual and physical needs of people.

▶ Facing great opposition and persecution they took the gospel across Asia to Yemen, South India, Ceylon, Samarkand and to China.

In the seventh century, China was the richest and most civilized nation on earth. Nestorians translated the gospel for the Chinese Emperor and took their outreach as far as Thailand.

By the fourteenth century Nestorians had organized 250 dioceses in China, India and throughout much of Asia. These contained fifteen million Christians, the result of a missionary enterprise unsurpassed in Christian history.

John Wycliffe in England, established strong movements of indigenous evangelism.

The poor preachers who followed John Wycliffe went further in preaching the gospel than did those who represented official church structures.

'**M**issionaries will convert the world by preaching, but also through the shedding of tears and blood and with great labour, and through a bitter death.'
RAMON LULL

From the Reformation to the present day: 1500–1993

KEY POINT

The emergence of the Protestant churches during the Reformation did not accelerate the cause of evangelism and missionary outreach.

A number of reasons can be given for this failure.

▶ The concern was to reform the church rather than to witness to the world.

▶ Church leaders were busy coping with the theological and ecclesiastical turmoil of their age.

▶ Many groups within Protestantism felt that the world was about to end.

▶ Protestant governments were indifferent to missionary and evangelistic outreach and their nations were usually at war with each other.

▶ There was an absence of missionary structures and organizations.

▶ European Protestants had little contact with avowedly non-Christian nations.

▶ Some emphasized a theology which pronounced that because 'the elect' would be saved anyway it made evangelism irrelevant.

▶ No major pioneering leaders of evangelism emerged at that time.

▶ Most denominations concentrated on countering each other!

For two centuries there was little concern among Christians to share their faith. Nor was there a commitment to evangelism and mission within the Protestant churches. This was not the case elsewhere!

In the Eastern Orthodox Church, Russian leaders pioneered evangelistic outreach into Siberia, throughout the Russian Empire, and even on to the American continent. We may never have heard of men like Cyril Suchanov and Ioasaf Bolotov but their contribution was enormous.

Meanwhile Slav Christians were sharing their faith and Christianity enjoyed considerable growth in their lands.

It was not until the eighteenth century that missionary and evangelistic concerns were fully married to evangelical theology. When that happened an explosion of life and growth took place.

A deep sense of the need for spiritual renewal in the lives of ordinary Christians prepared the ground for all that was to take place.

KEY POINT

This 'Pietist' movement of the seventeenth century emphasized the need for a personal faith. It contributed to the growth of the **Moravian** church which turned itself, as a whole unit, into one large missionary and evangelistic society. One family in every eight devoted themselves to missionary outreach, while the others supported them.

This spiritual commitment resulted in persecution. As a result Moravian refugees found shelter on the estates of Count Zinzendorf. There they established a prayer meeting which continued, non-stop, for one hundred years.

Moravian missionaries spread throughout Europe. One, Peter Bohler, convinced John Wesley and his brother, Charles, of their need to be justified by faith in Jesus Christ.

George Whitefield, arguably the finest preacher of the eighteenth century, moved out of church buildings and began to preach in the open air. Reluctantly John Wesley followed his example.

Theirs was not a lone endeavour. Many others

Case history

John Wesley had been a missionary in the Americas. He returned with a great overwhelming sense of failure. Although an Anglican clergyman he hungered to find God in a deeper and more personal way.

On 24 May 1738 he could finally write these words:

'I felt my heart strangely warmed. I felt I did trust in Christ, Christ alone for salvation; and an assurance was given me that he had taken away my sins, even mine, and saved me from the law of sin and death.'
The Journal of John Wesley, Volume 1

This experience proved to be the turning-point of his ministry.

■ He travelled a quarter of a million miles on horseback.

■ He preached over 40,000 sermons.

■ He challenged ordinary people, gathered in the open air, to turn from their sinful lives and to own Jesus Christ as their Saviour and Lord.

Despite severe criticism, opposition and persecution, John Wesley, George Whitefield and many others, preached the gospel to half the British population.

The Methodist Church grew out of the organizational structures which Wesley introduced for those who found faith at this time.

The missionaries

In 1742 the Scottish branch of SPCK sent **David Brainerd** as a missionary to the North American Indians. He was to die on his knees in the snow praying for the people he had grown to love.

His example was to inspire later missionaries such as the brilliant **Henry Martyn** who died in Persia, after translating the New Testament into Hindustani, Persian and Arabic. He was only 30 years old.

In 1792 a Northamptonshire shoe-mender, named **William Carey**, began the work on Baptist Missions worldwide. The Methodist, **Thomas Coke**, went as a missionary, and in 1799 the **Church Missionary Society** was established for Anglican outreach throughout the world.

Despite persecution, deprivation, hardship and death, missionary pioneers carried the gospel to far-off lands and Christianity was transformed into an actual, worldwide faith. The captain of the England cricket team, **C.T. Studd**, turned his back on fame and fortune. In his early twenties he sailed to China in order to begin a lifetime of missionary service.

Today the public face of missions has changed. Missionaries from the Two-Thirds World now outnumber those of Western nations. Many missionaries have to possess professional skills in order to enter other countries. Lives of public service in medicine, education or agriculture provide the opportunity for them to express the Christian gospel.

joined to proclaim the Christian message—in public meetings and in private conversation.

The eighteenth century

In view of this widespread growth in Christian belief, it is not surprising that eyes began to turn overseas. At the turn of the eighteenth century two major missionary societies began.

▶ The Society for the Propagation of the Gospel (1701)

▶ The Society for Promoting Christian Knowledge (1698)

This coincided with the development of a movement termed 'pan-evangelicalism'. This movement emphasized the unity of evangelicals and the potential for greater cooperation together. Anglicans and Free Churchmen began to work together—overcoming their denominational barriers.

   The challenge of pioneer missionaries like David Livingstone accelerated the momentum. From his own initiative emerged the Universities' Mission to Central Africa.

   Other examples were:

▶ The London Missionary Society

Case study

The founder of modern missions, William Carey was a humble shoemaker in Northamptonshire. Convinced of the importance of Christian mission, Carey taught himself several languages.

He coined the phrase, 'Expect great things from God and attempt great things for God'. He left his part-time pastorate and played a crucial part in establishing the Baptist Missionary Society.

Carey travelled to India and worked as a missionary. He:

■ Translated the whole Bible into Bengali

■ Translated parts of the Bible into twenty-four other languages and dialects

■ Founded the Indian Baptist Church

■ Established the Serampore College for training Indian clergy

■ Successfully campaigned against 'Suttee'—the burning of widows on their husbands' funeral pyre.

▶ The British and Foreign Bible Society

▶ The Religious Tract Society

▶ The China Inland Mission—founded by Hudson Taylor

This tremendous growth in Christian activism led to the eighteenth century being termed the 'Great Century of Christian Missions'.

The nineteenth century

In the nineteenth century, evangelistic fervour was matched with passionate social involvement.

KEY POINT

American evangelists like James Caughey, Phoebe Palmer and D.L. Moody existed alongside social reformers like George Muller, William Wilberforce, Lord Shaftesbury and Doctor Barnardo.

   The two streams united in the flamboyant independence of the Salvation Army and the caring missionary outreach of men like William Carey, Hudson Taylor and Henry Martyn.

   All were convinced evangelicals. They and thousands like them, acknowledged the impetus given by the 'Great Evangelical Awakening' of the eighteenth century.

The twentieth century

Twentieth-century society was changing. Popular support for the churches was challenged by:

▶ Scientific discovery

▶ Popular secularism

▶ The disillusionment created by World Wars

In the twentieth century the flames of the missionary movement began to die.

KEY POINT

▶ Non-evangelicals continued in their suspicions of the value of attempting to convert those of other faiths.

▶ Tolerance was demanded of 'other ways to find God'.

Evangelicals today have retained a commitment to preach Jesus to those of all nations and religions. Meanwhile domestic evangelism has concentrated on:

▶ Preaching

▶ Missions and special outreach events

▶ Personal witnessing

▶ A special emphasis on work among children and young people

Case history

Major campaigns associated with D.L. Moody and his soloist Ira D. Sankey had their twentieth-century counterpart in the 'crusades' of Dr Billy Graham and his musical director, Cliff Barrows.

When the Evangelical Alliance brought Billy Graham to Haringay in 1954 a fresh momentum was generated in British evangelism. Later visits to Britain by Billy Graham in 1955, 1961, 1966 and 1967 culminated in one million people attending his 'Mission England' in 1984.

Further visits in 1985, 1989 and the nationwide 'Mission Scotland' in 1991 have contributed to Dr Graham becoming well known nationally and globally.

KEY POINT

The latter half of the twentieth century has witnessed the growth of particular emphases within evangelism.

▶ Parachurch societies have sprung up to deal with specific issues, needs and sections of society.

▶ Major missions have largely replaced the emphasis on continuing day-by-day evangelistic witness within the local community.

▶ Greater concentration has been placed on supporting the skills of trained professionals rather than encouraging the involvement of all Christians.

▶ Prayer meetings have declined in popular recognition and attendance.

▶ Local churches have looked towards strategies for 'in-drag'—bringing people into church buildings and timetables—rather than 'outreach'—meeting people where they are.

Many now share a fresh determination to see Britain re-evangelized in this generation.

KEY POINT

Throughout the history of the church, it has only been at times when the Holy Spirit has created an army of 'ordinary people' to forge a major new direction that the church has truly prospered.

Case history Billy Graham

A farm boy from Charlotte, North Carolina, Billy Graham was not outstanding at school. He started working life as a door-to-door brush salesman, and became the world's best known and greatly loved Christian preacher.

As a nineteen-year-old, Billy Graham committed himself to God to help bring spiritual renewal to the American church and nation. After completing his studies he briefly pastored a church near Chicago. While there he came to prominence through a live weekly radio programme and his preaching at the local Youth for Christ rallies.

With a small team he spent six months in Britain in 1946–7 preaching 360 times in 27 different towns and cities in the process. However, it was his extended campaign in Los Angeles in 1949 that made him a household name in his own country and subsequently around the world.

In Britain, Billy is primarily remembered for his first major crusade at Haringey Arena in North London in 1954. He has been back many times as part of his international ministry which has seen him preach in most nations including China and the old Soviet Union, India, Brazil, South Africa, Japan and Korea where over one million people attended a single meeting.

A unique man of God. The history of the twentieth century would be different without him.

Many have waited for such a 'people movement' so that the dying years of the twentieth century might again see a fresh impetus on mission and evangelism.

Responding Through the Local Church

God has done great things throughout history. Never has the worldwide church been so large. Never has there been a better ratio of believers to unbelievers worldwide.

Nevertheless, the task has still to be completed.

The gospel has still not effectively been taken to every tribe and nation on the planet.

KEY POINT

It is at last possible to conceive this happening but whether it happens in our lifetime or not depends on each of us determining to play our part in its fulfilment.

Mission is out of fashion in the local church.

KEY POINT

After years of retrenchment at home it is difficult to seriously consider involvement in expansion abroad.

▶ **Secular opinion is strongly against mission.** We should tolerate those of other cultures and faiths—not try to change them.

▶ **Religious thought is strongly against mission.** If all religions are equal and if truth is merely a matter of personal choice, there is no reason to proclaim the gospel. If there is a God he will save everyone anyway.

▶ **Politically, experience is negative towards mission.** In nineteenth-century Britain it was considered our duty to export our civilization, including our religion. Today we are not even sure that we want to be part of Europe.

▶ **Traditional destinations for missionaries have changed.** China, India, much of Africa and South America have been replaced with new—less dramatic—locations, Belgium, France, Spain and Italy.

▶ **Glamour has been replaced by slog.** The dramatic Bible-smuggling to the oppressed peoples of the Communist bloc has been superseded by the need for training

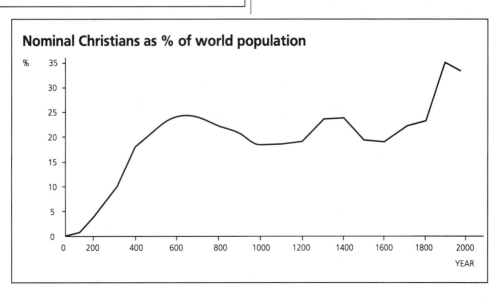

Nominal Christians as % of world population

Year (AD)	Total world population (millions)	People who do not claim to be Christians (millions)	People who call themselves Christians (millions)	Bible-believing Christians (part of column 3) (millions)	Non-Christians per believer (column 2 divided by column 4)	Unreached people groups
100	181	180	1	0.5	360 to 1	60,000
1000	270	220	50	1	220 to 1	50,000
1500	425	344	81	5	69 to 1	44,000
1900	1,620	1,062	558	40	27 to 1	40,000
1950	2,504	1,650	854	80	21 to 1	24,000
1980	4,458	3,025	1,433	275	11 to 1	17,000
1992	5,480	3,647	1,833	540	6.8 to 1	11,000

Non-Christians, column 2, means 'people who do not consider themselves to be Christians'. This number does not include people, column 3, who do consider themselves to be Christians and who have the Bible in their language but who may not truly know or believe the God of the Bible. Bible-believing Christians here means people who read, believe and obey the Bible, whether or not they are as active as they ought to be in world evangelization. The specific numbers here are correct within a small percentage, except for the earlier centuries. But the overall trend is what is unarguable, despite many gloomy statements to the contrary.

From *Mission Frontiers*, volume 14, numbers 5–6, US Center for World Mission, 1992

programmes, long-term workers fluent in the local language, legal literature-publishing programmes.

▶ **Churches have become happier with an emphasis on physical aid and social programmes.** This has been an important part of our proclaiming the comprehensive gospel of the kingdom of God—caring for the whole person. But it can lead to ignoring the task of proclamation and church planting.

KEY POINT

The urgent need is to change the attitudes in the local church and to initiate new programmes of mission.

Steps to Action

There are definite steps that must be taken if the task of evangelizing the whole world is to again become owned and acted on by the Church. These include:

▶ **Bible teaching on mission.** To renew our confidence in the unchanging nature of the great commission even if it is unpopular in an attitude of prevailing religious pluralism.

▶ **Mission education.** To inform the church of the nature of the need—dispelling the widespread ignorance of the spiritual state of the world, promoting what is already happening and advising of current needs.

▶ **Appoint a World Mission action group.** To implement the church's commitment to mission—gathering and distributing information, arranging visits and meetings, supervising the allocation of gifts, liaising with other groups. Their most important role should be to be the prime link to the missionaries sent out by or adopted by the church.

▶ **Link with at least one local church in**

another country. With modern communications much can be done to make this work. Monthly letters for public reading/display, telephone prayer requests, annual holiday excursion, youth exchange visits, inter-change of pulpits. Ideally, pair with an equivalent church for mutual benefit, perhaps in Western Europe or North America, and with a church needing a degree of outside aid—not necessarily in material goods—perhaps in Southern or Eastern Europe, Asia, Africa or South America. A development of the second relationship could be the adoption of and financial support of a pastor, Bible college student, evangelist, parachurch agency worker from that church.

▶ **Pray.** Build prayers around genuine relationships, with good quality information in a varied format and the use of different visual media. Integrate prayer like this into Sunday services, special prayer groups, part of the regular house-group programme and so on.

▶ **Use targets.** To help keep us on track to achieve our goals: financial goals, special projects, helping an adopted church build an extension, sending out young people on a summer evangelistic project (for example, Love Europe, YWAM Summer of Service, Oasis team and so on), 'arranging' one of the church leadership team to visit a new country/church/ worker/project.

▶ **Send out workers.** This need not necessarily be the traditional young, gifted, married couple. It could equally be an elder person or couple who have taken early retirement. Short-term workers are an important element in world mission. However, the relationship with those going short-term may not be as profound (or costly) as with those committing themselves indefinitely.

continued on page 80

Evangelism questionnaire

Personal information

Sex　　　　　male ☐　female ☐

Age　　　　　under 24 ☐　25–39 ☐　40–59 ☐　over 60 ☐

Marital status　single ☐　married ☐

Years committed Christian　under 2 ☐　3–9 ☐　over 10 ☐

Denomination　Anglican ☐　Baptist ☐　Methodist ☐
　　　　　Pentecostal ☐　New Church ☐　Roman Catholic ☐
　　　　　other ☐
　　　　　(specify) _____

Area you live in　urban ☐　suburban ☐　rural ☐

Were you raised in a committed Christian home?　yes ☐　no ☐

How did you come to faith in Christ?

Up to 3 answers, rated
1 = most significant
2 = next most significant
3 = next most significant

family	
witness of a friend	
local church activity	
Sunday school	
evangelistic meeting	
youth club	
personal crisis	
personal search for truth	
Christian literature	

At the time you made your commitment, what age were you?

under 11 ☐　12–16 ☐　17–24 ☐　25–39 ☐　40–59 ☐　over 60 ☐

Attitudes to evangelism

How important do you believe evangelism is?

extremely important ☐　very important ☐　important ☐
quite important ☐　not very important ☐

Is evangelism the task of . . .

everyone ☐　all mature Christians ☐
those with the gift ☐　full-time workers ☐　Holy Spirit only ☐

Do you enjoy sharing your faith?

always ☐　sometimes ☐　never ☐

Do you enjoy sharing your faith?

very much ☐　quite a bit ☐　not at all ☐

Do you want to evangelize?

yes ☐　sometimes ☐　don't know ☐　no ☐

Evangelistic activity

Does your church run evangelistic activities specifically with the aim of leading people to faith in Christ?

daily ☐　weekly ☐　monthly ☐　occasionally ☐　never ☐

Do you take part in any of your church's evangelistic activities?

always ☐　regularly ☐　often ☐　occasionally ☐　never ☐

Where are you happiest taking part in evangelism?

as close to home as possible ☐　in the locality ☐　as far away as possible ☐

Rate the importance of these activities:	Which of these activities are you personally involved in?
1 = vital; 2 = important; 3 = quite important; 4 = not very important; 5 = of no importance at all	1 = always; 2 = regularly; 3 = often; 4 = occasionally; 5 = never

	1 2 3 4 5		1 2 3 4 5
child evangelism		child evangelism	
Sunday School		Sunday School	
youth clubs (incl. scouts etc.)		youth clubs (incl. scouts etc.)	
open airs		open airs	
door-to-door		door-to-door	
marches of witness		marches of witness	
evangelistic celebrations		evangelistic celebrations	
street work		street work	
church-based missions		church-based missions	
interdenominational town-wide missions		interdenominational town-wide missions	
national campaigns		national campaigns	
overseas mission		overseas mission	
literature		literature	
concerts		concerts	
workplace initiative		workplace initiative	
lunches, banquets, etc.		lunches, banquets, etc.	
media (national and local)		media (national and local)	

How clear are you about the content of the gospel message?

very clear ☐　clear ☐　quite clear ☐　not clear at all ☐

What would help you most to be more active evangelistically?
1 = very much indeed; 2 = a lot; 3 = quite a lot; 4 = a little; 5 = not at all

	1 2 3 4 5
more practical training	
more Bible teaching on the subject	
more exhortation and challenge	
more personal encouragement	
more or better opportunities	
others to take a lead	
support from others	
better example from church leadership	
improved personal relationship with God	

▶ **Integrate international concerns.** Use media events to unite the so-called secular and spiritual world on the issue of mission. For example, the break-up of Yugoslavia and the Gulf War of 1991 have major implications for world evangelism. An informed church will be able to help direct prayer and practical support to Christians in these—and many other—situations.

▶ **Be positive.** Lead by example. Lukewarmness has killed the enthusiasm of others for world mission in countless churches. Too often international considerations are perceived as a threat to the efforts to raise money for the fabric fund/new hymn books/new minister and so on.

The past few years have produced a reaction to the current state of affairs. Increasingly Christian leaders have recognized the enormous size of the task that lies ahead. Yet there are valuable lessons that we can learn from the past. We can either:

▶ Sit and wait for a sovereign outpouring of God's Holy Spirit in revival power

▶ Venture out to fulfil our Lord's command and expect him to meet us as we act in obedience to him

FOUNDATIONAL READING

David Cohen and Steve Gaukroger, *How to Close Your Church in a Decade*, Scripture Union, 1992

Michael Green, *Evangelism Through the Local Church*, Hodder & Stoughton, 1990

Laurence Singlehurst, editor, *The Evangelism Toolkit*, CWR, 1992

FURTHER READING

David B. Barrett and James W. Reapsome, *Seven Hundred Ways to Evangelize the World*, New Hope, 1988

David B. Barrett and Todd M. Johnson, *Our Globe and How to Reach it*, New Hope, 1990

Paul Bassett, *God's Way*, Evangelical Press, 1981

John Benton, *One World, One Way*, Evangelical Press, 1992

Peter Brierley, *Christian England*, Marc Europe, 1991

E.H. Broadbent, *The Pilgrim Church*, Pickering & Inglis, 1931

David Burnett, *God's Mission: Heading the Nations*, Marc Europe, 1986

Jack Burton, *The Gap*, SPCK, 1991

Luis Bush, editor, *AD2000 and Beyond Handbook*, AD2000, 1992

Clive Calver, Derek Copley, Bob Mofett and Jim Smith, editors, *A Guide to Evangelism*, Marshalls, 1984

Wesley Carr, *Manifold Wisdom*, SPCK, 1991

Steve Chalke, *The Complete Youth Manual*, Volume 1, Kingsway, 1987

Ian Coffey et al., *No Stranger in the City*, Inter-Varsity Press/STL, 1989

Robert E. Coleman, *Evangelism on the Cutting Edge*, Fleming H. Revell, 1986

Robert E. Coleman, *The Master Plan of Evangelism*, Felming H. Revell, 1963

Gareth Crossley, *Everyday Evangelism*, Evangelical Press, 1987

M. Deanesley, *A History of the Medieval Church*, Metheun & Co., 1925

Tim Dowley, editor, *The History of Christianity*, revised, Lion Publishing, 1990

Declan Flanagan, *God's Move, Your Move*, Kingsway, 1988

Roger T. Forster and Paul Marston, *God's Strategy in Human History*, Highland Books, 1989

Roger T. Forster and Paul Marston, *Reason and Faith*, Monarch, 1989

Stephen Gaukroger, *It Makes Sense*, Scripture Union, 1987

Caughey Gauntlett, *Today in Darkest Britain*, Salvationist Publications, 1990

John Grayston, editor, *Care to Say Something?*, Scripture Union, 1982

Michael Green, *Evangelism in the Early Church*, Hodder & Stoughton, 1970

Michael Griffiths, *What on Earth Are You Doing?*, Inter-Varsity Press/STL, 1983

Leo Habets, *There is Hope*, Marshall Pickering, 1988

A. Harvey, editor, *Theology in the City*, SPCK, 1989

David S. Hasselgrove, *Communicating Christ Cross-Culturally*, Zondervan, 1978

David S. Hasselgrove, *Today's Choices for Tomorrow's Mission*, Zondervan, 1988

Monica Hill, editor, *How to Plant Churches*, Marc Europe, 1984

Roger T. Hooker and Christopher Lamb, *Love the Stranger*, SPCK, 1986

Bill Hull, *Jesus Christ, Disciple Maker*, Crossway Books, 1992

Todd M. Johnson, *Countdown to 1900*, New Hope, 1988

Arthur P. Johnson, *World Evangelism and the Word of God*, Bethany Fellowship, 1974

J. Andrew Kirk, *Loosing the Chains*, Hodder & Stoughton, 1992

Johan Lukasse, *Churches with Roots*, STL/BEM, 1990

Alister McGrath, *Explaining Your Faith*, Inter-Varsity Press/STL, 1988

Ruth March, *Europe Reborn*, OM Publishing, 1992

Michael Marshall, *The Gospel Connection*, Morehouse Publications, 1990

Jim Montgomery, *DAWN 2000*, Highland, 1990

Glenn Myers, *The World Christian Starter Kit*, WEC/STL, 1986

Lesslie Newbigin, *The Gospel in a Pluralist Society*, SPCK, 1989

J.I. Packer, *Evangelism and the Sovereignty of God*, Inter-Varsity Press, 1961

Maurice Sinclair, *Ripening Harvest, Gathering Storm*, Marc Europe, 1988

Ron Smith, *The A B C of Personal Evangelism*, Fishers Fellowship, 1984

John Stott, *Christian Mission in the Modern World*, Kingsway, 1975

Kim Swithinbank, *The National Touch*, Marshall Pickering, 1988

A.N. Triton, *Whose World?*, Inter-Varsity Press, 1970

G.S.M. Walker, *The Growing Storm*, Paternoster Press, 1961

David Watson, *I Believe in Evangelism*, Hodder & Stoughton, 1970

John Wimber and Kevin Springer, *Power Evangelism*, Hodder & Stoughton, 1985

Ralph D. Winter and Steven C. Hawthorne, *Perspectives on the World Christian Movement*, William Carey Library

Michael Wooderson, *The Church Down Our Street*, Marc Europe, 1989

John Young, *Know Your Faith*, Hodder & Stoughton, 1991

Not all of these books may be available at the event.

Eternity
Living in the Spiritual World

CONTENTS

Book of the seminar day:
Billy Graham, *Facing Death*, Word

Introduction

To quote George Bernard Shaw, 'Death is the ultimate statistic, one out of one dies.' What a morbid way to start.

Yet all true Christians are united to affirm, 'I believe in the resurrection of the body and the life everlasting.' We share a belief that anticipates eternal life, heaven and reigning alongside our Saviour, Jesus Christ.

But:

▶ How soon do we want this to happen?

▶ Where is heaven and what will we do there?

▶ Is hell really going to be 'like that'? And for ever?

▶ Where is science in all this?

▶ How should we cope with the reality of death?

▶ Should the fact of eternity make a difference to the way we live in time?

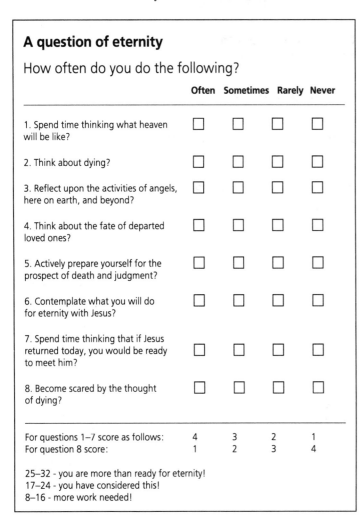

KEY POINT

Meanwhile, most people in our world live and behave as though time is all there is—and Christians are often little better.

For us, this is because:

▶ It is difficult to imagine what heaven or eternity could be like.

▶ Heaven does not appear on our horizons until life has ended. And few are prepared to think deeply about death before that moment arrives.

▶ We don't know what Eternity or Heaven - is really like. Apart from the New Testament the only accounts come from those who lack credibility in the Christian arena.

▶ There is the fear that it might all be just wishful thinking. Death may be the end, rather than a new beginning. There is the uncertainty that, if heaven should exist, at the last moment we might be rejected as unsuitable candidates.

How ready and aware are we to contend with eternity? This questionnaire may help to establish the answer.

The Significance of Eternity

These issues are important. If there is an afterlife then we must live our present life in the shadow—or searchlight—of the facts.

Recognizing eternal values:

▶ helps us to help and care for those who have been bereaved

▶ helps us to prepare Christians to face up to their 'golden years' and the challenge of death

▶ Equips us to cope with present fears:
Am I sure of salvation?
Will God accept me?
What about those things I have not yet accomplished?
Has God forgiven my secret sins?

Death and Bereavement

Death is the subject that the twentieth century does not talk about.

Each year, 660,000 people die in the United Kingdom. While, during an average week of television viewing, we can watch around forty-five violent deaths.

Yet, so far as the reality of death is concerned, our society ignores it, disguises it, jokes about it, fictionalizes it, and does anything rather than face up to it.

Gone are traditional signs of mourning:

▶ black ties and armbands

▶ drawn curtains

▶ black-edged correspondence

People no longer 'die':

▶ they 'pass over'

▶ we 'lose' them

▶ they 'kick the bucket'

We minimize periods of mourning and accelerate past a funeral cortège with impunity.

Bereavement should open up each of us to the reality of death and the questions that it raises:

▶ How will we endure any pain we might suffer?

▶ What will happen to those we leave behind?

▶ Will we arrive safely in heaven?

▶ What about the destiny of our friends and loved ones?

Besieged by such fears we are the reluctant witnesses of the death of others.

A question of eternity

How often do you do the following?

	Often	Sometimes	Rarely	Never
1. Spend time thinking what heaven will be like?	☐	☐	☐	☐
2. Think about dying?	☐	☐	☐	☐
3. Reflect upon the activities of angels, here on earth, and beyond?	☐	☐	☐	☐
4. Think about the fate of departed loved ones?	☐	☐	☐	☐
5. Actively prepare yourself for the prospect of death and judgment?	☐	☐	☐	☐
6. Contemplate what you will do for eternity with Jesus?	☐	☐	☐	☐
7. Spend time thinking that if Jesus returned today, you would be ready to meet him?	☐	☐	☐	☐
8. Become scared by the thought of dying?	☐	☐	☐	☐

For questions 1–7 score as follows:	4	3	2	1
For question 8 score:	1	2	3	4

25–32 - you are more than ready for eternity!
17–24 - you have considered this!
8–16 - more work needed!

'Death, we think, is something which only happens to other people.'
STEPHEN TRAVIS

KEY POINT

KEY POINT

What language do you use to talk about death?

Loss and Grief

A tragic by-product of this strange attitude to death is our lack of ability to cope with the experience of someone close to us dying. Or to be a help to those who have experienced bereavement themselves—a situation faced by two-thirds of a million families in Britain each year.

KEY POINT

The death of someone close to us creates a natural response from our emotions. God has made us that way—for our own good.

Bereavement can evoke:

▶ a self-centred response—'how will I cope?'

▶ a compassionate response for others—'how will they cope?'

▶ a sense of loss for the deceased—'I will miss them'

▶ a sense of concern—'Where are they now?'

None of this is wrong, but quite natural.

Grief is a gift from God to enable us to cope with the loss and change that the death of someone brings to us. Sadly, there are still Christians who believe that spiritual victory involves keeping a stiff upper lip. That is not a biblical view.

In his book *Pressure Points* (Kingsway), Peter Meadows points out that the concept of not grieving may be due to a wrong understanding of Paul's words 'We do not want you to … grieve like the rest of men, who have no hope' (Thessalonians 4:13). He explains, 'Paul is saying that their grief should be different to the grief shown by those who have no hope. He is approving grief but calling for it to be grief filled with hope.'

This can be seen from scripture:

▶ Confronted with the death of Lazarus we read that 'Jesus wept' (John 11:35). What was good for the Lord of life must also be appropriate for his followers.

▶ Jesus said: 'Blessed are those that mourn, for they will be comforted' (Matthew 5:4).

Stages of Grief

There are some common threads to the experience of bereavement.

It could never happen to us. Few prepare themselves for the reality of personal loss. As a result we feel shocked, and numbed by the awfulness of our loss.

How could God have allowed it? A reaction is to lash out at those around, or retreat into stunned silence. Because we do not understand why death should occur we often blame God for taking away someone we love.

Why should it be our family or friends? A tendency to self-pity: 'Why me? Why us? Why not them?' Thinking is distorted by emotion. It is impossible to know 'why?' Reason anyway cannot meet the pain felt.

The sense of personal loss and sadness. This is a deep anguish expressed in our innermost being. A gnawing sense that we have lost someone who can never be replaced; that things will never be the same again.

A conviction of remorse. A deep regret for all those things that we never said, or failed to do. This overpowering sense of guilt is often accompanied by physical reactions like shaking, heaving or sobbing.

The retreat into fantasy. We imagine all that might have been. This is focused on the good things in the past rather than the bad ones. A make-believe world where no angry word was ever spoken.

But it has happened. This is the moment of truth. Maturity begins when we not only acknowledge our loss but also begin the difficult process of accepting the fact.

Supporting the Bereaved

Someone who has been bereaved may experience a deep and lasting legacy of grief.

▶ They may have been thoroughly traumatized, and emotional scars will long remain.

▶ Memories may constantly trigger that feeling of loss and regret.

▶ Unresolved questions may linger.

▶ There may be a great sense of loneliness, frustration and even betrayal.

It takes time to learn how to live again, and it is here that caring support can be so significant.

The victim of personal tragedy or loss is often overwhelmed with kindness at the time—but later forgotten.

The moment a bereaved person is most in need of help—and best able to receive it—is usually long after the funeral is over.

Friends can contribute a sense of strength and hope. We need to help by offering contact and encouragement.

Talk and listen. It may be answers that they need—just the opportunity to voice their questions. Talk also about the person who has died and help to create a sense of fixed reality.

Tears. To cry with someone can be the most meaningful form of counselling and support in this situation.

Touch. A comforting arm, a shoulder to cry on, or a platonic embrace can say far more than volumes of words.

Friendship. The empty seat next to them in church, the lonely evenings or weekends at home, and the absence of casual conversation are all gaps where friends can help to fill the vacuum.

Our culture is geared to relationships between couples—something which can appear exceptionally cruel. Invitations to visit cease because 'three's a crowd!' We need to invite an individual in their own right, being prepared to split up our own 'twosome' for an evening, or work to make a threesome into a meaningful relationship.

Space. Some things can only be worked out alone, although this must not be an excuse for neglect.

Rebuilding a life. The trauma of bereavement can lead to hasty decisions. A caring friend is needed to advise or help keep options open.

Prayer. The emotional impact of loss can make it impossible for someone to pray for themselves. But they are reassured to know that others are praying on their behalf.

Are you ready to die?

KEY POINT

In Genesis 49:33—50:14 we have an account of the elaborate mourning of Joseph for his father lasting at least seventy days. How seriously should we treat this example?

What gifts, abilities, experiences and opportunities do you have to help the bereaved?

'**W**e only die once, and for such a long time.'
MOLIÈRE

'**I**t was a truly human tombstone which bore the inscription, "I expected this, but not yet." '
ANON

KEY POINT

'**T**he fence around a cemetery is foolish, for those inside can't come out and those outside don't want to get in.'
ARTHUR BRISBANE

In a Spring Harvest seminar in 1992 one guest in her fifties complained that for a whole year no one from her 'large, active, evangelical, charismatic church with a caring reputation' visited her after her bereavement. Her friends did not know how to react to her unexpected loss. How can this happen? Could it happen in your church? Why or why not?

Are you a good listener?

KEY POINT

KEY POINT

KEY POINT

Spiritual direction. Here there is a need for caution. Words can be terribly inappropriate. While part of our humanity means that we can get it wrong. Even when we think God is leading, the bereaved person may be too numb to either listen or understand.

The Bible and Eternity

It is not easy to cope with concepts of time—international date lines, time zones, periods of history. All these can create a sense of confusion and uncertainty. But if we struggle with time, how can we begin to understand eternity?

A mind that is limited by time, cannot fully understand eternity.

At best we can describe what can be known to the limits of our understanding—using images and analogies to describe, in familiar terms, that which is unfamiliar to us.

The main word for 'eternal' in the New Testament is αιωνιος (*aionios*) which 'describes duration undefined because endless' (W.E. Vine, *Expository Dictionary of New Testament Words*, Marshall Pickering, 1952). This word is applied to God, salvation, the gospel, Christ's future rule, and so on (John 3:15; Acts 13:48; Romans 16:26; Revelation 14:6).

Strictly speaking, in English, 'eternal' means 'without beginning or end'. Whereas 'everlasting' simply means 'without end'. In popular usage the words are used interchangeably.

The two words for time in the New Testament are:

▶ χρωνος (*chronos*), a space of time, whether shorter or longer. It implies duration or sometimes a date, past, present or future. It is primarily a term of quantity.

▶ καιρος (*kairos*), a fixed or definite period, sometimes an opportune occasion. It can be used to highlight the characteristics of a period.

In biblical times, the emphasis was not on the clock but on the wise use of time. Paul, quoting Isaiah 49:8, writes in 2 Corinthians 6:2, 'Now is the time (*kairos*) of God's favour, now is the day of salvation.' It was the *occasion* not the duration that was crucial. Some theologians, particularly Paul Tillich, claim that all of time is *chronos*—into which occasional moments of great significance (*kairoi*) occur. The greatest of these was the coming of Jesus.

Time itself, as we know it, is part of the created order.

Augustine of Hippo, back in the fifth century AD, said: 'God created the world *with* time, not *in* time.'

Time as we know it did not exist before God created the universe. God, of course, existed then in eternity.

This reminds us that eternity is more than time stretched indefinitely. It is of a different nature.

This means that all scientific debates about the beginning of the universe and the nature of time tell us nothing about the nature of eternity.

God, who inhabits eternity, also acts in specific ways within time and human history. This includes the unusual—signs and wonders—which are not unusual for God.

Death: The Final Frontier

Each of us has been born. Each of us will eventually die.

Scripture affirms that 'Sin pays a wage, and the wage is death' (Romans 6:23 NEB). Therefore death is no mere cosmic accident. Rather, it is an appointment which each of us must keep. As Paul reminds us, 'Sin entered the world through one man, and death through sin, and in this way death came to all men, because all sinned' (Romans 5:12).

To quote Peter Cotterell, 'Death isn't just physical, not just an accident that can be avoided... It has to do with our relationship with God.' (*I Want to Know What the Bible Says About Death*, Kingsway, 1979.)

Physical and Spiritual Death

The moment of death can be viewed from different perspectives.

▶ In purely physical terms death represents when the body no longer works. It occurs when:
1. There is irreversible destruction of brain matter, with no possibility of regaining consciousness.
2. Spontaneous heart beat can not be restored.
3. 'Brain death' is established by the EEG (electroencephalogram).

▶ In theological terms, death represents the parting of the body from the spirit. Life comes to a body when the spirit enters it and death arrives when the spirit departs. At death, the spirit then returns to God who gave it to us. The body has served its purpose and progressively disintegrates, returning to the dust from which it was formed.

From a physical viewpoint death is the final act—the conclusion of the story. But then, from a spiritual perspective, death represents the end of one chapter and the beginning of a new one!

Most people die as the result of the gradual deterioration of the body. Our bodies wear out. The body is like a tent (2 Corinthians 5:1)—which gradually falls apart.

Physical death is common to Christian and non-Christian alike. Christians, however, have received the gift of eternal life and are delivered from spiritual death (John 3:16).

Death was God's punishment for disobedience (Genesis 2:17). Man has two dimensions to his creation. Adam was made:

▶ physical—from the dust (Genesis 2:7)

▶ spiritual—in the image of God (Genesis 1:27)

As a result of the fall humankind was condemned to return to the dust (Genesis 3:19)—physical death—and lost communion with God (Genesis 3:23, 24)—spiritual death.

KEY POINT

The link between sin and death is fundamental to the whole of scripture (Ezekiel 18:4; Hebrews 9:27) and is at the heart of Paul's theology (Romans 5:12; 6:23; 7:13; 1 Corinthians 15:21).

Those who object to the concept of the fall of mankind have no option but to accept physical death as 'natural'. Mainstream evangelical Christian opinion rejects this belief because it would mean that God's creation was imperfect. Rather, just as death is alien to God, it must have been alien to his handiwork.

Some Roman Catholic theologians argue that humankind was created mortal but God then gave the gift of immortality to counteract this. Thus, the fall was limited to the spiritual dimension.

Others, for example A.M. Dubarle, mark the difference between the pitiful death we do experience as a result of the fall and a death as it would have been without sin. While yet another option is that humankind was created able not to die but lost that ability in the fall.

The various alternatives have often been offered in an attempt to harmonize an evolutionary theory with a theology of the fall of man. Often ingenious, they tend to blast the stark message of scripture. In particular, it is inconsistent to separate physical and spiritual death as a direct result of the fall. Our experience is that both physical and spiritual death are in us from birth. However, the gift of eternal life:

▶ Delivers us immediately from spiritual death

Death in the Bible

Death is the direct result of the fall. '...you will surely die' (Genesis 2:17).

We die as a result of our own sin. 'The wages of sin is death' (Romans 6:23).

Death has a spiritual as well as a natural dimension. 'As for you, you were dead' (Ephesians 2:1).

Death and judgment are linked. 'Man is destined to die once, and after that to face judgment' (Hebrews 9:27).

God is in ultimate control of life and death (Luke 12:20; Revelation 1:18) '...you must spare his life' (Job 2:6).

Satan still has the power of death and fear. '...him who had the power of death, that is the devil' (Hebrews 2:14).

Jesus defeated Satan and death. '...that by his death he might destroy him who holds the power of death' (Hebrews 2:14). 'Jesus, who has destroyed death' (2 Timothy 1:10).

We share in Jesus' death and resurrection. 'United with him . . . in his death . . . we will certainly also be . . . in his resurrection' (Romans 6:5).

Jesus literally died and rose again. 'he was raised' (1 Corinthians 15:4).

Eternal life is promised to us. 'If we died with Christ . . . we will also live with him' (Romans 6:8).

To die in Christ is like falling asleep—there is no sting. 'Those who have fallen asleep' (1 Corinthians 15:20).

God's victory over death is complete, removing the pain. ' "Death has been swallowed up in victory." "Where, O death, is your victory? Where, O death, is your sting?" ' (1 Corinthians 15:54–55).

Eternal life is resurrection of the body, not immortality of the soul. 'The body that is sown is perishable, it is raised imperishable' (1 Corinthians 15:42).

Our resurrected bodies will have a spiritual form (probably like Jesus' resurrected body—recognizable but not limited by natural constraints). 'It is sown a natural body, it is raised a spiritual body' (1 Corinthians 15:44).

Eternal punishment is not for believers. 'He who overcomes will not be hurt at all by the second death' (Revelation 2:11).

Eternal death is for all who reject Christ. 'If anyone's name was not found written in the book of life, he was thrown into the lake of fire' (Revelation 20:15).

Death itself will be abolished. 'There will be no more death or mourning or crying or pain' (Revelation 21:4).

(Romans 8:10).

▶ Changes the moment of physical death from being the end of life to the transition to another life (Romans 8:11; 1 Corinthians 15:53–54).

Speculation about the state of people if the fall had not happened is fascinating but inconclusive. Rival theories cannot be sustained conclusively from scripture about what is a totally hypothetical situation.

Life After Death

The Christian declares that while the body and the spirit are separated in death they will be reunited again. The day will come when each is resurrected to eternal life.

Luis Palau tells how the whole family gathered round the bedside of his dying father—who joyfully sang a hymn and passed into eternity. We often feel condemned at such stories of death with certainty. They are strange to our twentieth-century ears.

We wish that we possessed the same sense of security and conviction which should surely be the hallmark of every Christian. Yet we are painfully aware of our own weaknesses and deficiencies.

The Christian should equally live in the security of God's promises and the truth that Jesus has already been raised from the dead:

▶ If the resurrection of Jesus was not true then faith is deprived of its foundation (1 Corinthians 15:12–17).

▶ Since Christ has risen we have the promise that 'As in Adam all die, so in Christ will all be made alive' (1 Corinthians 15:22).

▶ Christians who have died are not lost (1 Corinthians 15:18) because, on the cross, Jesus destroyed the power and dominion of death (1 Corinthians 15:24–26; Colossians 2:15).

▶ A day will dawn when we will all be changed, the dead will rise, and the scripture will be fulfilled (1 Corinthians 15:51–53). At that moment, 'When the perishable has been clothed with the imperishable, and the mortal with immortality, then the saying that is written will come true: "Death has been swallowed up in victory" ' (1 Corinthians 15:54).

▶ When Jesus cried: 'It is finished' (John 19:30), his shout was one of triumph rather than anguish. For not only was his work concluded—so was the power of death—for ever!

Death and the Word of God

Scripture is full of confidence in describing the death of the righteous.

For those who have committed their lives to Jesus Christ there is the certainty of the promises that God has made about the death of his people.

▶ God will be with us, even as we pass into the shadows of death (Psalm 23:4).

▶ The Lord holds as precious and important the death of his saints (Psalm 116:15).

▶ Jesus has gone to prepare a place for us to be

'Because I could not stop for Death—He kindly stopped for me— The Carriage held but just Ourselves— And Immortality.'
EMILY DICKINSON

KEY POINT

'I am the resurrection and the life. He who believes in me will live, even though he dies; and whoever lives and believes in me will never die. Do you believe this?'
JESUS

'What is death at most? It is a journey for a season: a sleep longer than usual. If thou fearest death, thou shouldest also fear sleep.'
JOHN CHRYSOSTOM

'The foolish fear death as the greatest of evils, the wise desire it as a rest after labours and the end of ills.'
AMBROSE

'Whether you are a King or a clown, a Christian or an atheist, a person of substance or a pauper, a scholar or illiterate—it does not matter. Death is the ultimate equaliser.'
CLIVE CALVER

KEY POINT

with him forever (John 14:2).

▶ Jesus will return to take us to be with him (John 14:3; 17:24).

▶ God offers for the righteous a place of security and safety, even in death (Proverbs 14:32).

▶ In life or death we belong to Jesus (Romans 14:8); our death is merely our gain (Philippians 1:21).

▶ Heaven will be a place of rest for the believer (Revelation 14:13), because our home is not here; on earth we are but aliens and strangers (Hebrews 11:13).

▶ The death of the righteous is an end to be desired (Numbers 23:10), because then we will enjoy a perfect relationship with Christ, in glory (Philippians 1:23; Romans 8:23).

Death and the Christian

For the Christian, death represents the gateway to eternity.

Eternity provides a different body for us to inhabit. It is the invisible parts of our nature which the Holy Spirit invades at conversion and which are redeemed to spend eternity with Jesus Christ.

Scripture assures us that we consist of a material aspect ('flesh' or 'body') and a non-material aspect ('soul', 'spirit' or 'heart') (Hebrews 4:12; 1 Thessalonians 5:23).

Human beings are more than a collection of chemicals and glands, enzymes and hormones. We have this spiritual dimension. In the case of the Christian, at death, the soul and spirit have departed on the journey towards eternity with Christ.

In the light of this truth it is scarcely surprising that the apostle Paul could joyfully exclaim, 'Where, O death is your victory? Where, O death, is your sting.' (1 Corinthians 15:55)

The Return of Jesus

Death is not the only doorway through which we can anticipate eternity. There is also the promise that Jesus is to return to take the living in the eternity.

At the heart of the Christian message lies the expectation that Jesus is coming back.

▶ His first arrival was revealed to humble shepherds, his cradle a cattle trough and his home a carpenter's workshop.

▶ The second arrival will be visible to the whole of humankind and totally spectacular. Jesus will arrive 'in his Father's glory with the holy angels' and 'with great power and glory' in a day which 'lights up the sky from one end to the other.' (Mark 8:38; 13:26; 14:62; Luke 17:24)

What Will it Be Like?

This dramatic event will be:

▶ sudden (Matthew 24:37–44; 1 Thessalonians 5:1–6)

▶ visible (Matthew 24:30; Revelation 1:7)

▶ personal—not a 'spiritual' return (Acts 1:11)

▶ glorious (Matthew 25:31–32; Luke 21:27)

In his book *Dying to Live*, Jim Graham tells of asking a Christian doctor what differences he had observed in Christians and non-Christians as they were in the process of dying. The doctor replied that in his experience, occasionally there was a very marked difference, but often there was not! Why is this so?

'For me to live is Christ, to die is gain.'
PAUL

KEY POINT

'Like pilgrims to th'appointed place we tend;The world's an inn, and death the journey's end.'
JOHN DRYDEN

'Death was not God's doing, he takes no pleasure in the extinction of the living.'
WISDOM 1:13
(JERUSALEM BIBLE)

▶ in power (Daniel 7:13–14)

▶ decisive (1 Corinthians 15:24)

To paint the rest of the picture:

▶ Jesus will wind up the present age (1 Thessalonians 4:17)

▶ the dead will be resurrected (John 5:28–29)

▶ angels will accompany him (Matthew 16:27)

▶ the living believers will rise to meet him (1 Thessalonians 4:15–16)

▶ Jesus comes to deliver the church (Matthew 24:13)

▶ Jesus comes to judge the earth (Matthew 16:27)

▶ Jesus will destroy his enemies (1 Corinthians 15:22–28; Revelation 20:1–10)

▶ God's kingdom, in its fullest sense, will come (Luke 22:29–30; 2 Peter 3:13)

The return of Jesus will be to act as judge, and to receive his people to himself (2 Thessalonians 1:7–10; 2:3–12; John 14:3).

When Will it Be?

History is full of those who have confidently predicted specific dates for the return of Jesus. At the very moment in which this material is being prepared a leaflet has been delivered which boldly announces that Christians will be taken to live with Jesus on 28 October 1992.

Others have attempted to forecast key pointers to the end of time—such as who the antichrist is. The antichrist is the personification of evil in a human form, as opposed to Satan's angelic nature (1 John 2:18; 4:3). Saddam Hussein is the most recent to be so identified. The certainty of this conclusion was based on the grounds that he planned to rebuild the old city of Babylon. Past public figures similarly labelled as the antichrist include Mussolini, Hitler, the Pope and Henry Kissinger.

Similar identifications include the European Economic Community as 666, the mark of the Beast, Russia as Magog in the ultimate conflict, and the USA as God's prophetic answer to world problems. Europe is identified as the home of the ten-nation conspiracy symbolized by the ten-horned beast in the book of Daniel.

Jesus and a Thousand Years

In Revelation 20:2–3 there is a specific reference to a one thousand year period—a millennium—in which Satan is overthrown and held prisoner. This one

'After the resurrection of the body shall have taken place, being set free from the condition of time, we shall enjoy eternal life, with love ineffable and steadfastness without corruption.'
AUGUSTINE OF HIPPO

'Those who live in the Lord never see each other for the last time.'
GERMAN PROVERB

KEY POINT

Rapture on October 28 1992

'God created the universe in six days and rested on the seventh day, and sanctified the seventh day to be His day' (Gen 2:3). According to 2 Peter 3:8 'with the Lord one day is a thousand years, and a thousand years as one day'. One day can be interpreted as a thousand years therefore, human history will end in six thousand years, and Jesus will reign in the last thousand years, a total of seven thousand years of history. Adam to Jesus was four thousand years, and in the year 1999 six thousand years of human history will end. If we subtract seven years of the Great Tribulation, Jesus' second coming (rapture) must take place in the year 1992.

We do apologise that you were not warned earlier!

> '*P*robably the mark of the beast will not be enforced until the beast (Antichrist) has a power base from which to operate. He first rules the ten nations of Revived Rome, later the whole world. In the meantime a physical, scannable mark could be offered by various banks or governments. Most likely in free nations it would be suggested as a convenient option. Take it or leave it. My advice? Do not accept a physical identity mark on your body (especially your right hand or forehead). This does not apply to a temporary invisible ink rubber stamp mark for passage in and out of Disney World or Six Flags over Texas'
>
> DAVID ALLEN LEWIS, *PROPHECY 2000*, NEW LEAF PRESS, 1990

The above is not reproduced in order to endorse it, but to illustrate the kind of book now readily available from many of our Christian bookshops in this country.

What do you believe about the millennium? Does your church have a corporate view on this subject? Does it matter?

KEY POINT

KEY POINT

mention has produced four major views as to the sequence of events that lead up to the end times.

The non-literal view denies there will be a literal, personal return of Jesus Christ to planet earth. This liberal view rejects scripture at its face value and insists that Christ's return is fulfilled in a spiritual sense variously by:

▶ the presence of God with his people after Pentecost

▶ the destruction of the temple in Jerusalem in AD70

▶ the gradual growth of the church throughout the world

The post-millennial view affirms the second coming of Jesus Christ will occur post (after) the thousand year period.

The millennium is viewed as a literal one thousand year period of universal peace and righteousness, where the gospel is preached and received throughout the whole world. This will provide a clear demonstration of the establishment of the kingdom of God, the conversion of the Jews and the binding of Satan.

At the close of this period Jesus will return, following a short time of persecution and trouble for the church. At Christ's coming there will be a general resurrection.

The amillennial view holds that the literal second coming of Jesus will not be followed by a literal one thousand year reign of Christ on earth.

The one thousand year period is understood to be a symbol of the complete period from the resurrection of Jesus Christ until his second coming.

All the Old Testament promises given to Israel are seen as being fulfilled in the church.

The premillennial view takes a literal interpretation of scripture and places Christ's second coming before the millennium. The Old Testament prophecies concerning the restoration of Israel and her future glory are fulfilled when Jesus establishes his Messianic kingdom on earth, reigning from Jerusalem.

Throughout the years of church history different views concerning the millennium have been dominant.

Churches in the past have been divided and relationships damaged by a concentration on issues such as this—about which we cannot be certain. Today there is a growing reluctance among British evangelicals to be dogmatic about this.

But one thing unites evangelical Christians—we share the conviction that Jesus will return.

The subsequent sequence of events will prove which theory was right, and which was wrong.

The Last Days

Confusion may be caused by misunderstanding the biblical expression 'the last days'. This does not refer specifically to the *immediate* period of time before the second coming of Christ but the whole period from the day of Pentecost until that event. Different references refer to different aspects of this period. For example:

▶ the day of Pentecost itself (Acts 2:17)

▶ the destruction of Jerusalem in AD70 (Matthew 24:15)

▶ the run-up to Christ's return (Luke 17:26–30)

▶ the actual return (Acts 2:20)

▶ or the whole era (Jude 18; 2 Timothy 3:1; 1 Peter 1:20)

There are two similar expressions which must be noted:

▶ 'the last day'—used of the resurrection of the dead and future judgment (John 6:39, 44, 54; 11:24; 12:48)

▶ the last days of Israel—which are prophecies of the nation's future, not necessarily linked to the current era (Isaiah 2:1–5; Micah 4:1)

The Signs of His Coming

The Bible affirms that Jesus will come back unexpectedly, like a thief in the night, especially to those who are not eagerly awaiting his return (Matthew 24:36–51; 25:13; Mark 13:32–37; 1 Thessalonians 5:1–11; 2 Peter 3:10).

While we are not to know the timetable, there will be certain warning signs. These include:

▶ National disaster, earthquakes, famines and plague (Luke 21:11, 25)

▶ Religious apostasy (Mark 13:5–6)

▶ International conflict (Mark 13:8)

▶ A godless, hedonistic society (2 Timothy 3:1–4)

▶ Disruption of family life (Mark 13:12)

▶ Dread of disaster (Luke 21:26) particularly focused on the city of Jerusalem (Luke 21:20–24)

▶ Persecution (Mark 13:9, 13)

▶ Worldwide witness of the church (Mark 13:10)

The New Testament writers are in no doubt that Jesus is coming back (1 Thessalonians 1:9–10; 4:16–17; Titus 2:11–14). Even outside the book of Revelation there are more than two hundred verses in the New Testament which refer to the second

Do you personally think Jesus is coming back soon? Does it make a difference to your lifestyle? Should it do so?

KEY POINT

> '*F*or ever with the Lord!
> Amen, so let it be!
> Life from the dead is in that word;
> 'Tis immortality.
> Here in the body pent,
> Absent from Him I roam;
> Yet nightly pitch my moving tent
> A day's march nearer home.'
>
> JAMES MONTGOMERY

coming of Jesus Christ.

The entire canon of scripture concludes with the promise, 'Yes I am coming soon', along with the author's passionate response, 'Amen. Come, Lord Jesus' (Revelation 22:20).

Eternity and the Judgment

KEY POINT

When Jesus returns it will not only be as Saviour and King—he will also come back as Lord and Judge.

This will be the final episode of Jesus' work on earth. On his first visit he came to save—he will return to judge the earth (John 5:22, 27–30).

The nature and character of a holy and righteous God mean that he cannot receive unforgiven sinners and remain true to himself. The whole purpose of the life, death and resurrection of Jesus Christ is the provision of salvation, a key part of which is that one day he would return in judgment (Acts 17:31; 2 Timothy 4:1).

▶ This authority has been given to Jesus by his Father (John 5:22, 27).

▶ The verdicts of Jesus will be true and right (John 5:30).

▶ God himself has decreed that his Son will judge everyone (Acts 17:31; Romans 2:16), both the living and the dead (1 Peter 4:5–6).

▶ At the Judgment, everything hidden will be exposed, and justice will be done (1 Corinthians 4:5).

There is to be a day of judgment (Acts 17:31; Romans 2:16; 2 Peter 3:7), and it applies to Christians and non-Christians alike (2 Corinthians 5:10; Romans 14:10).

People will be divided into:

▶ 'the wicked' and 'the righteous' (Matthew 13:49)

▶ 'the sheep on his right' and 'the goats on his left' (Matthew 25:33)

▶ 'his holy people' and 'those who do not know God' (2 Thessalonians 1:8–10)

All will be either 'blessed' or 'cursed' (Matthew 25:34–41), and will depart to either heaven or hell.

KEY POINT

The Christian's Reward

KEY POINT

All believers will appear at the judgment seat to give an account of their works (1 Corinthians 3:11–15; 2 Corinthians 5:10) and receive their reward (2 Timothy 4:8; Revelation 11:18).

This judgment does not relate to our salvation—which was settled on the cross (John 3:16–18). It is a judgment of our work and service for the Lord Jesus (1 John 4:17; 2 Corinthians 5:10–11).

In ancient Greece, at the conclusion of the athletics competition, the competitors assembled in front of the 'judgment seat' where the judge awarded the laurel crown to the victors. Some of the contestants would not receive a crown, because they had failed to win an event.

Jesus promised:

▶ That our faithfulness, stewardship and application of the 'talents' he gives his people would ultimately be rewarded (Matthew 25:20–23; Luke 19:12–19).

▶ Our reward will be in heaven (Luke 6:23) and given to us by Jesus himself (Revelation 22:12).

We have no precise information as to the nature of the rewards of a righteous man, of prophets, of saints, nor of servants who honour Jesus' name (Matthew 10:41–42; Revelation 11:18).

Jesus promises rewards both now and in the age to come, for those who put him before home, family, children and possessions (Matthew 19:29; Mark 10:29–30).

KEY POINT

What we are told is that the believer's rewards include:

▶ the crown of life (James 1:12; Revelation 2:10) especially for those who have suffered or have been martyred for their Lord and Master

▶ the crown of glory (1 Peter 5:2–4; Hebrews 2:9) especially for faithful shepherds

▶ the crown of righteousness (2 Timothy 4:8) especially if we lead holy lives

▶ the incorruptible crown (1 Corinthians 9:25–27) for all believers

▶ the crown of rejoicing (1 Thessalonians 2:19–20) especially for those who lead others to Christ

Jesus wants us to persevere and overcome—in order to arrive with boldness at the day of judgment and not be ashamed on the glorious day of his return (1 John 4:17; 2 Timothy 4:1–8; Revelation 11:18).

So we are urged to look after our crowns! (Revelation 3:11)

The Unbeliever's Judgment

It was never God's plan that any should perish. This is why Jesus came—bringing a message of repentance and hope (Luke 13:3, 5).

He wants all to enjoy eternal life (John 3:15), and for that purpose he died and rose again (John 3:16–18). Yet there is a just punishment for those who reject God's free offer of life in Christ Jesus. That penalty is one of eternal and final separation from God (Matthew 8:12; 25:46).

This is not because Jesus desires it, but because justice demands it.

The final judgment for unbelievers takes place before the great white throne (Revelation 20:11–15):

▶ Even those who have rejected the claims of Jesus must bow their knee before him, and every tongue will have to confess that 'Jesus Christ is Lord' (Philippians 2:10–11).

▶ They will be judged according to their works (Jude 14–15).

▶ They will face everlasting separation from God because of their sin (Matthew 10:28; Hebrews 10:29).

▶ They will receive the just reward of their disobedience and rejection of God (2 Thessalonians 1:7–10).

These verses deliver the solemn warning that 'They

KEY POINT

KEY POINT

KEY POINT

will be punished with everlasting destruction and shut out from the presence of the Lord and from the majesty of his power on the day he comes to be glorified in his holy people and to be marvelled at among all those who have believed' (2 Thessalonians 1:9–10).

Those Who Have Never Heard

'What about those who have never heard the gospel? Will they be saved?' There are two basic groups to whom this applies.

▶ Those who live where there is no existing church and the Christian message has yet to reach.

▶ Babies, young children and those suffering from extreme disabilities who are unable to respond to the gospel before they die.

Dogmatic answers are not possible in individual cases. But we can rely on certain principles:

God is always just and merciful in his judgments (Genesis 18:25; Revelation 19:1–2; Jeremiah 32:19).

▶ People are judged according to the light they have received (Romans 2:12–16).

▶ God has made himself known through his creation and through our conscience (Romans 2:1–16).

▶ The major problem is that while many recognize God's existence because of what they see in the beauty of creation, none can live up to the standard of their own conscience.

None of us do what we know we should and must, if forced, condemn ourselves as guilty. This explains why Paul declares that preaching the gospel provides an opportunity for their salvation (Romans 15:20–21; 1 Corinthians 9:16).

However, Jesus also made it clear that once people have heard the truth it is their responsibility to respond.

The degree of judgment depends on the light we have received (Luke 12:47–48; Hebrews 10:26–29):

▶ Jesus said that the inhabitants of Bethsaida and Korazin would face greater judgment for their rejection of him than would those who lived in Tyre and Sidon (Luke 10:13–14).

God can and does intervene supernaturally to reveal himself to earnest seekers by dreams, visions and other means (for example, Cornelius in Acts 10:3–6). This may or may not be followed by an opportunity to hear the gospel.

Those We Love Who Are Not Christians

There is a natural concern for those who are special to us and who face eternity without Christ. Here, two things are particularly important:

▶ Our knowledge of an eternal destination should create an obligation and desire for us to share that certainty with those we know and love.

▶ Heaven will contain many surprises for us. Ultimately, God is the final judge, not ourselves. There are those who, in the last flickering moments of life, finally surrender to their creator.

Our prayers for loved ones can be answered—even though we may never make that discovery until we are reunited in heaven.

The Judgment of Satan and His Cohorts

Jesus is to pass final judgment on his enemy, Satan. This has been made certain by Christ's victory on the cross (Colossians 2:15; Hebrews 2:14). Now:

▶ Satan will be cast into the lake of fire for eternity (Revelation 20:10).

Similarly his vast army of evil spirits:

▶ have been reserved for judgment in everlasting chains (2 Peter 2:4; Jude 6)

▶ have been made subject to Christ (1 Peter 3:22)

▶ will join their master in his final destination (Matthew 25:41)

The Final Destination

What happens when we die? Do we decompose back to the dust from which humankind was first created, and then there is nothing? Or are we actually heading somewhere? How are the biblical promises of eternal life to be understood?

Those who wrote the New Testament did so from the context of their own culture and understanding. It is therefore helpful to understand the traditional Jewish and contemporary Greek thinking which was familiar to them.

Death in the Old Testament

Most evangelicals believe that we can trace a developing understanding of death through the Old Testament. It is seen as:

▶ the conclusion of a person's physical existence. 'Like water spilled on the ground, which cannot be recovered, so we must die' (2 Samuel 14:14).

▶ the end of life. '... return to the ground, since from it you were taken; for dust you are and to dust you will return' (Genesis 3:19).

▶ being cut off from God. 'I am set apart with the dead, like the slain who lie in the grave, whom you remember no more, who are cut off from your care' (Psalm 88:5).

▶ a part of life. 'There is a time for everything... a time to be born and a time to die' (Ecclesiastes 3:1, 2). It is accepted.

▶ accepted and inevitable (Psalm 89:48).

The Jews initially did not regard death itself as divine punishment. They believed man was not created immortal. The curse in the Garden of Eden—'You shall surely die'—was seen as a premature death, not an end to immortality.

It was God who prevented Adam and Eve from achieving that state by denying them access to the fruit of the tree of life so they would not 'eat and live forever' (Genesis 3:22). Only later was death itself seen as the result of sin.

The place of the departed was 'Sheol'. Thus man

did not totally cease to exist.

▶ Sheol was the shadowy abode of the dead, almost a land of not being (Psalm 88:1–5).

▶ God's lordship reached to Sheol (Psalm 139:8).

Jewish thinking developed particularly after the exile in Babylon and, to some extent, after contact with Persian thought.

▶ God was seen as having a purpose for the individual beyond death.

▶ The hope of resurrection was introduced.

▶ The body might perish but the soul could be redeemed and there would be life in God's presence (Psalm 49:14–15; Ecclesiastes 12:7).

This would be achieved by the Messiah (Psalm 16:8–11).

As understanding developed further it became clear that there must be a difference between the just and the unjust.

▶ God's fairness demanded a future day of reckoning (Daniel 12:1).

▶ The day of reckoning comes through God (Joel 3:14–16) and the Messiah (Isaiah 9:7).

▶ Ultimately, a catastrophic judgment awaited the earth before the inauguration of a new heaven and earth (Isaiah 65:17–23; 66:24).

Death Between the Old and New Testaments

In inter-Testament literature the Greek influence can be clearly seen.

▶ The soul was seen as immortal, remaining in the heavens after death, awaiting resurrection.

▶ Martyrdom was seen as heroic.

▶ The influential Jewish thinker, Philo, saw the body as evil; at death the soul was liberated from its prison of passion and evil desire.

Death in Greek Thought

In Greek thought the most important influence was that of Plato and his disciples. For them:

▶ What was of supreme importance was true wisdom from which stemmed wise actions. The immaterial 'soul' is the residence of these ideas.

▶ Reality and virtue are in the soul and therefore it must be eternal.

▶ Death follows life as the seasons follow each other.

▶ Death is not to be feared as at that moment the soul is released.

▶ The wicked are cast into torment; the wise go to a higher existence.

▶ Those not particularly bad or wise have to undergo further purification.

The immortality of the soul is its natural property because of its 'divinity'.

All the influences on the writer help us to understand the New Testament teaching on the subject. Throughout scripture we have a gradual unfolding of the truth of God. However, this process did not happen in a vacuum. Each writer was a child of his time, subject to his own culture, traditions and understanding of the world.

As God revealed truth to the prophets and other authors of scripture he did not by-pass their minds but directed them so that, clothed in the language and thinking of their time, eternal truth was written as scripture.

This means that viewed from our culture some passages of scripture seem confusing until something of the background is explained and the original meaning made clear.

The New Testament is set against a background of Greek culture. Paul and the other writers were well versed in Greek thought, although they rejected much of it as being incompatible with their scriptures (the Old Testament).

However Paul and John in particular reflect some of the insights of the Greek philosophers which constitute a further stepping-stone to the full picture the Holy Spirit inspired in their writings.

On the subject of life after death Paul rejected most of Plato's teaching on the immortality of the soul—which would have been the understanding of the non-Jewish readers of his letters—although he integrated some ideas of immortality into his prime teaching of the resurrection of the body.

A Christian View of Life After Death

The New Testament teaching on life after death focuses on the resurrection of Jesus.

KEY POINT

In 1 Corinthians 15, Paul lays out the heart of Christian belief. In this chapter, Paul:

▶ argues that the resurrection of the Lord is 'of first importance' (v. 3)

▶ shows that if there is no resurrection of the dead, our hope would be in vain (vv. 13–14)

▶ describes Christ's resurrection as 'the first fruits of those who have fallen asleep' (v. 20)

▶ points to the resurrection of Jesus as the means of our own resurrection (vv. 21–22)

▶ says that at the return of Jesus he will receive the rest of the fruit which belongs to him (v. 23), but will then even destroy death itself (v. 26)

Paul goes on to describe the nature of our resurrected bodies.

▶ When a seed is planted, it must die before new life in a totally different form can appear (v. 37).

▶ There is both continuity and change. Earthly forms and heavenly forms are different (v. 40).

In verses 42 to 44, Paul makes these contrasts.
It can be seen that:

▶ From the first man, Adam, we inherited our natural bodies with their characteristics (v. 45).

▶ The last Adam, Jesus, gave us our spiritual lives as a subsequent inheritance, which is added to the first (v. 46).

▶ To the substance of the dust is added the substance of the spirit (v. 48).

▶ We will possess the likeness of Jesus (v. 49; compare 2 Corinthians 3:18).

▶ Only redeemed humanity, the imperishable, can inherit the kingdom of God (v. 50).

The body

Earthly	Resurrection
Perishable	Imperishable
Dishonourable	Glorious
Weak	Powerful
Natural	Spiritual

▶ Only the dead will be resurrected, but all, including those alive at the time of Christ's coming, will be transformed (v. 51).

▶ This transformation will be instant, at the sound of God's trumpet, the symbol of both the end of the era and of celebration (v. 52).

▶ The nature of this transformation, will be to endow the righteous with immortality and a body that will not perish (v. 53).

▶ After this, death will be beaten, having lost its hold on mankind (v. 54).

We are not told in scripture exactly what our resurrected existence will be like.

KEY POINT

All we can confidentially affirm is that:

▶ It is the gift of God (Romans 8:11; 2 Corinthians 5:1)

▶ It is a spiritual body, the natural home of the redeemed spirit, and free from all the effects of sin (John 3:6; 6:63; 1 Corinthians 15:45, 46).

▶ It will be imperishable, glorious and powerful (see box above—1 Corinthians 15:42–44).

▶ It will be—like that of angels—inappropriate for marriage and without need of food (Luke 20:34–36).

▶ Its natural home is in heaven (1 Corinthians 15:40; 2 Corinthians 5:2) which is associated with light (Colossians 1:12).

▶ Its pattern will be the glorious body of Jesus (Philippians 3:21).

The relationship between our present bodies and our future spiritual bodies is unclear. But for resurrection to have real meaning, there must be an element of continuity as well as change.

It is also unclear what our transformed personalities will be like. Our present state is one of imperfection and a tendency to sin (Romans 8:14–25). But Christ died to make us perfect (Hebrews 10:14). Although, right now, in God's eyes we are regarded as righteous (Colossians 3:3), it is only through the transformation promised at the second coming, or the resurrection of the dead, that we will be truly perfect.

Hell

There are few words in the English language that are as evocative as—hell. It conjures up images of fire, demons, suffering, blackness and torment.

The modern mind treats such concepts as myth and fantasy. As a word, 'hell' is no more than a casual exclamation, while comedians find it a constant source of material.

Nevertheless, the popular media constantly use the word when describing places of great pain and carnage.

The Bible treats the subject of hell with great seriousness.

Hell is the place of punishment after the judgment. Jesus used the word 'Gehenna' for this location (Matthew 5:22, 29–30; 10:28; 18:9; 23:15, 33; Mark 9:43, 45, 47; Luke 12:5).

Gehenna is a transliteration of the Old Testament expression 'valley of Hinnom'. This:

▶ Was a ravine located on the south side of Jerusalem and had once been a centre for idol-worship and child-sacrifice (2 Chronicles 28:3; 33:6; Jeremiah 32:35).

▶ Later became the Jerusalem rubbish dump.

'Hades' is a word also used. Normally this refers to the abode of the dead, righteous and unrighteous alike (the equivalent of the Hebrew 'Sheol'). Its prime meaning is the temporary place of the dead before the judgment, and has no sense of either pain or pleasure.

In the Authorized Version, 'Hades' was unfortunately mistranslated 'hell' which has caused some confusion.

It has been likened to a waiting room, or the ante-room to either heaven or hell following the judgment.

Little wonder that, when King Josiah smashed down the idol shrine in the eighth century BC, the place became the sewage pit of Jerusalem. The corpses of animals and criminals and all general rubbish was thrown into the valley and set on fire.

▶ Fires there burned continuously in order to consume the filth and impurity of the place.

▶ The fires were fed by brimstone, creating a terrible stench.

▶ Worms fed on the garbage out of reach of the fires, and vultures watched on as the stench and smoke rose up continually (2 Kings 23:10; Isaiah 30:33).

No wonder the place became a symbol for the fires of hell.

The Bible describes hell as:

▶ a lake of fire or of burning sulphur (Revelation 19:20; 20:10–15).

▶ a place of retribution and punishment where people are separated from God for eternity (2 Thessalonians 1:8–9).

▶ where all contact with God is removed and

Purgatory

There is no reference in scripture to a place called purgatory, which the Roman Catholic Church defines as, 'the place or state in which, after death, the soul is purified from sin'.

Nor is there any indication in scripture of a 'second chance' process for the purging of sins.

The concept of purgatory was discussed by Augustine, the great early church Father, in his book *The City of God*. His conclusion was: 'I do not reject this theory, for it may be true.'

It was not until the Council of Florence in 1439 that purgatory became an official doctrine of the Roman Catholic Church. But by the time of the Reformation gross and corrupt practices had sprung up exploiting the vulnerable on behalf of their departed loved ones.

The doctrine of any possible purification through punishment between death and the final judgment was rejected by the Reformers as unbiblical. It remains the official teaching of the Roman Catholic Church.

KEY POINT

consequently those there live in absolute darkness (Matthew 8:12; 22:13).

▶ a place of punishment for the wicked (Matthew 23:14–15, 33), for those whose names are not written in the book of life (Revelation 2:11; 21:8).

▶ a place of horrible torment (Luke 16:22–24).

▶ a fire that will never be extinguished (Mark 9:43–49).

▶ a place of continually ascending smoke, a fiery furnace (Matthew 13:42, 50; 25:41–46).

▶ A valley of human despair for those who have rejected God's sacrifice in Jesus and whose conscience will never die. They will be tormented by thoughts of past guilt and rejected grace (Isaiah 66:24; Matthew 5:30; 18:9; Luke 12:5).

▶ an eternal jail for wicked humankind but originally prepared for Satan and his angels (Isaiah 66:22–24; 2 Peter 2:4; Revelation 14:9–11).

▶ a place of eternal shame and contempt (Daniel 12:2).

Despite the clear evidence of scripture, evangelicals often fail to speak about hell.

To some extent the reasons are understandable:

▶ Nagging doubts over the question—'How could a God of love and compassion ever allow such a situation to exist?'

▶ A society that is obsessed with thoughts of 'now' and has little concern for eternity.

▶ A fear of repeating the mistakes of past generations, when preachers 'dangled people over the fires of hell' in attempts to frighten them into the kingdom.

▶ The reluctance of our rationalistic society to take seriously even the possibility of the existence of hell.

If hell is the awful destiny for those who die apart from Christ then surely we should live life with a greater sense of urgency.

If we accept the Bible as truth, we should be committed to sharing the truth in a way that will:

▶ warn rather than scare

▶ attract people to heaven rather than repel them from hell

Heaven

Heaven is the place to which we are ultimately travelling. In this world we are strangers and pilgrims. It is only one staging-post on our road to eternity (Psalm 119:19; 1 Peter 2:11). Heaven is our final destination.

While researching the material for these seminar notes, two things became clear:

▶ There is a multitude of books that concentrate on God's timetable for the end times, the closing stages of human history.

▶ There is hardly any which deals with the nature and content of heaven.

The millennium was clearly a popular theme, heaven was not!

The Bible and Heaven

The Bible does have a great deal to say about heaven.

▶ The Hebrew word used is *shemayim*—a plural word meaning 'heavens, or something lofty, high up'.

▶ The Greek word is *ouranoi*—a word used in both the singular and plural, translated 'the heavens, the skies'.

The same words are used of:

▶ the physical heavens—the air (Matthew 6:26; James 5:18)

▶ sky and space (Matthew 24:29; Mark 13:25; Hebrews 11:12)

▶ the dwelling place of God (Matthew 5:16; 12:50; Revelation 3:12; 4:1–2)

The Bible declares that:

▶ The heavens were created by God (Genesis 1:1; 1 Chronicles 16:26, 31; Job 9:8).

▶ This present physical universe is to be transformed and replaced by 'new heavens and a new earth' (Isaiah 65:17; 66:22; 2 Peter 3:10–13; Revelation 21:1).

▶ Heaven is an actual place (Genesis 2:1, 4; Deuteronomy 10:14).

▶ Heaven is the home of God himself (1 Kings 8:30; 2 Chronicles 30:27; Job 22:12; Psalm 123:1; Isaiah 66:1; Luke 11:2; Acts 7:49).

▶ God looks down from heaven (Deuteronomy 26:15). God is ruler, Father and God of heaven (Jonah 1:9; Matthew 5:45; 7:21; Ezra 1:2).

▶ But God is not alone in heaven. He is worshipped there by angelic hosts (Nehemiah 9:6; Mark 13:32).

'Heaven' is also used alternatively for 'God' himself.

▶ The prodigal son confesses to sinning against heaven when it is actually against God that he has sinned (Luke 15:18–21).

▶ Matthew constantly substitutes the phrase 'kingdom of heaven' for the term 'kingdom of God' which is used by Mark and Luke. The two are apparently identical.

What Will Heaven Be Like?

We don't know what the structure of heaven will be like. But we do know:

▶ It will be the city of God, needing no sun or moon, because God and the Lamb will fill it with the light of their glory (Revelation 21:22–23).

▶ All the attention of believers will be focused on Jesus.

▶ Our worship will centre around him alone (Revelation 21:22).

▶ Heaven will be like a wedding feast (Luke 12:35–38; Matthew 12:1–10). Where:
We are the bride,
Christ is the bridegroom,
God will be the host.

For the Christian, heaven will possess four basic characteristics:

KEY POINT

Heaven will be a place of release.

The illnesses, evil and suffering of earth will all be lost in heaven.

▶ There will be no sorrow or death, no crying or pain, and no curse or night (Revelation 21:4; 22:3–5).

▶ Immortality will be the gift of heaven because death has been finally conquered (Hebrews 2:14; 1 Corinthians 15:26, 54; Revelation 20:14).

▶ God himself will wipe away the tears from our eyes (Isaiah 25:8; Revelation 21:4).

▶ Insecurity and evil practices will be obliterated and the old will pass away (Hebrews 12:28; Revelation 20:10; 21:4, 27).

This release will not merely be seen in the removal of negative factors, it will also be witnessed in the introduction of a positive weight of glory.

▶ We will be with Jesus (Colossians 3:4).

▶ Our transformed bodies will be like his for we will have traded the old one for an eternal model (Philippians 3:21).

▶ We will reign as co-heirs with Jesus and will share his glory (Romans 8:17; Colossians 3:4).

▶ We will shine like the sun in God's kingdom (Matthew 13:43).

▶ We will be honoured by the Father, and witness the glory of the Son (John 12:26; 17:24).

▶ We will be in a far better place than we enjoyed here on earth (2 Corinthians 5:8).

▶ All our sufferings will have been worthwhile (Romans 8:18).

▶ Our resting place in heaven will last for eternity (2 Corinthians 4:17; 2 Timothy 2:10).

Heaven will be a place of community.

We will not merely be absorbed into a vast amorphous whole. We will retain our individuality—but within the community of the redeemed.

▶ The vast multitude will be drawn from those of every tribe, language, race and nation (Revelation 5:9).

▶ We will still possess identity, for Jesus could name individuals in the kingdom of heaven (Matthew 8:11).

▶ We will enjoy perfect unity, for no unrighteous person will be there (Revelation 21:27; 22:15).

Heaven will be a place of activity.

In heaven:

▶ We will not know hunger, thirst or physical discomfort (Revelation 7:16).

▶ We will never die (Luke 20:36).

All this could sound rather boring. And it would be for those who do not love God. But the world to come is no EuroDisney with free rides to occupy our leisure time.

Heaven is a place of loving and serving God forever. Where God is loved and his will performed. That can scarcely be a static experience for those of us who have known his love and made our own surrender to him.

An intriguing aspect of New Testament teaching is the concept of us reigning with Christ (Luke 22:28–30; Romans 5:17; 2 Timothy 2:12). This is an exciting prospect although 'who' we are going to rule and 'how' is not made clear. It does, however, seem to be a future benefit for those who suffer now for Christ and yet endure.

The biblical imagery of heaven is vibrant and exciting. Heaven will abound with creativity, action, community and relationship.

We do not understand all that this will mean—but one day we will! (1 Corinthians 13:12)

Heaven will be a place of worship.

▶ Above all the activity of heaven will be worshipping the Lamb who was put to death instead of us (Revelation 5:9–10).

Paul speaks of the continuity of our personalities through death into resurrection in 1 Corinthians 15. The same is paralleled with our culture in Revelation 21:26.

This suggests that the wealth of art, beauty and human creativity is not lost at death but is carried through into heaven—with the impurities removed.

Worship of God in his heaven, and of our beloved Lord Jesus, will not be a dull routine but an expression of ultimate spiritual reality.

The Westminster Shorter Catechism declared that we were made to 'glorify God and to enjoy him forever'.

In heaven we will fulfil our destiny. We will do that for which we were designed and made.

We will enjoy him, in his presence, and the myriads of angels will gaze in wonder at the worship of the redeemed.

We too often become obsessed with the realities of the here and now. As creatures of space and time we live with the anxieties and priorities of life within our world.

But there is another dimension ahead. We always need to remember that heaven is not life with Jesus now, it will be life with Jesus for eternity.

Between Death and Resurrection

The teaching of scripture is that the day will come for the resurrection of all believers who have died before the return of Jesus Christ (Mark 12:24–27; 1 Corinthians 15:35–58). That same moment will witness the inauguration of our eternal reign with him.

Is immortality a state which is not natural to us, but a gift of God who chooses to share his immortality only with those people who belong to him (2 Timothy 1:10; 1 Corinthians 15:50–54)? Or, as Christians have traditionally believed, is the soul immortal—whether redeemed or not? The answer to this question is directly connected to our view of hell which is discussed on pages 91–92.

There are two other questions raised:

▶ What happens to us between death and resurrection?

▶ Do unbelievers share the same immortality in their separation from God as those who will

'*T*he Swiss theologian Karl Barth was once asked, ''Will we see our loved ones on the other side?'' He answered, ''Yes, but with others too!'' '

QUOTED IN STEPHEN TRAVIS, *I BELIEVE IN THE SECOND COMING OF JESUS*, REPRODUCED BY PERMISSION OF HODDER & STOUGHTON LTD, 1976

'*L*ove of Heaven is the only way to Heaven.'

JOHN HENRY NEWMAN

'*W*e can afford to suffer now, we'll have a long Eternity to enjoy ourselves.'

A.W. TOZER

spend eternity in heaven?

It is at Christ's return that the believers on earth and all who have died in the faith are to receive new bodies and become inhabitants of heaven.

Until that time:

▶ Heaven is populated only by God himself and his angelic creatures.

However:

▶ Jesus said to one of the thieves crucified with him, 'Today you will be with me in paradise' (Luke 23:43).

In the same way, Paul expresses two different views within one epistle:

▶ Paul expects to be with Christ when he dies (Philippians 1:23).

▶ He refers to the resurrection taking place when Jesus returns (Philippians 3:20–21).

So where are believers between death and the return of Jesus?

Jehovah's Witnesses, Seventh-Day Adventists and others believe in 'soul-sleep'. The idea is that there is a time interval for the dead person between their death and the ultimate resurrection. This period is spent in unconsciousness or 'sleep'.

It is true that 'sleep' is occasionally used as a picture of death. However, the bulk of biblical teaching leads to a different conclusion.

Most orthodox Christians believe that, in the interval between death and the return of Jesus Christ, the dead are 'with Christ', but in a disembodied form (Philippians 1:23; Luke 23:43). So when Jesus returns all his people will receive their resurrection bodies.

Some believe that we will be in an unconscious state, as when asleep. From the moment of death until our next conscious moment at the return of Christ. However, is this compatible with the story of Dives and Lazarus (Luke 16:19–31) or Paul's expressed desire to be with Christ (Philippians 1:23)?

Alternatively, the answer may lie in our understanding of time and eternity.

▶ For those in earth-bound time there is clearly a gap between the death of an individual and Christ's return. We conceive of a dead person as being in a kind of airport transit-lounge anticipating take-off!

▶ For God, time and eternity unite. 'A thousand years in your sight are like a day that has just gone by' (Psalm 90:4).

Is Punishment Eternal?

Christians take no pleasure in the belief that unbelievers are condemned to eternal torment. This is simply what they understand the Bible to teach. However, there are also Christians who tentatively suggest that this is not the only conclusion that can be deduced from scripture.

There are seven major views of hell and its eternal nature. Many of these views inter-link.

Universalism This denies that God could ever allow

anyone to be excluded from heaven. It is a view which began in the cults.

The concept is that a God of love will ultimately draw everyone to himself. The texts quoted in its defence—John 12:32; Ephesians 1:10; Philippians 2:10–11; 1 Corinthians 15:28—are all open to an entirely different interpretation when read in their context. God is not only a God of love but also of justice. The God of all the earth has to be true to his character, doing that which is right—even if it breaks his heart.

Reformation By this theory people may be originally punished for their sin, but eventually their suffering will purge their guilt and they will be restored to the joys of heaven. In other words, hell becomes a redemptive form of purgatory.

The early church Father, Origen, and modern writer William Barclay held this view. Supporters appeal to Matthew 19:28; Acts 3:21 and Ephesians 1:9–10. However, these scriptures, in the light of the rest of the New Testament, are best understood as speaking of Christ's ultimate triumph over all things and the whole of creation being subject to his order.

Annihilation Assuming that immortality is a gift from God, would he give the potential for eternal suffering to any human being?

So, while God offers his people eternal life, everyone who has rejected him is eternally separated from him. At the judgment day God either unites people to himself, or condemns them to extinction. The effect of the punishment may be everlasting, but the experience of it is not.

It appeals to texts such as Philippians 2:10–11, Ephesians 1:9–10 and 1 Corinthians 15:28, but draws different conclusions from other views which use the same texts.

Oblivion This is linked closely with annihilation in its initial argument, suggesting that death rather than the judgment is the end and that it is only believers who are resurrected to face judgment and eternal life. The unrighteous stay dead.

Those unbelievers who are still alive when Christ returns will be judged, but their punishment is death. Those unbelievers who have already died just remain dead.

This uses the same scriptures as annihilation but dates the end of existence from the earlier moment.

Punishment The fact that sinners should face punishment is not contested by this perspective; but the duration of the punishment is.

The argument is raised as to whether or not immortality is conditional on belonging to Christ. If God does not give immortality to unbelievers then he can punish them in hell for a period of time, and ultimately consign them to extinction.

This is an attempt to reconcile the need for judgement and retribution with a dislike of God punishing people for ever. It appeals to ideas of judgment tempered by mercy. Ultimately, it is another variant of annihilationism as it denies eternal conscious punishment. It has the virtue of appealing to traditional passages about hell but has the difficulty of verses such as Revelation 14:9–11 and 20:10 which imply an unending state.

Partition This suggests that hell involves endless suffering for demons, but annihilation for

'*I* do not dogmatise about the position to which I have come. I hold it tentatively. But I do plead for frank dialogue among Evangelicals on the basis of Scripture. I also believe that the ultimate annihilation of the wicked should at least be accepted as a legitimate, biblically founded alternative to their eternal conscious torment.'

JOHN STOTT

'*T*wo things fill the mind with ever new and increasing wonder and awe, the more often and the more seriously reflection concentrates upon them: the starry Heaven above me and the moral law within me.'

IMMANUEL KANT